GREEK TRAGEDY
IN NEW TRANSLATIONS

GENERAL EDITORS
Peter Burian and Alan Shapiro

FOUNDING GENERAL EDITOR
William Arrowsmith

FORMER GENERAL EDITOR
Herbert Golder

THE COMPLETE EURIPIDES, VOLUME II

The Complete Euripides, Volume II

Iphigenia in Tauris and Other Plays

Edited by
PETER BURIAN
and
ALAN SHAPIRO

OXFORD
UNIVERSITY PRESS

2010

OXFORD
UNIVERSITY PRESS

Oxford University Press, Inc., publishes works that further
Oxford University's objective of excellence
in research, scholarship, and education.

Oxford   New York
Auckland   Cape Town   Dar es Salaam   Hong Kong   Karachi
Kuala Lumpur   Madrid   Melbourne   Mexico City   Nairobi
New Delhi   Shanghai   Taipei   Toronto

With offices in
Argentina   Austria   Brazil   Chile   Czech Republic   France   Greece
Guatemala   Hungary   Italy   Japan   Poland   Portugal   Singapore
South Korea   Switzerland   Thailand   Turkey   Ukraine   Vietnam

Electra Copyright © 1994 by Janet Lembke and Kenneth J. Reckford

Iphigeneia in Tauris Copyright © 1973 by Richmond Lattimore

Orestes Copyright © 1995 by John Peck and Frank Nisetich

Iphigeneia at Aulis Copyright © 1978 by W. S. Merwin and George E. Dimock, Jr.

Compilation Copyright © 2010 by Oxford University Press, Inc.

Published by Oxford University Press, Inc.
198 Madison Avenue, New York, New York 10016

www.oup.com

Oxford is a registered trademark of Oxford University Press

Library of Congress Cataloging-in-Publication Data
Euripides.
[Selections. English. 2010]
Iphigenia in Tauris, and other plays / [Euripides] ; edited
by Peter Burian and Alan Shapiro.
    p. cm. — (The complete Euripides ; v. 2)
(Greek tragedy in new translations)
Includes bibliographical references and index.
ISBN 978-0-19-538868-8; 978-0-19-538869-5 (pbk.)
1. Euripides—Translations into English.
I. Burian, Peter, 1943– II. Shapiro, Alan, 1952–
III. Title.
PA3975.A2 2010
882'.01—dc22   2010013884

EDITORS' FOREWORD

"*The Greek Tragedy in New Translations* is based on the conviction that poets like Aeschylus, Sophocles, and Euripides can only be properly rendered by translators who are themselves poets. Scholars may, it is true, produce useful and perceptive versions. But our most urgent present need is for a *re-creation* of these plays—as though they had been written, freshly and greatly, by masters fully at home in the English of our own times."

With these words, the late William Arrowsmith announced the purpose of this series, and we intend to honor that purpose. As was true of most of the volumes that began to appear in the 1970s—first under Arrowsmith's editorship, later in association with Herbert Golder—those for which we bear editorial responsibility are products of close collaborations between poets and scholars. We believe (as Arrowsmith did) that the skills of both are required for the difficult and delicate task of transplanting these magnificent specimens of another culture into the soil of our own place and time, to do justice both to their deep differences from our patterns of thought and expression and to their palpable closeness to our most intimate concerns. Above all, we are eager to offer contemporary readers dramatic poems that convey as vividly and directly as possible the splendor of language, the complexity of image and idea, and the intensity of emotion and originals. This entails, among much else, the recognition that the tragedies were meant for performance—as scripts for actors—to be sung and danced as well as spoken. It demands writing of inventiveness, clarity, musicality, and dramatic power. By such standards, we ask that these translations be judged.

This series is also distinguished by its recognition of the need of nonspecialist readers for a critical introduction informed by the best recent scholarship, but written clearly and without condescension. Each play is followed by notes designed not only to elucidate obscure references but also to mediate the conventions of the Athenian stage as well as those features of the Greek text that might otherwise go unnoticed. The notes are supplemented by a glossary of mythical and geographical terms that should make it possible to read the play without turning elsewhere for basic information. Stage directions are sufficiently ample to aid readers in imagining the action as they read. Our fondest hope, of course, is that these versions will be staged not only in the minds of their readers but also in the theaters to which, after so many centuries, they still belong.

A NOTE ON THE SERIES FORMAT

A series such as this requires a consistent format. Different translators, with individual voices and approaches to the material at hand, cannot be expected to develop a single coherent style for each of the three tragedians, much less make clear to modern readers that, despite the differences among the tragedians themselves, the plays share many conventions and a generic, or period, style. But they can at least share a common format and provide similar forms of guidance to the reader.

1. *Spelling of Greek names*

Orthography is one area of difference among the translations that requires a brief explanation. Historically, it has been common practice to use Latinized forms of Greek names when bringing them into English. Thus, for example, Oedipus (not Oidipous) and Clytemnestra (not Klutaimestra) are customary in English. Recently, however, many translators have moved toward more precise transliteration, which has the advantage of presenting the names as both Greek and new, instead of Roman and neoclassical importations into English. In the case of so familiar a name as Oedipus, however, transliteration risks the appearance of pedantry or affectation. And in any case, perfect consistency cannot be expected in such matters. Readers will feel the same discomfort with "Athenai" as the chief city of Greece as they would with "Platon" as the author of *The Republic*.

The earlier volumes in this series adopted as a rule a "mixed" orthography in accordance with the considerations outlined above. The most familiar names retain their Latinate forms, the rest are transliterated; -os rather than Latin -us is adopted for the termination of masculine names and Greek diphthongs, as in Iphigen*eia* for Latin Iphigenia. (In this collected volume, however, we have given the two plays that bear her name their traditional titles, *Iphigenia in Tauris* and *Iphigenia at Aulis*, while otherwise respecting the translators' preferred orthography.) Some of the more recent translations continue the practice of mixed orthography, but where translators have preferred to use a more consistent practice of transliteration or Latinization, we have honored their wishes.

2. *Stage directions*
The ancient manuscripts of the Greek plays do not supply stage directions (though the ancient commentators often provide information relevant to staging, delivery, "blocking," etc.). Hence stage directions must be inferred from words and situations and our knowledge of Greek theatrical conventions. At best this is a ticklish and uncertain procedure. But it is surely preferable that good stage directions should be provided by the translator than that readers should be left to their own devices in visualizing action, gesture, and spectacle. Ancient tragedy was austere and "distanced" by means of masks, which means that the reader must not expect the detailed intimacy ("He shrugs and turns wearily away," "She speaks with deliberate slowness, as though to emphasize the point," etc.) that characterizes stage directions in modern naturalistic drama.

3. *Numbering of lines*
For the convenience of the reader who may wish to check the translation against the original, or vice versa, the lines have been numbered according to both the Greek and English texts. The lines of the translation have been numbered in multiples of ten, and these numbers have been set in the right-hand margin. The (inclusive) Greek numeration will be found bracketed at the top of the page. The Notes that follow the text have been keyed to both numerations, the line numbers of the translation in **bold**, followed by the Greek lines in regular type, and the same convention is used for all references to specific passages (of the translated plays only) in both the Notes and the Introduction.

Readers will doubtless note that in many plays the English lines outnumber the Greek, but they should not therefore conclude that the translator has been unduly prolix. In most cases the reason is simply that the translator has adopted the free-flowing norms of modern Anglo-American prosody, with its brief-breath-and-emphasis-determined lines, and its habit of indicating cadence and caesuras by line length and setting rather than by conventional punctuation. Even where translators have preferred to cast dialogue in more regular five-beat or six-beat lines, the greater compactness of Greek diction is likely to result in a substantial disparity in Greek and English numerations.

ABOUT THE TRANSLATIONS

The translations in this series were written over a period of roughly forty years. No attempt has been made to update references to the scholarly literature in the Introductions and Notes, but each volume offers a brief For Further Reading list that will provide some initial orientation to contemporary critical thinking about the tragedies it contains.

THIS VOLUME

The plays collected here all stem from the later phase of Euripides' career, but, more important, they are united thematically. This volume might be entitled "Agamemnon's Children." In these plays, Euripides puts on stage the final generation caught up in the waves of crime and vengeance that engulf the House of Atreus. Unlike Aeschylus in the great Oresteian trilogy, however, Euripides makes no attempt to dramatize a vast swath of legendary history as a way of making sense of (and bringing closure to) the story as a whole. Rather, each of these four plays revisits a specific moment of the story in ways that open up questions of meaning and closure, defamiliarizing in various ways the now familiar figures and actions. *Iphigenia at Aulis* and *Electra* are Euripidean "rereadings" of two of the most famous episodes of Atreid history: Agamemnon's sacrifice of his daughter Iphigeneia, and Orestes' and Electra's revenge killing of their mother and her lover for the murder of their father Agamemnon. *Orestes* and *Iphigenia in Tauris*, by contrast, are almost novelistic in their invention of plots that imagine, respectively, what happens to Orestes after the matricide and before he leaves Argos on his Fury-driven flight, and how Orestes, in flight, meets Iphigeneia, miraculously saved from her apparent sacrifice, and is himself rescued from death by her. The plays might also be read as pairs of linked stories, *Orestes* dramatizing the madness of its hero after the matricide of *Electra*, and *Ipigenia in Tauris* constituting a salvific sequel to the sacrifice of *Iphigenia at Aulis*. In this volume, the plays are simply presented in their apparent chronological order.

Electra is Euripides' setting of the one subject for which we happen to have dramas by all three Athenian tragedians, and we can thus compare it to the others directly and in detail. This is not the place for such a comparison, but a few points will suggest how innovative and disturbing Euripidean treatment of Electra's and Orestes' matricide is. Aeschylus, in *Libation Bearers (Choephori)* is at pains to show that this deed, necessitated by the immutable force of *dike* (justice understood as the restoration of a balance disturbed by a preceding offense), mandated by Apollo, and placed entirely in the hands of Orestes, a young man with no motivation beyond righting a terrible wrong, is nonetheless a horrible crime that cries out for its own vengeance. Only then, in the third drama of his trilogy, *Eumenides*, does Aeschylus give us a way out of the exchange of blow for blow and blood for blood. This solution goes beyond individual motivation and guilt to involve the very fabric of society. A court of law, designed to strengthen, not destroy, the community takes the prosecution of *dike* out of the hands of the offended party. The court, weighing claims and counter-claims, reaches a decision that brings the dispute to an end, and all parties in the end accept the decision as final.

The *Oresteia* was first produced in 458; the *Electras* of Sophocles and Euripides came, in all probability, something less than half a century later. Unfortunately, we have no precise date for either and cannot specify which came first; all we can say is that they seem to be responding one to the other. Both plays give the central role to Electra, a marginal character in Aeschylus; both insist on the difficulty of her situation and character. And yet, if Euripides' world is not that of Aeschylus, it is also far from Sophoclean. Sophocles' Electra suffers but endures, rejecting any compromise and willing to act by herself if need be. And when Orestes returns, there is nothing agonized in the killing of their mother, or even climactic, since (in a reversal of Aeschylus) she is killed first and the drama ends with Orestes' killing of Aigisthos, cheered on by Electra, sure that her vindication is now complete. Euripides, on the other hand, gives us an Electra married to a mere peasant and more affected by the misery of her circumstances as she perceives them, more concerned with her own status, than obsessed with the need to take vengeance on her father's killers. Euripides' Orestes is both more craven and more brutal than his counterpart in Sophocles (to say nothing of Aeschylus). Orestes stabs Aigisthos in the back while he is sacrificing at an altar, and Electra lures their ostensibly monstrous, heartless mother to her death—with, of all things, an invitation to the naming ceremony of a fictional grandchild. After the deed is done, both are overcome with remorse and doubt, and with their sorrow hardly assuaged by the appearance of their divine cousins, the Dioscuri, they depart in tears to their separate exiles.

Whether Sophocles' or Euripides' *Electra* came first, the contrast between the two remains striking, as the Introduction to the translation in this volume points out. Either Euripides is answering the integrity of the harsh heroism in Sophocles, or Sophocles is challenging Euripides' deheroized world and ambiguity about what constitutes noble action. The settings of the two plays by themselves tell a great deal about their difference of tone and atmosphere. Sophocles' drama (like that of Aeschylus) takes place before the palace of the Argive kings. Euripides sets his at the modest house of a peasant to whom Electra has been given in marriage. This yeoman farmer is by far the most agreeable character of the drama. He shows his understanding of his place by respecting the virginity of his princess bride, and in general is a beacon of decency and good sense. But for Electra, of course, the poverty of his world and her own reduction of status are intolerable. When, for example, the lively village maidens of the Chorus invite Electra to a festival of Hera, she complains, in effect, that she has nothing to wear; they offer to loan her a dress, which she of course refuses. When the Farmer invites two strangers (still unrecognized as Orestes and Pylades) to a meal in his humble abode, Electra reproaches him for daring to offer such simple fare as he has to people obviously of higher rank. When an old family retainer reports that he has seen evidence (borrowed from Aeschylus) of Orestes' unannounced return, Electra rejects it with scorn because it suggests "that my

courageous brother would crawl here / in secret because he fears Aigisthos" (**541–42** / 525–26). But that is precisely what Orestes, in all caution, has done.

Iphigenia in Tauris, by contrast, presents Orestes and his sister Iphigeneia in a more positive light as together they escape peril in a barbarian land. Iphigeneia's rescue from Aulis at the hands of Artemis and translation to the land of the Taurians was a story at least as old as the *Cypria,* an epic of the Trojan Cycle. Furthermore, the Temple of Artemis at Brauron in Attica (Iphigeneia's destination at the end of the play) already had a strong association with Iphigeneia through the hero shrine dedicated to her there. What Euripides adds is Orestes' part in the story, which turns it into a drama of recognition, rescue, and escape. (Lattimore's Introduction to the translation in this volume points out how much the plot has in common with that of Euripides' *Helen,* securely dated to 412 B.C. Like the majority of scholars, he believes that *Iphigenia in Tauris* is slightly earlier, giving it a probable date of 414.)

In many ways, *Iphigenia in Tauris* is a rite-of-passage drama. Both Orestes and Iphigeneia have been removed from their accustomed surroundings and subjected to terrible trials. Iphigeneia has been rescued from death only to preside as priestess of Artemis over the sacrificial slaughter of foreigners who arrive on the Taurian shore. And Orestes, in this version of the story, is still being pursued by a group of his mother's Erinyes, unwilling to accept the acquittal at law in Athens that, in Aeschylus' *Oresteia* at least, ended his suffering. Apollo has told Orestes that to win final release from the madness and pain, he must seize the ancient image of Artemis from her Taurian temple and bring it to Attica. When we first encounter Orestes, he sees only the difficulties and dangers of this task, and his friend Pylades must counter the nervousness and self-doubt engendered by Orestes' ordeal. His precarious state is confirmed by a herdsman, who reports to Iphigeneia and the Chorus that he has seen two young men, one of whom in an obvious fit of madness attacks the herds, thinking them Erinyes, the other protecting him from the herdsmen's volley of stones. Once overcome, the two foreigners are delivered to King Thoas, who sends them to Iphigeneia for sacrifice. Iphigeneia has dreamt of Orestes' death, a vision that has cast her into despair and made her more willing to accept her terrible role, wishing that it were Helen and Menelaos

that she could sacrifice. At the same time, she expresses her disapproval of any god who could demand human sacrifice, as Artemis apparently does among the Taurians.

In this emotionally fraught and complex situation, the encounter of Iphigeneia with Orestes and Pylades becomes an equally fraught and complex recognition scene. When the reunion is finally accomplished, however, and the action moves to rescue and escape, and the emotions of dread, doubt, and then joy yield to the exciting externals of plot, and to suspense as we wait to see how the young heroes of the tale will win their way home, bringing the rite of passage to successful completion. In the event, there is both the satisfaction of seeing the cruel barbarian king taken in by Greek cleverness and the *frisson* of an unexpected reversal: an adverse wind brings the escaping Greek vessel back to port and Greeks themselves into the hands of the irate king. Euripides creates this final obstacle only to have it removed by Athena, the goddess who earlier saved Orestes at his trial in Athens and to whose land the appropriately purified cult of Artemis will now be transferred. The point appears to be both to effect the assent of King Thoas to the will of the gods and to vindicate the gods themselves: Apollo's advice was good, Artemis escapes the barbarity of her Taurian cult for a new civilized home on Attic soil, and Athena proves her lasting concern for Orestes and his clan. She even sees to the return home of the Greek maidens who sang so longingly of home in their second stasimon (1067–1128 / 1089–152). No other Euripidean "happy ending" is so free of shadows.

Orestes, like *Iphigenia in Tauris*, is a kind of novelistic embroidery on legends presumably known to all the Athenians gathered in the theater of Dionysus in 408, the date of its first performance. Orestes, pursued by the Furies, was forced to leave Mycenae, seek purification at Delphi, and finally rewin his freedom in Athens (in Aeschylus' version by acquittal at the hands of the Areopagos court). But what happened to Orestes between the initial onslaught of the Furies and his departure? Euripides develops an elaborate and exciting plot that defies tradition by making it seem impossible for Orestes even to escape from Argos, until Apollo, appearing at the last moment as *deus ex machina*, sets everything to rights, which is to say, puts the play back on the proper mythological track.

The focus early in the play is very much on Orestes' sufferings and Electra's loving care of her brother. She recounts the troubles they have had since the killing of their mother, while Orestes sleeps in utter exhaustion from attacks of madness, or rather (as he perceives them) of Clytemnestra's Furies. When he awakes, we see direct evidence of his illness and of the mutual devotion of the siblings. The situation is desperate, since the Argives have decided to shun them entirely, and on this very day the assembly will meet to decide whether to execute them both by stoning for their mother's murder. Personal suffering thus bcomes political as well. Their only hope comes from the belated return to Argos of their uncle, Menelaos. A sympathetic Chorus of Argive women arrives to express concern, and indeed everything here conspires to make the young royals appear to be victims who deserve our sympathy.

Menelaos' appearance on the scene does not bring the hoped-for aid, since in the end he can only suggest that the people's mood may change and that he will try to aid that change with gentle persuasion; in short, he offers no help at all in these circumstances. More passionate and more disturbing, however, is the intervention of Tyndareos, Clytemnestra's father, which Euripides has devised as an interruption of the colloquy between Orestes and Menelaos. Tyndareos in no way defends his errant daughter, but insists that Orestes was wrong to murder his own mother: if nothing else, he should have had recourse to law. Here Euripides differentiates the world of his play further from that of the Aeschylean *Oresteia*, in which it is Orestes' very deed that leads to the establishment of the first court of law. The political world of Euripides' play recontextualizes Orestes' crime, but his long defense of his matricide takes no account of the difficulty this presents, nor does he do so when he defends his deed before the Argive assembly as the exemplary killing on behalf of all men of a woman who betrayed her husband.

After the condemnation to death by the Argive assembly of Orestes and Electra (the only concession being that they be allowed to kill themselves), the play takes an entirely different turn. Urged on by Pylades, Orestes decides to use his sword to kill Helen, rather than himself. As Pylades points out, it is the perfect crime: revenge against Menelaos for his refusal to help his kin, and against Helen on behalf of all the Greeks who died on her account. Electra then adds the suggestion that Helen and Menelaos' daughter Hermione

(who appeared briefly in the prologue, on her way to pour libations at Clytemnestra's tomb) be kidnapped, as a hostage against any threats from Menelaos. There follows a complex and confused sequence of events (Helen escaped, but what exactly happened doesn't come clear, despite a bizarre "messenger speech" in the form of a monody sung by a Phrygian slave in a kind of pidgin Greek as he flees the palace), at the end of which the stage and the myth are decidedly out of joint. Menelaos appears and bangs on the palace doors, which remain closed as Orestes appears on the roof, with his sword at Hermione's throat and flanked by Electra and Pylades and carrying torches. Orestes threatens to kill Hermione and burn down the palace, Menelaos orders his men to break into the palace—and then the action stops: Apollo appears *ex machina*, suspended above the roof of the palace.

Apollo ends the struggle quickly and definitively. He announces that it is he who snatched Helen from Orestes' sword at Zeus' command, for she is to become a goddess. He tells Orestes what he must do to win acquittal in Athens and adds that he will then marry Hermione, "the woman / at whose throat you hold that sword" (1721–22 / 1653–54). Pylades will marry Electra, Orestes will rule in Argos, and Menelaos in Sparta, with a new wife to replace the deified Helen, who after all gave him nothing but grief. Everything is settled in the most satisfactory way for all concerned; familial, dynastic, and political problems are solved in one spectacular *coup de théâtre*, but with none of the sense of fitness and satisfaction that accompanies the "happy end" of *Iphigenia in Tauris*. The myth has been saved, but at a moral and human cost that can only raise questions about the meaning of the rescue operation.

A scholion (ancient annotation) to Aristophanes' *Frogs* informs us that *Iphigenia at Aulis* was produced after Euripides' death by his son, along with the lost *Alcmaeon in Corinth* and the surviving *Bacchae*. Any assessment of *Iphigenia at Aulis* must come to terms with the strong possibility that it was left unfinished by Euripides and its conclusion patched together for its first, posthumous performance, or alternatively that it was transmitted in an incomplete or mutilated state and patched up later. Nevertheless, even those who do not share the confidence that George Dimock expresses in his Introduction regarding the soundness of the transmitted text, the

outline of Euripides' drama is clear. Like *Orestes*, *Iphigenia at Aulis* treats a crucial moment of the Troy saga as a kind of family drama, played out against the background of the larger world of political realities, here represented by an army on the move, the great force gathered from every corner of Greece to avenge the abduction of Helen. An angry Artemis has stalled the Greeks at Aulis, stilling the winds and denying the ships further passage until the virgin daughter of Agamemnon has been sacrificed to placate her wrath.

A characteristic feature of this drama is the number of times that its characters change their minds—or are forced to. Agamemnon, as the play begins, tells an old servant that when he learned that Artemis could only be placated by the sacrifice of his daughter, his immediate reaction was to say, then we'll all go home, but Menelaos convinced him to agree to Iphigeneia's death, and he wrote to Clytemnestra with a lying tale about betrothing their daughter to Achilles, and ordering her to come with the child. Now he has changed his mind again, and wants to send a second letter countermanding the first. And this of course will not be the final change.

Menelaos (on whose behalf the expedition had been launched) intercepts the letter and enters into a lengthy argument with his brother, who refuses to budge from his new decision. But after a messenger arrives to announce the imminent arrival of Clytemnestra with the supposed bride-to-be, Menelaos finally observes his brother's anguish and somewhat surprisingly changes his mind about the sacrifice. At this point, in a further reversal Agamemnon, though grateful for the solidarity of his brother, concludes that he no longer has a choice, since once the army hears of Artemis' demand and his broken promise, they will enforce the sacrifice whether he is willing or not. He continues the charade of the marriage until Clytemnestra, encountering Achilles, learns that he knows nothing of a marriage to her daughter, and Agamemnon's old servant reveals the terrible truth to them both. At this point, Achilles, who had originally come full of fervor for battle at Troy to express to Agamemnon his own and his troops' impatience at the long delay, decides that his honor demands resistance to the sacrifice even more than the winning of glory in battle. He, too, however, will discover that the greatest heroic valor is no match for the wrath of an entire army.

With the failure of Achilles' resistance comes the most striking and significant change of mind in the entire drama: Iphigeneia's decision no longer to plead for her life, but to embrace her death as a voluntary sacrifice, for her own glory and to permit the Greeks to show their superiority over barbarians. Aristotle criticized this change (*Poetics* 1454a31f.) on the grounds of inconsistency between the earlier and later character of the heroine, but even if we see this change of character as consonant with the shifting attitudes that characterize this play and natural enough in a young idealist facing certain death, we are left to interpret its significance. Consider two very different answers to this question: George Dimock, whose Introduction offers a coherent interpretation of the play as "Euripides' last attempt to confront his fellow-Greeks with a picture of their tragic folly" (p. 278) in pursuing the disastrous Peloponnesian War, sees Iphigeneia's reversal as a depressing act of self-deception rather than heroic self-sacrifice:

> As she leaves the stage singing a hymn to Artemis in which she pictures herself as Troy's sacker and the preserver of the freedom of Hellas from barbarian rape, we are left desolate. If even under such circumstances as we have witnessed, Iphigeneia cannot be saved, and if youthful idealism such as hers can be made to accept, as it only too evidently can, such crude jingoism as her hymn implies, hope for mankind is dim indeed.
>
> True, the play has often been read quite differently, as though Iphigeneia's unselfish adoption of her father's belated attempts to justify the war against Troy suddenly made it legitimate. But a closer look makes it hard to see how this can be. How can we forget what we so gladly welcomed in Agamemnon at the beginning of the play: his perception that it is wrong to kill his daughter in order to win a war over a worthless woman? He and his daughter have both submitted to the sacrifice on the assumption that it is a bowing to necessity, a poor second choice compared with what they know to be most desirable (p. 281).

The original publication of this translation featured a foreword by the founding editor of the series, William Arrowsmith, who begged to differ on this crucial point:

> So far as I can see, there is only one person in this play who has an instinctive and passionate intuition of freedom; that person is, unmistakably, Iphigeneia. One may regret that she decides to offer her life in order that her barbarous and slavish father may prosecute his war against the Trojans. But in a play in which bad faith is persistently displayed by those who have the power to act, the importance of Iphigeneia's assertion of freedom, while under constraint, cannot be too strongly stressed. Her death may be futile (for what can be the end of a war led by such men as Agamemnon?), but this does not diminish the

significance of the freedom she asserts. And *that* freedom, that responsibility, even that nobility (for generosity is, in Euripides, however naive, always noble), are essential not only to this corrupt society but to all human culture. Alcestis' free sacrifice of her life may be, given Admetos' character, naive; but it is, as the final epiphany of Alcestis as peer of Herakles and Orpheus shows, heroic, a free and responsible, a *noble*, confrontation with death. Whether Iphigeneia dies of her own free will or under constraint, the war against Troy will go on; for that war, *pace* Professor Dimock, she has no responsibility whatever. Her glory is that she alone asserts the hunger for freedom that is instinct in the species, until prevented by bad faith in those who govern or "lead," and especially visible in the young. In this respect she is simply the last in the long line of Euripides' self-sacrificing young people—but in the girls above all, for surely significant reasons—a line which begins with Alcestis, Makaria, Polyxena, and the others. Like the others, she *teaches* the freedom and *arete* she embodies.

Taken together, these two comments represent the poles in interpretation of Iphigeneia's change of mind, and indeed of this strong, moving, passionate play. It is up to every reader (or spectator) to decide how to understand both this crucial gesture and the drama that makes it so complex and equivocal.

The plays in this volume were originally published between 1973 and 1995. The late RICHMOND LATTIMORE was widely honored as a rare amalgam of poet, translator, and scholar. In addition to several volumes of his own verse he translated much of the surviving poetry of archaic and classical Greece. Best known, perhaps, are his *Iliad* and *Odyssey* and Aeschylus' *Oresteia*. Equally noteworthy are his translations of the major poems of Hesiod, the *Odes* of Pindar, the volume of *Greek Lyrics*, and Aristophanes' *Frogs*, which won the Bollingen Translation Prize in 1962. Most audaciously, he published his own version of *The Four Gospels and the Revelation*. The other plays of Euripides translated by Professor Lattimore are *Alcestis, Trojan Women, Helen,* and *Rhesus*. JANET LEMBKE, best known for her numerous books of essays on the natural world and the place of humans and other animals in it, is also a poet and a translator from Latin (*Bronze and Iron*, a splendid volume of fragments from early Latin poetry, and more recently Virgil's *Georgics*) and Greek. For this series she has also translated Euripides' *Hecuba* (like *Electra*, in collaboration with Kenneth Reckford) as well as two plays by Aeschylus. W. S. MERWIN is one of America's best-known and best-loved poets and an eminent translator of poetry. Over his long and prolific career, Merwin has published two dozen volumes of poetry and nearly as many of translations, as well as several prose works. His poetry has won (among many other prizes) the National Book Award in 2005 and two Pulitzers, the first in 1971, the second for the *Shadow of Sirius* in 2009. As a translator, Merwin has ranged widely, from such classics as the *Satires* of Persius, *The Song of Roland*, the *Poem of the Cid*, and Dante's *Purgatory* to works by important twentieth-century poets in at least half a dozen languages. JOHN PECK is a distinguished American poet whose learned, nuanced, and passionate work has won a devoted following and many honors. Among his books are *The Blockhouse Wall*, which won the Prix de Rome, *Poems and Translations of Hi-Lo, Argura, Selva Morale, M and Other Poems, Collected Shorter Poems, 1966–96, Red Strawberry Leaf, Collected Poems, 1994–2001*.

An equally distinguished and sensitive trio of scholars collaborated on these translations. The late GEORGE E. DIMOCK was perhaps best known for his work on the *Odyssey*, including the much admired 1956 article "The Name of Odysseus," published in *Hudson Review*, and *The Unity of the "Odyssey"* (1989), but he also wrote important essays on Euripides' *Helen* and *Hippolytus*. FRANK NISETICH is a scholar-translator of note, author of much-praised translations of two of the densest and most difficult Greek poets, Callimachus and Pindar (to whom he also devoted the monograph *Pindar and Homer*), and most recently of the complete epigrams of the newly discovered poetry book of Posidonius. KENNETH J. RECKFORD is a versatile classical scholar and one of today's subtlest, widest ranging, and most humane critics of Greek and Roman literature. Reckford's books include *Horace, Aristophanes Old and New Comedy*, and most recently *Recognizing Persius*. His other translation for this series, Euripides' *Hecuba*, was also the product of collaboration with Janet Lembke.

CONTENTS

CONTENTS

ELECTRA

Translated by

JANET LEMBKE

and

KENNETH J. RECKFORD

INTRODUCTION

A revenge play gone askew, Shakespeare's *Hamlet* has misled number-
less theatergoers, readers, and critics into seeking some definite answer
to what seemed the obvious question: why doesn't Hamlet get on with
the job? After Hamlet learns from his father's ghost how Claudius
poisoned his brother the king and stole his queen-wife (Hamlet's
mother), and after Hamlet confirms that tale by staging the play-murder
and play-seduction, all he need do is kill his uncle. Surely Elsinor will
support him, so why delay? Is it because Hamlet has a flawed character?
Is he overly intellectual and given to melancholy brooding? Or is it
because his Oedipal strivings lead him to identify unconsciously with
Claudius?

All these possibilities may be correct, for Shakespeare gives wide
scope to directors, actors, and critics to superimpose their own interpretation. But this odd tragedy of hesitation, of vengeance delayed, has other
underlying motivations. Shakespeare's Hamlet is no hothead, no
Laertes. He is a thoughtful, self-aware person in a thoughtless world.
Uneasily he finds himself cast in what might have been—in what in an
earlier period was—the typical revenge play, where the hero outwits and
kills the usurper. Hamlet rushes into nothing. He probes and tests. Very
sensibly he demands reassurances that his informant was an honest
ghost, not a tempting devil. Wisely, too, he forbears killing a villain at
his (seeming) prayers. Certainly his mind is clouded—by shock, by
sexual disturbance, and by a madness only half feigned; it only clears
in Act 5, when resolution is still outpaced by events. But he has also been
thinking all this time—about himself, about family and friends, about
Denmark, and about what Maynard Mack has called the "pervasive
inscrutability" of things. It is not just that Hamlet is unready for revenge,

3

but that, for this intelligent and sensitive hero, the call to revenge opens up a host of questions that require but do not receive a simple answer.

Euripides' *Electra*, by contrast, is a tragedy of nonhesitation. Electra, if not Orestes, is entirely decisive, and the two accomplish their business of revenge with marvelous efficiency and ease. So why does this play (much more than *Hamlet*) leave such a bitter aftertaste?

To Euripides' audience the rightness of revenge at Argos must have seemed self-evident. It had almost scriptural authority, for Zeus himself, early in the *Odyssey*, cites Aigisthos' murder of Agamemnon as a paradigm of human wrongdoing and folly. Aigisthos was warned, says Zeus, but he ignored the warning, and was rightfully killed by Orestes, Agamemnon's son and avenger. Later, indeed, Orestes' revenge is held up to Telemachus as a model of right conduct, but fortunately Penelope proves faithful, unlike Clytemnestra, and so Odysseus enjoys a paradigmatically successful Return and Revenge (with disguise, reconnoitering, and various recognitions) and order is restored to Ithaca. By contrast, Orestes' revenge evolves into guilt and pain, for in post-Homeric lyric narrative and in Attic tragedy he must kill Clytemnestra as well as Aigisthos, bringing down a mother's Furies upon himself. And yet, with Apollo's and Athena's help he is purified and acquitted of crime, and the old rule of Mycenae is restored. Few Greeks can have doubted that Orestes' revenge, albeit painful, was finally necessary and right.

But Euripides, as ever, has doubts; and he continually forces us to consider the "pervasive inscrutability" of a world in which traditional mythic assumptions about the morality of revenge are contradicted by ordinary human feeling and experience. Yet Euripides' characters lag behind their author in sensibility. Orestes hesitates before killing his mother but remains feeble and irresolute; his stronger sister drives him on, even guiding his hand in the killing stroke. Like Hamlet, Electra is impulsive and more than a little mad, but she utterly lacks Hamlet's self-awareness (which emerges, not least, in flashes of sympathy with others). Instead, her moral and spiritual nearsightedness connives with the dark side of that inscrutable universe to create new evil. It is only after the last murder that Electra's and Orestes' eyes see clearly; only then do they acknowledge their deed, asking whether Apollo's oracle may have been a voice of evil.

With Electra, as with Hamlet, reductionist explanations are tempting. We can say that Electra has a father fixation, that she has become deranged through pathological grief and isolation. "She is quite mad," we say, a forerunner of that unattractive lunatic in the Strauss–von Hofmannsthal opera. But this is to evade the issue. For Euripides, like Shakespeare, shows us a world where good and bad people alike fail, and where the moral differences are not, in the end, so very clear. There is something wrong at bottom—and not just with Argos (or with Denmark). The time is out of joint.

The crucial theme in *Hamlet* is performance. Hamlet uses a troupe of players to test court appearances. He is also aware of himself as performing a part in a play where his understanding and control of things are inadequate, and where playing, rather than clarifying life, drives him deeper into chaos. By contrast, Electra puts on a performance as though it were her very skin. Her grievances and anger have become her life. She neither reflects nor gives Orestes the necessary time to reflect. Awareness comes too late, even though (like Hamlet) this brother and sister survive for what in another world might have been a happy ending.

II

Aeschylus' *Oresteia* (458 B.C.) told the later story of the House of Atreus in three consecutive plays, as in three acts. In *Agamemnon*, that hero returns triumphant from Troy with captives and spoils. Clytemnestra dominates the play; she has laid her plans carefully; she lures her captive, Agamemnon, into the palace, where he and Cassandra are killed. When the queen, on reemerging, proclaims and defends her act over the two bodies, and Aigisthos, the weak usurper, joins her, we feel how much the moral and political order has been subverted, and we can foretell that, despite Clytemnestra's prayer, the troubles of the House will not stop here. In *Libation Bearers*, Orestes returns secretly. Aided by Electra and the Chorus, he lures Aigisthos to death, then kills Clytemnestra. Apollo ordained these killings and will stand by Orestes, even though at the play's end Orestes turns to flight, pursued by the Furies. In *Eumenides* he comes to Athens, still pursued by the Furies and defended by Apollo; and in a cosmically decisive trial with human judges, but presided over by Athena, he is acquitted of murder. After the verdict Orestes goes off and Athena appeases the Furies, who are transformed into the Eumenides, "benevolent" underworld deities.

The *Oresteia* moves through suffering to release. It offers no easy moral: "Great tragedy," as someone has said, "is closer to the altar than the pulpit"; but there is a discernable movement from complication to resolution, from division (especially male vs. female) to reconciliation, from darkness to light, and from servitude to freedom. The entanglements of the cursed House, evoked in choral song and in Cassandra's darkly visionary pronouncements, are given their full weight of tragic repetition, of crime breeding crime. It began with Tantalos, the arch-sinner, who served up his son Pelops to the gods. (Pelops was saved, only his shoulder was replaced with ivory. He grew up to seize the rich kingdom of Mycenae by fraud and violence.) Atreus, Pelops' son, struggled with his brother Thyestes for sovereignty; his unfaithful wife, Aerope, connived with Thyestes, but Atreus regained power and served up Thyestes' two older children to him at a banquet ("Thyestes' Feast"). A third son, Aigisthos, seduced Clytemnestra and joined with her to kill Agamemnon (who had incurred further guilt by sacrificing his daughter, Iphigenia, leading Greeks to die at Troy, and sacking that city's holy shrines). So when Orestes in turn stands over the two bodies, we have to ask: Will the chain of disasters ever be broken? The trilogy, through its last act, gives a positive answer. Not an easy one: for much remains unsettled, and there are hints of arbitrary violence underlying the establishment of human and divine justice; yet, at both levels, a satisfying resolution is achieved. The law court, divinely sanctioned, supplants the vendetta. The very spirits of blood-vengeance are transformed. Whether at Athens or upon Olympus, progress comes violently and painfully, but it does come.

We return to *Libation Bearers*, that second act against which Euripides' *Electra* is specifically played. The play's first movement is from mourning to recognition. Orestes enters with his faithful friend Pylades; he watches as Electra and the Chorus of servingwomen bear ritual offerings to the tomb, mourn for Agamemnon, and cry out for help and vengeance. Electra discovers signs: a lock of hair, a footprint like her brother's. Has he really come? She wavers between hope and despair; but quickly and joyfully—and with a third, finally convincing recognition-token, a piece of her weaving—Orestes reveals himself to her. He is confident of Apollo's backing but driven also by a threat of Hell—his father's Furies, if he fails to avenge him. The second movement is lyrical, intense. The Chorus, Orestes, and Electra pray to the powers of heaven, the underworld, and the dead man (his will is still potent, only needing to be aroused). Power and right, they and we feel, are on their side. Vengeance follows, with trickery. Orestes, posing as a stranger, brings a false story of his own death. Aigisthos arrives. He is directed inside and killed. Clytemnestra realizes her danger, calls for an axe (she is still dangerous), but Orestes stops her. She pleads for mercy; he hesitates; and Pylades, heretofore silent, urges him on in three tremendous verses that might have been spoken by Apollo himself. Orestes drags Clytemnestra inside, to kill her. Now the Chorus celebrates. "Justice guided his hand." "Now we can see the light." Orestes comes out, displays the two bodies, and reaffirms the justice of his actions, guided by Apollo. As he departs, pursued by the Furies, for Delphi and

Athens, the Chorus awards him final praise—though it also asks, "Where will it end?"

Taken in isolation, *Libation Bearers* is an exercise in fear. We keep watch in the shadow of one murder, waiting, like Clytemnestra, for another. Old anger exacts new vengeance with almost ritual precision. It is harsh and frightening, and we sense more suffering to come; but Aeschylus allows little doubt about the necessity of Orestes' act. Apollo ordained it; Apollo will see the process through. And retributive justice (*dikē*), once completed, will restore the light of freedom to Argos. The Chorus is reassured and reassuring. Electra, a sympathetic figure, leaves the stage midway. All Orestes need do is act, suffer, and endure. Neither he nor his acts of killing are finally isolated; all signs point to a larger pattern of meaning, and of redemption. In Euripides' *Electra* things will seem less clear.

III

As a single play, Euripides' *Electra* isolates the killing of Aigisthos and Clytemnestra from any larger, Aeschylean development. We are not shown their past wrongdoings at firsthand, nor do we watch as powerful deities negotiate a more promising future. The action is entirely human until the epilogue. As in Aeschylus' *Libation Bearers* (though not in Sophocles' *Electra*), it builds to the emotionally more disturbing murder of Clytemnestra; but Euripides gives Electra a large share in this killing, somewhat replaying the earlier Clytemnestra and isolating for us the merely human question: What sort of persons, and in what frame of mind, would kill their mother?

But first, a surprise. The scene is shifted: away from palace and tomb, into a pleasant country setting among distant hills. The prologue introducing the play's first movement (1–447 / 1–431) gives largely familiar mythic background, but with a twist: it is delivered by the Farmer to whom Electra has been married off in order to make her potential offspring ineffective. The rural setting conveys Electra's double isolation, of body (she considers this exile) and of spirit. Her life is unnatural. She is a princess turned farmer's wife, a maiden married in name only. At the same time, the somewhat idealized ordinariness of country life—here represented by the decent, gentle-natured Farmer, the Chorus of cheerful young women of the neighborhood, and (later in the play) a faithful old retainer—shows up with irony and humor every false note in the world of tragic heroics that Electra constantly invokes. Aeschylean conventions that once supported high tragedy now prove impotent. The old revenge plot forfeits its accustomed nobility, its basic rightness. What remains is altogether perverse.

In *Hamlet* the hero's suit of inky black, though incongruous at the bright court, was justified. It was the others who had, too quickly, forgotten the dead. Hamlet's performance rings true, as theirs does not. By contrast, as we watch Electra's act with cropped hair and water-jar on head and as we hear her voice her grievances, we come to feel, together with the patient Farmer, that this has been going on for years. It all belongs, so to speak, in some tragic opera—not here in the beneficent countryside. As the Farmer points out, with very gentle irony, Electra need not draw water on his account: they do have help; and if she insists—well, it isn't very far to the spring, anyway. And then there are those friendly young women who invite Electra to join them in celebrating Hera's festival. Her refusal, her insistence on mourning, might seem understandable, even after all those years; but when she relapses into complaints ("I *never* go out, I *never* have anything to wear. If I didn't make all my own clothes, I would go *naked!*"), we cannot help remembering how the Chorus offered to lend her party dresses and jewelry a few minutes earlier. Her isolation from society, even from the gods, is partly of her own making.

Orestes, too, seems out of place in this quiet setting. His business should have been at the palace. He is not the strong Aeschylean hero, moving prudently, steadily, and confidently toward his divinely ordained goal; still less is he the swan-knight of Electra's dreams who will return to rescue her from all this. "My courageous brother," she will say indignantly, would never "crawl here in secret" for fear of Aigisthos—but that is exactly what Orestes has done. From the first, he is timid, indecisive. He is prepared to skip across the border if things go badly. On seeing the "slave girl" he panics. Even after eavesdropping and discovering that she is Electra, he still hesitates for an intolerably long time, telling her a false story, and saying things like "Oh, dear" and "What would Orestes say?" as she goes through her Cinderella performance. When the Farmer returns, his straightforward hospitality shows up Orestes by contrast as a snobbish, patronizing young aristocrat who, underneath all those pseudosophisticated comments on true nobility, may be deeply insecure. Orestes goes on and on, playing for time. By contrast, the Farmer exhibits a gentleman's naturalness and ease, even when, in a very funny scene, Electra scolds him for inviting important people to dinner when he knows they don't have enough food.

Both sister and brother play a self-conscious part. Electra, especially, plays to the gallery: to the gods, to show how much she is mistreated; to the "absent" Orestes, to convey how greatly Agamemnon and his chil-

dren are abused. And Orestes, though less intelligent, is also disingenu-
ous. In a deeper sense, neither one is self-aware. Each is caught up in a
performance that, in this country setting, must seem unnatural and
artificial. The dissonance is often comic; there is more laughter to
come. It undercuts our expected sympathy with this tragic pair.
More important, it helps Euripides distort the revenge plot into something unnatural and evil. At the same time, it relaxes our minds and
sensibilities, much as Shakespeare's lighter scenes can do, so that we are
caught off guard when, finally, the kitchen knife is set to the victim's
throat.

IV

The second movement of *Electra* (448–903 / 432–872) carries us through
a happy recognition and a successful act of revenge, each culminating in
a high moment of hope and joy.

After a choral ode pits mythic good against evil, culminating in the
prophetic threat that Clytemnestra will pay in blood for her evildoing,
the Old Man's entrance starts a comic scene. His ordinariness, his slow
climb, his presents of food and drink, including a lamb, return us to that
cheerful, relaxed mood in which high tragedy must seem misplaced.
(This lamb will contrast wonderfully with the Golden Lamb, legendary
emblem of rivalry, seduction, and murder.) A hilarious failure of Aeschylean recognition-tokens follows. The lock of hair, the footprint, the
piece of child's weaving—all are demolished scornfully by Electra, who
is well armored against false hope; but then the Old Man sees the scar on
Orestes' forehead and reveals his identity. We might wonder why Electra
never noticed it. Perhaps she was preoccupied. Or we might think of
Homer, of the scar on Odysseus' thigh that gives him away to the nurse,
and almost to Penelope. It was inflicted by a wild boar, in Odysseus'
adolescent *rite de passage*. (The Homeric echo goes with many others,
such as Odysseus' stay with the good swineherd before he comes to the
palace, to kill the suitors.) But where did Orestes' scar come from? He
fell, chasing a pet deer around the yard. It all seems rather silly. Orestes is
no Odysseus. Nor is he the gleaming savior of Electra's dreams.

Their reunion is nonetheless joyful, a high moment marked by
embraces and by choral dance and song. But it is brief. Orestes turns
quickly to planning revenge. How to attack Aigisthos? The diffident hero
is easily discouraged by obstacles ("You can't even get *near* the palace!").
He snatches eagerly at the Old Man's suggestion that he catch Aigisthos
in the open, at sacrifice. With stronger determination and a power of
command ironically reminiscent of the Aeschylean Clytemnestra, Electra announces that *she* will deal with her mother. It will be easy to trap

9

and kill her, playing on her pity. After brief prayers (they will seem perfunctory, indeed, to anyone who recalls the great invocation scene in Aeschylus), the troops depart. Electra proclaims "Victory or Death." With a sure sense of melodrama, she will hold a sword in readiness against bad news.

The intervening time is marked by a second choral ode, less bright and happy this time: the crimes of the House, centering on that Golden Lamb, culminate in Clytemnestra's murder of Agamemnon. Even as they sing, the treacherous Aigisthos is being killed by Orestes. And what a killing it is! The messenger's report is a masterpiece of black humor. Even Aigisthos, it seems, is not like Aigisthos: we never see him for ourselves, but he is described as an amiable, easygoing person who, on seeing the strangers, quickly invites them to join in the sacrifice and feast. (Agamemnon, in Homer's version, was slaughtered at a feast.) We may be deceived; that smiling villain, Claudius, could be genial, too. Still, the abuse of hospitality is unsettling; and, still more, the perversion of sacrificial ritual. Hamlet had better intentions when he declined to kill Claudius at his prayers. Orestes has no such scruples; it is enough for him to keep his hands unwashed. Invited to show his skill with the cleaver, he smashes it down (attacking from the rear, of course) through his host's backbone. It all works splendidly, and without time for reflection, we are caught up in the general mood of celebration as the Chorus proclaims victory, joy, and hope. It is the last happy moment in the play.

V

The third and climactic movement of *Electra* (904–1276 / 873–1232) begins with a moral descent. Orestes and Pylades enter, to be crowned with wreaths like victorious athletes; and before we know it, Electra is insulting Aigisthos' corpse. However justified her hatred, this is clearly hubris, on a par with Aigisthos' insults to Agamemnon's tomb reported earlier. Even the Chorus seems uneasy, although it reaffirms the justice of this revenge. Victory is losing its moral luster. And then, appropriately, Clytemnestra is sighted, and Orestes asks in panic, "What should we do? Must we kill our mother?"

This is (differently from Aeschylus' staged confrontation of Orestes and Clytemnestra) the decisive scene. We feel the pressures. Orestes knows what a mother is; he cries out that Apollo's bidding must be wrong. (Is it "a damned ghost that we have seen?") What forces him on is not Pylades this time, speaking awesomely for the god, but Electra's iron will. She feels no qualms, parries every objection. We sense the tension within her: to hesitate now is to lose everything. Her final, most effective appeal is to Orestes' manhood. Ironically, he is overborne by a woman—precisely as Aigisthos had been (in Electra's own contemptuous words). Orestes gives in, although, as he says, killing is no longer sport. He goes in, to await his second victim.

A fanfare of trumpets, and Clytemnestra enters in her carriage with a rich entourage. (Today it would be a long black chauffeured limousine.) Although the scene echoes that other famous scene of Agamemnon's return and moral entrapment, we are meant to see what Electra cannot, that Clytemnestra is a person, a woman who has aged and weakened and may even feel remorse. (Impressions are subjective, but we were told earlier, in the prologue, that she once saved Electra's life.) All the same, the lady protests too much. Her overrehearsed arguments seem unconvincing: how Agamemnon killed Iphigenia in a bad cause; how he brought a mistress, Cassandra, home with him. She even tries humor, appeals to female solidarity against irresponsible males. But Electra has taken on her mother's earlier hardness. Her rebuttal (surely also much rehearsed) is cold, sarcastic, brilliantly effective. She strips away her mother's pretenses, to reveal the shameful adulteress, destroyer of family bonds. Yet her intense anger is there, and once she almost gives away the game:

> ...And if blood
> calls for blood in the name of Justice, I will kill you—
> I and your son Orestes—to avenge our father.
>
> (*stepping back*)
>
> If death was just there, here it is also just.
> (1130–33 / 1093–96)

At the last moment she covers her tracks with commonplaces.

We might (if we listened thoughtfully) be surprised when Clytemnestra answers with soft words. Her forbearance, her genuine sorrow, might even lead us to see her as a person, to ask why, after all, she must be killed. But Electra refuses to listen, or to look. "Too late to lament. There's no cure now" (1146 / 1111). She forces a quarrel, angers her mother, and makes her hurry inside—Clytemnestra now wanting, with understandable impatience, to be done with this wretched scene and (more irony here) to rejoin her husband at the sacrifice.

So she goes in. Electra follows. And Clytemnestra is killed, very quickly, even while the Chorus recalls the killing of Agamemnon and asserts once more that justice has been carried out. But when the killers reappear, spattered with blood, everyone sees what has happened as though for the first time. Orestes foresees an exile, Electra an isolation, far worse than before. They see, and lead us to imagine, the killing as it really happened: Clytemnestra's plea; Orestes' driving his sword through her living flesh, in a horrible parody of Perseus and the Gorgon; Electra's guiding his hand. "Too late to lament," Electra had said. "There's no cure now." With sorrow and respect, they cover the body; and Electra asks (we have a sense of déjà vu) that the ills of the House end here.

VI

We may ask, at this moment of retrospection just before the epilogue, how the actions, songs, and judgments of the Chorus should themselves be judged. Have these sympathetic young women become accomplices, even cheerleaders, in the actions of revenge? They have helped lure the last victim and have helped justify (and obscure) new killings by keeping old ones before our eyes. To put it simply, they believe that they are living in an Aeschylean world where *dikē* (justice, payment for wrongdoing, satisfaction rendered) is gradually reinstituted under the supervision of heaven. Even after Electra abuses Aigisthos' corpse, they perceive his dreadful fate as balancing his dreadful deeds. So, too, they invoke measure for measure as Clytemnestra is killed. Only afterward does their judgment shift (like ours?), and only in part: to decry the ongoing misery of the House and to blame Electra, as she now blames herself, for the evil she willed earlier and for her dreadful compulsion of her brother.

Our imagination, like that of the Chorus, has traveled far since that first lovely ode with Achilles' ships escorted to Troy by leaping dolphins and dancing Nereids; with Chiron, the good centaur, who nurtured that prince of heroes; with the blazing sun and dancing stars, emblems of brilliance and cosmic order, at the center of Achilles' shield; and with depictions of legendary combats, Perseus and the Gorgon, Bellerophon (on Pegasus) and the Chimaera. In this familiar world of bright heroes slaying monsters killing is easily justified, and the Chorus looks forward confidently to a time when the avenging sword of justice will let blood from Clytemnestra's throat.

On closer inspection, recent critics have argued, the ode betrays hints of latent violence and of the dusty death to which even great Homeric heroes come. What matters more is our growing sense of a discrepancy between the traditional, somewhat romanticized world of heroic legend and the quite ordinary life of the Argive uplands where Electra and now Orestes find themselves. The contrast makes for surprise and laughter. It may also shock an audience into facing human realities. In legend Perseus' killing of the Gorgon Medusa was a victory of humanity, backed by bright gods, over dark and monstrous evil. Accordingly, in Aeschylus' *Libation Bearers*, the Chorus urges the unseen Orestes to "hold the heart of Perseus in your bosom" and to kill Clytemnestra blamelessly, as one might a "loathsome Gorgon" (827–37). But in Euripides' play, after Orestes (aided by Electra) kills Clytemnestra in the manner of Perseus, holding a cloak before his eyes as he stabs her flesh, the difference between slaying a monster and murdering one's mother becomes appallingly clear.

In the second choral ode (724–71 / 699–46), myth approaches history. Once again Euripides begins with images of loveliness, of music and pastoral beauty; but the Golden Lamb, emblem of sovereignty, soon becomes a symbol of deception, violence, and cruel revenge—of wrong breeding wrong. Thyestes' seduction of Atreus' wife Aerope, his deceitful seizure of power, foreshadow Aigisthos' seduction of Clytemnestra and their murder of Agamemnon; Thyestes' horrific fall (not here detailed) should have been a lesson to Clytemnestra, had she "remembered." But memories are selective. So are interpretations of myth, and of history. Even as the Chorus sings of justice rendered, its own interpretation of things is selective and misleading; and so, perhaps, is ours.

When Zeus, in this second ode, turned back the sun, was he confirming Atreus' rule despite the stolen lamb? Or was he proclaiming universal horror at the escalation of evil, the unnaturalness of "Thyestes' Feast?" We do not know. The Chorus, less naive than earlier, professes skepticism. Still, it seems more than ordinarily portentous when the sun, that fixed center of brightness and order, alters his course. The world is changed and, in this version, changed forever. Which is to say, that the time in which the Chorus sings, and in which we live, is still, radically, out of joint; and there is little chance that further killing in the name of justice will set it right.

VII

Although the stage is thick with corpses at the end of *Hamlet*, the ending brings some consolation, some promise of order. Horatio will live to report Hamlet's story aright. Fortinbras proclaims his nobility. There is a suggestion that, with the usurper dead, the poisonous corruption of Denmark has been expelled; perhaps Hamlet served as sacrificial victim so that the state might return to normality and health. The cannons shot off now to honor the dead prince, not to amuse a drunken usurper, seem finally reassuring.

The epilogue of *Electra*, by contrast, is intentionally somewhat lame. Certainly, the Dioskouroi mean well. Castor, their spokesman, tries to bring us back into an Aeschylean world of meaning and resolution, and even to provide a happy ending all around; but his effort somewhat miscarries, raising more questions than it solves. Castor gives the impression of a decent but minor figure in the heavenly bureaucracy who, although disapproving privately, cannot criticize the misjudgments of his superior, Apollo, in public. Needless to say, nothing like a convincing Aeschylean theodicy is forthcoming.

Certainly, Castor tries. He tells how Orestes, pursued by the Furies, will travel to Delphi for purification and to Athens for acquittal (which is familiar and Aeschylean); how Electra will marry Pylades; how the Farmer will be rewarded. But where are the civic and cosmic solutions, so familiar from Aeschylus? There is no suggestion that Orestes will return to Argos, that the old political order (did it ever exist?) will be restored. As for divinity: the Furies must be subdued in this version, not appeased; nor is it reassuring to learn of Zeus only that he planned the Trojan War to solve the population problem. That Helen is absolved of guilt (for human beings may be pardoned their blind actions in an irrational world) seems less than consoling.

All Castor wants is to finish his prepared speech on an upbeat note of promised happiness and release from toil (1284–337 / 1238–91), and then, not waiting for questions, to move on to the next crisis on the Sicilian Sea. He does not get off so easily. First Orestes and then Electra pose unanswerable questions. Why all this horror? Why couldn't the Dioskouroi have helped their sister Clytemnestra? It was Apollo, says Castor, and fate, and the accumulated disasters of the House of Atreus binding their victims in common misfortune. Whether or not they accept these answers, the human actors now turn to each other one last time to share their sorrow and their love. What awaits them is pain, separation, and unending exile. Castor looks on with pity, too, even though he closes on a new authoritative note: The good are rewarded by heaven; the bad are left to their misery. The Chorus comments on this in the play's last words: happy the life that does not sink beneath misfortune.

What are we left with, finally, when the actors and Chorus have departed? With less reassurance, surely, than at the end of *Hamlet* when the cannons shoot. For we have not, despite Castor's valiant efforts, been restored to that Aeschylean world where patterns of meaning, growth, and justice can be discerned behind human suffering, and where the order, not just of the polis but of the very gods, evolves over time and space. But neither are we in the world of Sophocles, where heroes and heroines struggle with intolerable loneliness and pain, yet achieve final nobility and worth, and sometimes even victory, through endurance and the paradoxical connivance of amoral gods. The heroine of Sophocles' *Electra* is difficult (like Antigone) but thoroughly admirable. She endures; she rejects oppression and helplessness; she will act, if only by herself—but Orestes, who counterfeited his own death, has returned alive to kill Clytemnestra and Aigisthos (in that order; the agony is not here, but in Electra's prolonged horror of loneliness and despair). Perhaps—we do not know—Sophocles' play came first. If so, Euripides wrote against *two* predecessors, degrading Sophocles' heroine while restressing, more finally than Aeschylus, the evil of matricide. Or perhaps Sophocles wrote last, to vindicate human nobility (as ever) under extreme pressure. Whatever the order, the contrast remains impressive: between the integrity of heroism in Sophocles, which challenges us to become greater than we are, and the disintegration, the sheer vulnerability of character and human life in Euripides, who insists on our basic helplessness to do anything lastingly great or good.

What Euripides leaves us with is compassion, the keener for lost reassurances. We learn to pity not just Agamemnon's mistreated children but also the ruinous adulterers, killers, and usurpers. This is not to forget that Aigisthos and Clytemnestra are dangerous still. They set their spies, hold Electra suspect, and would kill Orestes if they caught him returning to Argos. But more than that, they are vulnerable, like ourselves. Their flesh is weak, and their blood, once shed like an animal's, cannot be recalled. In the end, the common fate of mortals unites them beyond the passing distinctions of good and bad, noble and base, right and wrong.

It remains true that the pity evoked by our shared humanity can be ineffective, delusory, or positively dangerous as a guide to action, especially when it comes too late, as it so often does in Euripides' plays. Electra especially uses pity as a weapon: to spur Orestes on, to lure Clytemnestra to her doom. And when Orestes speaks of the heightened sensitivity from which uncommon people like himself must necessarily suffer—

> Harsh words. My god, how just hearing of miseries
> endured by others can sink sharp teeth into a man....
> Pity, impossible for lowborn brutes, comes
> only to those who inherit noble feelings.
> But even they pay dearly to scruple overmuch.
> (302–3 / 290–91, 306–8 / 294–96)

We might reflect, if we had time, not just that Orestes' talk rings hollow, but that the world's wrongs might not be healed even today by that heightened sense of compassion that Euripidean tragedy still evokes in educated people like ourselves. It never was easy to do good.

Nevertheless, the ending of *Electra* speaks powerfully for the importance of pity, if not for its everyday efficacy. For even if the Dioskouroi arrive late and accomplish little, they still bring with them some heavenly brightness, and some binding up of wounds; and it is no small consolation that the gods themselves feel pity, not scorn, for human suffering;

> Pain, such pain in your words that even
> gods hear its anguish.
> I and my heavenly kind know
> pity for men who must suffer and die.
> (1374–77 / 1327–30)

Castor's Olympian perspective briefly suggests what Euripides' spectators might have felt, or might have been meant to feel, as they looked down from their benches in the theater of Dionysos on the victims turned killers and the killers turned victims. And perhaps, from out of the anger and hatred, the bitterness and sharp divisions of war-torn Athens, they might momentarily have imagined what it would have been like to live in a kinder, happier world, where the ordinary gifts of life such as wine, cheese, lamb, and flowers shine with new beauty, and where, in Virgil's later words (and he was much influenced by Euripides) "there are tears for things, and the common fate of men touches the heart" (*sunt lacrimae rerum et mentem mortalia tangunt*).

JANET LEMBKE
KENNETH J. RECKFORD

ON THE TRANSLATION

Pleasure and pain kissed: for Euripides' audience, as it was brought through a "pleasure of many tears" (*polydakryn hadonan*) by the playwright's art; and again, just now, for ourselves as translators. To read Euripides closely means to become increasingly aware of the fragility of human life, and of the human spirit. But we also experienced what is too easily forgotten, the sheer excitement of the play as a play—its pace, surprises, and musicality, its sureness of artistic construction and effect—as we rehearsed Greek verses back and forth in the summer greenness of Chapel Hill or on a porch, refreshed by the sea breeze, in Beaufort, North Carolina.

It is never easy for *readers* to catch Euripides' interplay of joy and pain. When, for example, the Chorus invites Electra to Hera's festival, the joyful rhythms of the many-voiced invitation bring out, by contrast, Electra's stark isolation, and her refusal in turn recalls the real possibility of human happiness from which she feels forever excluded. Or again: the beauty and joy of the "Nereid" lyrics is not just delusory, not just a foil to everyday unhappiness and failure. Joy is as real as pain. Knowledge of joy, or of the possibility of joy, enhances our sympathy for suffering and misfortune, even the extreme wretchedness into which Euripides' heroines and heroes are so regularly cast.

Our shared sense, as translators, of the pace, structure, and impact of *Electra* has been reinforced greatly by two dramatic readings: first, by Theater Wagon of Staunton, Virginia, in August 1986, directed by Rick Hite and produced in the generously theatrical house of Margaret and Fletcher Collins; and, second, by the UNC Playmakers of Chapel Hill, directed by David Hammond, in January 1987. A good dramatic reading opens one's eyes—and ears and feelings—to much. This is not to argue that modern recreations can *prove* anything about ancient plays. We could not prove (to take a difficult problem) that Aigisthos' head was separated from his body—though it *works*. But we did see things that the casual reader ignores, like the stage presence of the silent, sinister, masked Pylades accompanying Orestes, and the way he is echoed by the silent, masked Pollux accompanying Castor in the epilogue. Much, too, that we had sensed in the reading emerged strongly and clearly in performance: Orestes' athletic handsomeness; Electra's edge of hysteria; the Farmer's quiet dignity and humor, shared with the audience in an easy, familiar way; the broad comedy of the scene when the Old Man prowls around Orestes, peering at him, to his great disquiet; the *still* audible shock of the audience when Electra calls her mother a slut. We could go on. But, above all, these dramatic readings confirmed and enhanced our impression of how the play *moves*, in two senses. For Euripides takes us rapidly and masterfully through numerous quick scenes of wide-ranging contrasts, which not only surprise but also throw us constantly off balance; and we, the translators, who knew what was coming, felt silenced and shocked as much as the others by the killing of Clytemnestra when it came, and by the grief, the remorse, and the universal feeling of human pain in the last scenes. It is, even more than we realized, an extremely disturbing play.

What is also remarkable is how not just the sedentary translators but the directors and actors felt that they were in the hands of a master. We remember, admiringly, that Euripides was more than a playwright. He was director, producer, choreographer, and musical director. It takes many hands to do the job today, and our usual failure to recreate the singing, dancing, and music of *Electra*, as of other Greek tragedies, inevitably results in a considerable loss of pleasure, balance, and overall effectiveness.

It remains to give thanks. Our explorations of *Electra* were eased by James Diggle's fine 1981 Oxford Classical Text of Euripides, volume 2, which we mainly follow; by the still invaluable 1939 commentary of J. D. Denniston; by many outstanding articles and chapters on *Electra*;[1] and by the advice and encouragement of John Herington and David Kovacs. Gifted graduate students at Chapel Hill joined us in attacking textual and interpretive problems. We are grateful, too, for the watchful care of our twin editors, William Arrowsmith and Herbert Golder, as they continue to protect "Greek Tragedy in New Translations" from untimely shipwreck.

A longer debt is to our spouses, who stood by us and encouraged us through this enterprise, and sometimes made fun of us. To Adrian Stanley and to the memory of Mary Reckford, we dedicate this translation.

J.L.

K.J.R.

1. We single out as especially helpful the work of James Halporn, Katherine King, Masaaki Kubo, Michael O'Brien, Friedrich Solmsen, George Walsh, and Froma Zeitlin. Ann Michelini's *Euripides and the Tragic Tradition* (1987) includes the best chapter on *Electra* we have seen.

A NOTE ON STAGING

The scene shows a farmhouse, with perhaps a statue of Apollo in front of it and an altar. It is a poor, isolated farm in the uplands. No clear stage directions are given for the many places of offstage action mentioned in the text, which include:

the Farmer's fields
a spring
Orestes' country of exile (= Pylades' homeland)
Agamemnon's tomb
the city of Argos
the Old Man's encampment
fields where Aigisthos sacrifices to the Nymphs
a barn in which Clytemnestra's horses are stabled
Athens

Let the Farmer's fields lie in the one direction, stage left. Then the spring will lie in the other direction (stage right); and so, further on, will Aigisthos' fields, Agamemnon's tomb, and the great town of Mycenae on the Argive plain (which Euripides rather casually identifies with the modern town of Argos). Orestes and the Old Man enter from the same direction as the tomb, which lies well outside the town. Orestes will depart for Athens in the opposite direction from which he came.

J.L.
K.J.R.

ELECTRA

Translated by

JANET LEMBKE

and

KENNETH J. RECKFORD

CHARACTERS

FARMER   Electra's husband

ELECTRA

ORESTES   Electra's brother

PYLADES   a mute character, Orestes' friend and son of Orestes' protector Strophios

CHORUS   of young, unmarried peasant women

OLD MAN   former tutor to Agamemnon

MESSENGER   Orestes' servant

CLYTEMNESTRA   mother of Electra and Orestes, widow of Agamemnon

THE DIOSKOUROI   Castor and Polydeukes, sons of Zeus, brothers of Clytemnestra

Servants to the Farmer
Men attending Orestes and Pylades
Trojan slave women attending Clytemnestra

Line numbers in the right-hand margin of the text refer to the English translation only, and the Notes beginning at page 75 are keyed to these lines. The bracketed line numbers in the running heads refer to the Greek text.

A farm in the mountain of Argos. In the background center, a small farmhouse.

The FARMER *enters from the farmhouse.*

FARMER Age-old valley of my shining land, how your rivers
gleamed as they saw war launched in a thousand ships
when Lord Agamemnon sailed against Troy.
And after he'd killed Troy's ruler, Priam,
and burnt and leveled that famous city,
he came back to Argos to hang many spoils
seized from those barbarians high on our temple walls.
Away from home he found good luck, but in his own house
he was killed by Clytemnestra's treachery
and the hand of Thyestes' son Aigisthos.   10

A long line of kingship was broken when he died.
Now Aigisthos wears the country's crown
and holds both Agamemnon's scepter and his wife.
When the king sailed for Troy, he left at home
the baby Orestes and his little girl Electra.
Orestes would have died by Aigisthos' hand,
but his father's old tutor smuggled him away
and gave him to Strophios in the north for protection.
Electra stayed in her father's house.
When her youth reached its flower,   20
the foremost young men of Greece came courting.
But, terrified that she'd bear princely sons
to avenge Agamemnon, he held her under house arrest,
Aigisthos did; and denied her any marriage.

Yet, when he planned to kill her out of great fear
that she might take a highborn lover in secret
and bear him sons, her mother—a savage woman—
did save her from Aigisthos' hand. Reason is,
Clytemnestra had excuses for her husband's death
but dreaded blame for murdering her children.   30
Aigisthos answered with a new design:
by public decree he offered gold to the man

23

who'd kill Agamemnon's fugitive son.
Then he gave me young Electra to have
as my wife. My forefathers, Mycenean, highborn—
in them I can't be faulted, for my lineage
shines though we never had much money, a fact
that puts paid to the benefits of noble birth.
So, to sap the power of his fear, he gave her
    to me, a powerless man.   40
You see, if she'd married someone of position, he
    would have
waked Agamemnon's murder from its sleep, and then
Aigisthos would have paid the penalty.
Yet I never—Aphrodite, bear me witness—
never shamed Electra's bed. She is still a virgin.
It would shame me, a man born poor,
to do such outrage to any rich man's girl.
It hurts to think that my kin in name only,
Orestes the exile, might come back to Argos
and find his unlucky sister married to me.   50

But anyone who says I'm foolish—receiving
a virgin in my house but not once touching her—
uses a worthless standard to take the measure
of self-control, and he's the fool.

        ELECTRA, *bearing a water-jar on her head, enters*
                           from the farmhouse.

ELECTRA Black night, brood-nurse of golden stars,
        wrapped in your darkness I walk bearing this jar
        to draw fresh water from the spring,
        but not because need bends me to such menial work.
        No! I'd show the gods how Aigisthos insults me.
        And I cry my grief through wide air to my father.   60
        Listen! Tyndareos' daughter—my mother
            who spoils all she touches—
        drove me from home and heritage to please her new
        husband. She slept beside him, bore him other children.
        She casts Orestes and me from our own house.

FARMER   My poor lady, why wear yourself out for me?
         You weren't brought up for heavy labor.
         Why not listen when I tell you let it be?

ELECTRA You are a friend I respect as I do the gods,
         for in my troubles you have not once mocked me.   70
         What providence for anyone beset by ills
         to find a healing comfort such as you.
         So, at no one's bidding, I *must* use my strength
         to make your labors lighter, easier, and share
         the work. You have more than enough to do
         out there in the fields. Keeping house is my domain.
         And when a working man comes in at dusk,
         he likes to find order and his supper ready.

FARMER   Go then, if that's what you want. The spring's not far.
         Soon as daylight comes, I'll yoke the oxen,   80
         drive them to the fields, and get on with planting.
         No man can keep himself alive by mouthing
         idle prayers to the gods. It takes hard work.

         ELECTRA *and the* FARMER *exeunt to spring and fields,*
                                         respectively.

         ORESTES *and* PYLADES *enter with their attendants.*

ORESTES Pylades, you are the one man on this earth
         I count as loyal—my friend, my host. You alone,
         of all my friends, continued to admire me
         when I suffered, as I still do, from the deadly
         acts of my father's killer and my mother
              who spoils all she touches.
         Now I come from Apollo's oracle at Delphi.   90
         He ordered me home, where no one suspects my presence,
         to exchange murder for my father's murder.
         So, last night I went to my father's tomb,
         wept, offered a fresh-clipped lock of hair,
         and cut a sheep's throat over the altar,
         all without being caught by those who lord it here.

25

Nor do I mean to set foot inside city walls.
Two goals, clear in sight, keep me near the border—
one, swift access to a safer country
if some king's man should spy me out;   100
the second, finding my sister—they say she lives
married to someone, she's no longer maiden.
I'd plan and work revenge with her, and through her
learn exactly what goes on inside those walls.

Sun's coming up—time to change course and leave
this path well used by daytime travelers.
Some man off ploughing his fields, some housemaid
at her errands might be able to tell us
if my sister lives anywhere near.

Look, here comes a servant,   110
jar of water on her shorn head—
somebody's slave. Pylades, let's find
a place to sit. We may overhear some
answers to the questions that brought me home.

> ORESTES, PYLADES, *and their attendants conceal*
> *themselves to eavesdrop.*

> ELECTRA *enters bearing a jar of water on her head and*
> *keening.*

ELECTRA *(singing and dancing)*
Speed your step, season I wait for, O
come quickly, come wailing, come howling grief!
    Come now, now!
I was fathered by Agamemnon,
born to a queen, Clytemnestra,
a woman inviting hate.   120
Now citizens add "poor thing"
to Electra's name.
Cruel, how cruel my troubles!
How hateful my life!
Father who lies in death's darkness

26

your wife and Aigisthos made you their sacrifice—
    O Agamemnon.

Come, raise the dirge from its ghostworld.
Lead into light the pleasure of tears.

Speed your step, season I wait for, O   130
come quickly, come wailing, come howling grief!
    Come now, now!
City or household—where
has wandering led you, poor brother,
leaving a grief-stricken sister
locked fast in the women's rooms
of her father's house?
Return, put an end to my troubles,
release me from grief.
God, O God, stop your wandering. Come home   140
to Argos, to our murdered father's blood.
    Help me avenge him.

ELECTRA *takes the water-jar from her head and puts it on*
the ground. As she sings and dances, she enacts the ges-
tures of mourning mentioned.

Down with this weight that I carry, for only
at dawn can I cry out the dirges
    that catch in my throat night-long.
Wailing, words, the full music of death—
Father, to you in the dark earth
all of my body sings dirges.
Day after day I offer
tears pouring out and fingernails   150
raking my cheeks till they bleed,
hands gripping a head shorn of hair
    because you are dead.

(*beating her head*)

    Drum, my hands, drum!
And as a cygnet

stranded by a river
keeps rasping its calls to the father it loves
trapped and lifeless in treacherous mesh,
so I keep crying, crying out to you,
    poor Father,   160

caught by surprise as you bathed, your body
now cold within death's earthen bed.
    And my cries find no rest.
Sharp the axe-blade that cut you, and sharp,
Father, the schemes that were laid
while you journeyed from Troy.
Your welcome home, no laurels,
no crown, but a sword's double edge
and your wife designing the crime
that she helped Aigisthos commit   170
    so he'd lie in her bed.

       The CHORUS *enters singing and dancing joyfully.*

CHORUS (*severally*)—Daughter of Agamemnon,
    Electra, I've run all the way
    to your home in the wild hills.

    —A man came, a man who drinks milk for wine
    came with his herd through these mountains.

    —He tells of a proclamation.

    —Three days from now, the festal sacrifice
    at Hera's temple.

              —All would-be brides   180
    are asked to celebrate her holy rites.

ELECTRA (*singing*) No longer, my friends, do I go forth
    lighthearted, dressed in gleaming robes
    and necklaces of gold.
    In my sorrow I cannot lead

the songs of your bridal choir
nor step with you lightly in circling dance.
In tears I spend my nights.
Day after day the tears
come streaming from swollen eyes.   190
Look at me—raw stubble on my head,
my robe more holes than cloth.
Are such things fit for Agamemnon's
royal daughter? Fit for my father
whom Troy remembers well
as the man who brought her low?

CHORUS (*severally*)—The goddess works wonders. Come.

—Borrow the fine things you need. Please
let me lend you a soft cloak.

—A robe.   200

          —Gold to make everything gleam.

—Your tears do not honor the gods.
Do you think that tears can defeat
your enemies?

          —Worship the gods
with prayers, not wails, and then
you shall know brighter days.

ELECTRA No god gives heed to my battle cries.
Heaven disdains me and has long forgot
my father's sacrifice,   210
though I wail for the dead and wail
for one alive, the wanderer
who somewhere in a strange land
discovers warmth and rest
only at peasants' fires—
and he the son of a far-famed king.
And I must live in a poor man's house,
my spirit wearing thin,
exiled from home and heritage

to mountain crags while my mother   220
settles a new mate
in her murder-bloodied bed.

CHORUS LEADER (*speaking*)
For bringing evil days to Greece and to your house,
your mother's sister Helen bears the blame.

ELECTRA (speaking)
Oh look! No time for more tears.
Women, look—strangers near the house,
men ready for ambush. Quick!
Run down that path. I'll slip inside.
Give them no chance to rob or rape us.

> ORESTES, PYLADES, *and their attendants emerge from*
> *hiding.*

> ELECTRA *freezes at the strangers' approach while the*
> CHORUS *retreats and stops, watching.*

ORESTES Stay. Don't be afraid of me.   230

ELECTRA Apollo, don't let me die!

ORESTES I'd rather kill someone I hate.

> ORESTES *reaches toward* ELECTRA *but does not touch*
> *her.*

ELECTRA (*flinching*) Go! Don't paw. No need to paw me.

ORESTES I have just reason to touch you.

ELECTRA Why lurk in ambush with a sword?

ORESTES Stay. You won't regret it.

ELECTRA I have no choice. You're stronger than I.

ORESTES But why should Aigisthos so insult you?

ELECTRA Because children born of this marriage would be powerless.

ORESTES Because—indeed!—such children would not seek
                                                            vengeance?

ELECTRA His very scheme. May he pay me a just price.   280

ORESTES Does he know you're still a virgin?

ELECTRA He does not know. We've kept our silence.

ORESTES (*indicating the* CHORUS)
        Are they your friends, these women with open ears?

ELECTRA Friends, oh yes, who keep their lips closed.

ORESTES What should Orestes do *if* he comes home?

ELECTRA You ask this? He must come! It's time to act.

ORESTES *When* he comes, then, how might he kill your father's
                                                            murderers?

ELECTRA Daring against them what they dared against my father.

ORESTES And with his help would you dare kill your mother?

ELECTRA Yes! And with the same axe that destroyed my father.   290

ORESTES Do I tell him this? Will you stand firm?

ELECTRA I'd die to let blood from my mother's throat.

ORESTES Fierce!
        If only Orestes could hear you.

ELECTRA Stranger, I wouldn't recognize him.

33

ORESTES No wonder—separated when you were young.

ELECTRA Only one of my friends would know him.

ORESTES The one who concealed him to prevent his murder?

ELECTRA Yes, my father's tutor, an old man now.

ORESTES Was your father's body granted a decent tomb?   300

ELECTRA Granted as he was granted expulsion from his own house.

ORESTES Harsh words. My god, how just hearing of miseries
         endured by others can sink sharp teeth into a man.
         But tell me more so I may bring your brother
         the news, however joyless, that he needs to hear.
         Pity, impossible for lowborn brutes, comes
         only to those who inherit noble feelings.
         But even they pay dearly to scruple overmuch.

CHORUS LEADER My heart has the same urge.
         Far from the troubles of the city and her people,   310
         I know nothing. But I want to learn.

ELECTRA If talk is needed, I will tell you as a friend
         how heavy fortune has weighed on me and my father.
         But now that you force my words, I beg you, stranger,
         tell Orestes of the wrongs done both of us,
         that I wear robes fit for a cowshed
         and bend beneath filth and under a roof like this
         spend my days—I who came from a royal house—
         I, callusing my fingers at the loom to weave cloth
         so that my naked body has some shred to wear;   320
         I, bowed by the weight of water on my head.
         Without one holiday to lead these girls in dance,
         yet must I shun other wives because I am a virgin
         and stand ashamed before Castor, now one of the gods,
         whom I was meant to marry, my kin, my own kind.
         Meanwhile, my mother in Oriental luxury

lolls on the throne waited on by Asian
slaves my father took as spoils of war.
They wear vests of fine soft wool fastened by gold.
My father's blood has gone black, still rotting   330
beneath that roof, while the man who killed him
exults, careering headlong in the chariot
my father drove, and clutches in his murderous hand
the scepter once wielded to command the Greeks.
And Agamemnon's tomb—no honor paid,
not one libation, no myrtle sprig,
the altar bare of any ornament.
Sodden with strong drink, my mother's husband—
the Glorious they call him—staggers on the grave
and flings rocks at my father's memorial stone   340
and rants against us with a reckless mouth:
"Where *is* Orestes? Where? How well your son's presence
guards your tomb." Thus does he mock my absent brother.

But, stranger, I beg you, tell him this, too.
Each part of me sends him its message,
hands and tongue and spirit in distress,
my cropped head, my grief for the one who fathered him.
Shameful if the son whose father leveled Troy
cannot himself kill one lone man.
But my brother is young and strong and nobly born.   350

The FARMER *enters.*

CHORUS LEADER Electra, look there—at your husband, I mean.
He's left the fields. He's on his way home.

FARMER (*to* ELECTRA) Well! Who are these strangers at my door?
Why come to the gates of this farm? What
do they want from me? Shameful—and you know it—
for women to dally in the company of young men.

ELECTRA My dear, don't put me under suspicion
before you know the facts. The strangers came
bringing me news of Orestes.

35

(to ORESTES *and* PYLADES*)*

Strangers, forgive his outburst.   360

FARMER What do they say? He's alive?

ELECTRA Alive, so they tell me. They seem worth trusting.

FARMER Does he remember the wrongs done you and your father?

ELECTRA I hope so, but a fugitive is powerless.

FARMER What do they tell you about Orestes?

ELECTRA He sent them to observe firsthand the wrongs done me.

FARMER Aren't some plain to see? And you've told them all the rest?

ELECTRA They know everything. Nothing was held back.

FARMER Shouldn't our doors have been opened long before now?

(to ORESTES *and* PYLADES*)*

Please come inside. In trade for good news   370
you'll find the food and drink my house
stores for its guests.

(to the attendants, who obey)

[Take in their gear.]

(to ORESTES *and* PYLADES*)*

And don't refuse me. Sent by a friend, you come here
as my friends. Though I must live by my sweat,
I'll never show myself ill-bred in manners.

ORESTES *(to* ELECTRA*)* My god, is this the man who does not
consummate your marriage lest he shame Orestes?

ELECTRA He is called poor Electra's husband.

ORESTES So!   380
There's no precise mark for recognizing worth.
Appearances confuse. I have seen the son
of a noble father existing as a nothing,
and able children born of bad stock,
and famine in a rich man's spirit,
and fine conscience in a poor man's frame.

How does one find the right criterion?
Wealth? But that's a sorry test.
Lack of property? But being without brings
madness; sheer need turns man into monster.   390
Shall I consider arms? What soldier confronting
a spear thinks it indicates the spearman's courage?
But enough of such speculation.

Witness this man, not great among his countrymen,
not puffed up by his family's rank. He's one of the crowd,
but I find him a natural aristocrat.
Isn't it senseless to be led astray
by preconceived notions and not judge good breeding
by a man's company and his manners?

[Such people bring credit to city   400
and family. But flesh empty of purpose
is a statue set to decorate a public square.
Nor does holding a spear distinguish strength from weakness.
Only character matters, and courage.]

But, for Agamemnon's deserving son
who is not here, yet here through me, we accept
your hospitality.

                    (*to the attendants, who obey*)

                Forward now, it's your duty,
into the house.

37

(*to* ELECTRA)

Better a poor man who's willing   410
than a rich man as my host.
I have only praise for the welcome found here.
Still, I could wish your brother knew good fortune
and were now leading me into a house more fortunate.
As I come, so may he. Though human prophecies
may be dismissed, Apollo's oracle speaks true.

ORESTES *and* PYLADES *exeunt into the farmhouse.*

CHORUS LEADER Now, Electra, as not before, joy
lights my heart. Fortune, slow in her coming,
may take a stand here for the best.

ELECTRA (*to the* FARMER)
You reckless man, you know the house lacks everything.   420
Why receive guests who far outrank you?

FARMER Why not? If they are noble—as they seem, won't they
be satisfied by any food, plain or fancy?

ELECTRA Because you lead a plain life, you miss the point.
Go to the old man who brought up my father.
He's banished from the city. You'll find him
herding his flocks near the river
that marks the boundary between Argos and Sparta.
Give him my order that he come to your house
bringing food to entertain our guests.   430
He will be pleased, oh yes! He'll thank the gods
to hear the boy whose life he saved is living still.
My mother, as you know, would give us nothing
from my father's house, and bitterness would fill her
brimming over should she learn Orestes lives.

FARMER Then, as you wish, I'll take the message to the old man.
Best hurry to the house and tidy it, begin

your preparations. Improvise. We have much
a woman needs to fix a hearty meal.
I'm sure the house stores forage enough   440
to fill their bellies for at least one day.
But whenever I give such matters any thought,
I think that money grants a man power
to treat guests handsomely and preserve his own body
when he gets sick. But a day's worth of forage
costs little. Rich or poor, a man can eat
only so much before he's satisfied.

The FARMER *exits to fetch the* OLD MAN.

ELECTRA *exits into the farmhouse.*

CHORUS (*singing and dancing*)
Once, the famed ships sailed eager toward Troy,
oars beyond count pushing them onward
escorted by Sea-Nymphs dancing their songs,   450
and a dolphin loving the flutes
leaped and rolled round and around
the dark beaks of prows
while decks echoed under the unresting strides
of Achilles, Thetis' son,
who, with Agamemnon, surged to Troy,
that fortress rising where its river meets the sea,

and Sea-Nymphs leaving their sheltered coves
carried the burden Hephaistos forged
on his loud-ringing anvil—arms wrought of gold—   460
up over Pelion's cliffs,
up holy Mount Ossa where the Nymphs
made search from high crags
for the boy whom the Centaur-father brought
into manhood, Thetis' son,
the sea-child born with quick strides to be
a light for Atreus' sons and all of Greece.

And I heard in Nauplia's harbor
from someone who'd fled out of Troy

a firsthand account, Achilles,   470
of your famous shield, its pulsing designs—
gold come alive!—wrought to bring Trojans
down to their knees in fear,
and quick on the roundshield's rim
Perseus the throat-cutter
flying on winged heels above churning seas
brandishes the Gorgon's head
in the presence of Maia's son,
country-bred Hermes,
the messenger of Zeus himself,   480

and wheeling in shield's very center
the sun drawn by winged horses
blazes out noon's white-hot light
and stars in bright chorus hum as they whirl—
Pleiades, Hyades, frightening fires
too bright for Hector's eyes,
and crouched in the helmet's gold
Sphinxes work talons
deep into prey lured close by their crooning,
and on the body-armor, flames   490
roar on the Chimera's breath
and her claws harrow earth
as she runs from Pegasus' flying hooves,

and around the murderous sword-blade, war-stallions
gallop, their hooves raising clouds of black dust.
The commander of spear-hurling Greeks—

(*turning, addressing the absent* CLYTEMNESTRA)

you killed him—you, his wife,
Tyndareos' daughter, driven by malice.
For that the gods in heaven
will send you to your death.   500
And may I see your throat beneath the knife.
And may I see your life's blood pumping out.

The OLD MAN *enters carrying a lamb and other gifts.*

OLD MAN (*speaking*)
Where can she be? Where's the young lady I've served—
Agamemnon's child? I brought her up.
How steep the path to her house—
no easy going for a wrinkled old man.
No matter. To reach a friend I won't be
hindered by my hunched back and these shaky knees.

ELECTRA, *hearing him, enters from the farmhouse.*

My daughter, here you are!
See what I've brought you from my flock—   510
a lamb that was still on the teat, and here,
crowns of flowers, and cheeses fresh from my press,
and this treasure from Dionysos, not much
but aged well, has a fine bouquet, enough
to make a sweet cup when it's mixed with weaker wine.
Have someone take these inside for your guests.
And here I stand in worn-out robes
wanting to wipe the tears from my eyes.

ELECTRA   Old man, why are you crying? Do you still,
after all this time, remember my troubles?   520
Or do you mourn Orestes, a helpless fugitive,
and mourn my father? You held him when he was a baby,
taught him as he grew—and for what?

OLD MAN   For nothing. But this is what I really could not bear—
his lonely tomb. On my way to you, I stopped there
to prostrate myself and weep. No one saw me.
I loosened the wineskin brought for your guests and poured
a hasty libation. Then I put myrtle around the tomb.
And there on the altar I saw black fleece,
a sheep sacrificed, its blood still fresh,   530
and a curl of chestnut hair cut from someone's head.
Child, I wonder at such recklessness.
No Argive dares approach that tomb.

41

But someone came in stealth—perhaps your brother,
home and shocked by a father's neglected grave.
Go there. Inspect the curl. Compare it with your own
cropped hair. See if the colors match.
There's often a natural resemblance
in children of the same father's blood.

ELECTRA It does not become an old man wise as you to joke,   540
suggesting that my courageous brother would crawl here
in secret because he fears Aigisthos.
And that snip of hair—how can it match mine?
Cut for the wrestling school, a man's hair grows out coarse;
combing keeps a woman's soft and fine. No comparison!
Old man, many have hair of the same texture,
same color, yet share no drop of common blood.

OLD MAN Yes but, child, go see the bootprints on the path.
Perhaps those feet and yours measure out alike.

ELECTRA Now how can a footprint be made on stony ground?   550
But if such prints exist, a sister's foot is
not equal to her brother's, nor a woman's
to that of a man. Male feet grow bigger.

OLD MAN Is there not—supposing your brother *has* come home—
a piece of your weaving you'd know him by,
something he wore when he was smuggled from his death?

ELECTRA Don't you recall how young I was when Orestes
was taken away? Supposing I *had* made clothing
that fit him as a child, could he wear it now?
Or did the cloth grow along with his body?   560
No! At the tomb some stranger, struck by pity,
cut his hair, or some native outwitting the spies.

OLD MAN Strangers—where are your guests? I'd like
to see them, ask them about your brother.

ELECTRA Just leaving the house to come our way..

42

ORESTES *and* PYLADES *enter from the farmhouse.*

OLD MAN Wellborn, I'd say, but first impressions don't always
ring true. Many a wellborn man is worthless.
No matter. I'll pay my respects to your guest.

ORESTES Sir, my respects.

(*to* ELECTRA)

To which of your friends, Electra,   570
does this ancient remnant of a man belong?

ELECTRA Stranger, he brought up my father.

ORESTES What! Is he the man who smuggled out your brother?

ELECTRA The very man who saved his life—if he still lives.

ORESTES Oh!
Why does he squint at me as if examining
a bright new silver coin? Do I look like someone he knows?

ELECTRA Perhaps in you he sees Orestes. You're the same age.

ORESTES He was fond of Orestes. But why is he shuffling around
me?

ELECTRA Stranger, I don't know. He surprises me.   580

OLD MAN My lady, pray! Daughter, pray to the gods!

ELECTRA Pray for what? Something absent, something here?

OLD MAN God makes treasured hope come true. Reach! Hold it fast!

ELECTRA Gods in heaven! What are you saying, old man?

OLD MAN Child, look at the one you love best.

ELECTRA Are you so old you've lost your good sense?

OLD MAN Lost my good sense, have I, telling you your brother—

ELECTRA What do you mean? Old man, I can't hope for such news.

OLD MAN —Orestes, Agamemnon's son, stands here before my eyes?

ELECTRA Convince me. By what mark should I know him?   590

OLD MAN The scar over his eyebrow. He got it by tumbling—
          remember?—when he chased with you after a fawn.

ELECTRA With me? Yes, I do see the cut—long healed.

OLD MAN Then why hold back? The brother you love—embrace
                                                    him!

ELECTRA No more delay. Dear man, your evidence
          persuades my heart.

                              (*embracing* ORESTES)

                    At last, you—here, real!
          I'd lost all hope.

ORESTES   And I hold you at last.

ELECTRA I never thought it possible.   600

ORESTES   Nor did I hope.

ELECTRA You *are* he?

ORESTES   Yes, your one and only ally.
          I look for a net to land our catch,
          and it *shall* be found. Else, why believe in gods
          if wrong is not punished but rewarded?

CHORUS (*singing and dancing*) You come, come at last,
          O day we were helpless to speed.

You dawn with new light. You blaze on the city
signaling one whose long-ago flight   610
sent him homeless, defeated, to spend the slow years
wandering in exile.
Now, our time has come. A god, friends, a god
brings victory to us.
Raise your hands high,
    raise voices high,
        send prayers to the gods
that by some fortune that conquers misfortune
your brother will enter the city in triumph.

ORESTES (*speaking*)
May that day come. This day I know the sweetness   620
of my sister's arms. And we'll embrace again, later.
And you, old man, you've come at the right time
to tell me how I repay my father's murderer
and my mother, his partner, his unhallowed wife.
Do I have one friend who wishes me well?
Or has misfortune made me bankrupt of friends?
With whom can I join? By night or by day?
What road can I take against my enemies?

OLD MAN Child, misfortune leaves you no friends.
It's rare good luck, I'll tell you, to find   630
anyone who stands by through good times and bad.
But you—completely stripped of friends,
no hope of friendship left—come, listen to me.
In your hands you hold all the fortune you need
to repossess your heritage and your people.

ORESTES And how may we accomplish this?

OLD MAN By killing Thyestes' son and your mother.

ORESTES I've come for just this crown. But how do I win it?

OLD MAN You won't if you enter the city.

ORESTES Defended by a well-armed garrison?   640

OLD MAN Of course. He fears you. He gets little sleep.

ORESTES So. Tell me how to proceed.

OLD MAN I just now thought of something. Listen to this.

ORESTES Go ahead. I'll listen if it's worthwhile.

OLD MAN Aigisthos—I saw him as I came here.

ORESTES You have my attention. Where?

OLD MAN (*gesturing*) Over in the meadows where his horses graze.

ORESTES Doing what? I begin to see hope.

OLD MAN Preparing a feast, I think, for the Nymphs.

ORESTES In thanks for living children or one not yet born?   650

OLD MAN I know only that he was making ready for sacrifice.

ORESTES Were free men there? Or was he alone with his slaves?

OLD MAN No citizens, just his household staff.

ORESTES Is anyone there who'd recognize me?

OLD MAN No, only slaves who never saw you as a boy.

ORESTES If I win, will they give me allegiance?

OLD MAN Slaves know who's master. That's to your advantage.

ORESTES How—and when—may I edge close to him?

OLD MAN Go where he'll see you when he makes the sacrifice.

ORESTES The road, then, skirts the meadow?   660

OLD MAN Yes. He'll see you there and invite you to the feast.

ORESTES If god so wishes, he'll find his share tastes bitter.

OLD MAN Then, as the dice fall, make your next play.

ORESTES Good advice. And where is my mother?

OLD MAN In town, but she'll join her husband for the feast.

ORESTES Why did she not go with him?

OLD MAN She trembles at the blame on people's tongues.

ORESTES Yes, she must know the whole nation accuses her.

OLD MAN Exactly. They hate that ungodly woman.

ORESTES How do I kill them both?   670

ELECTRA I myself will arrange my mother's death.

ORESTES And fortune will neatly dispose of him.

ELECTRA (*indicating the* OLD MAN)
         Let him serve both of us in this.

ORESTES As you wish. How will you seek our mother's death?

ELECTRA (*to the* OLD MAN) Go to Clytemnestra, old friend.
         Announce that Electra has borne a male child.

OLD MAN Some time ago or recently?

ELECTRA Ten days ago. It's time for the postpartum rites.

OLD MAN Does this have bearing on your mother's death?

47

ELECTRA My mother shall come when she hears I've borne a son.   680

OLD MAN But why, my child, would she concern herself with you?

ELECTRA She'll come. She'll weep about my son's high rank.

OLD MAN Perhaps. But what are you really saying?

ELECTRA When my mother comes, she shall be killed.

OLD MAN Oh! Let her enter these gates, then.

ELECTRA And won't she find she's at the gates of death?

OLD MAN If only I might see this before I die!

ELECTRA (*indicating* ORESTES) Take him now to the right place.

OLD MAN Where Aigisthos prepares for sacrifice?

ELECTRA When you meet my mother, give her my message.   690

OLD MAN As if you'd spoken it yourself.

ELECTRA (*to* ORESTES) You have your task: take first turn at killing.

ORESTES As soon as my guide points the way.

OLD MAN I'm more than willing to escort you.

ORESTES, ELECTRA, *and the* OLD MAN *pray.*

ORESTES O Zeus of our Fathers, be Router of enemies.

ELECTRA And pity us, for we have suffered pitifully.

OLD MAN Have pity on those who sprang from your seed.

ELECTRA And Hera whose power kindles flames on our altars,

ORESTES give us victory if you find justice in our prayer.

OLD MAN Give it for him they justly avenge.   700

ORESTES I call to your earthen house, Father godlessly murdered.

ELECTRA (*kneeling and beating on the ground*)
         Earth, holy queen, I give you these hands that would
                                            wake him.

OLD MAN Wake, wake to defend the children you love.

ELECTRA (*rising*) Now rise, bring the legions of dead as our allies,

ORESTES the dead you commanded whose spears brought Troy ruin,

OLD MAN who hate those defiled by ungodly crimes.

                                   The prayer ends.

ORESTES You, forever wronged by our mother, can you hear?

OLD MAN I'm sure your father hears your prayers. Our time draws near.

ELECTRA Yes, quite sure.

                                   (*to* ORESTES)

                  Be the man you need to be.   710
         [It cannot be put too strongly: Aigisthos must die.
         If *you* fall losing the contest and your life,
         I, too, would die. No, don't tell me I'd be saved.
         My hand would drive a sword right through my heart.
         No matter what happens, I shall be ready.]
         If news should come that fortune favors you,
         victory cries will ring through the house. But if you die—
         silence, absolute. That's all I need tell you.

                                   (*to the* CHORUS)

Women, do this for me: at contest's end, let voices
blaze to signal the outcome. I shall be waiting,   720
my arm raised and ready to plunge home the sword.
No enemy of mine will ever celebrate
his victory by raping me.

ELECTRA *exits into the farmhouse. The* OLD MAN *exits,*
followed by ORESTES, PYLADES, *and their attendants.*

CHORUS (*singing and dancing*)
How tender the lamb as it suckled its mother!
Now only old men know stories of Pan
but this tale still rings through the wild hills.
Listen—the pipes breathe a reedy
sweetness! Pan the divine shepherd
plays to his flock as he lifts up
the lamb—grown, fleeced with fine gold—   730
and carries it off. From a high, rocky
ledge, a herald shouts to the valley:
"Assemble, assemble, nobles
of Argos! Heaven sends a portent
to make you shiver.
It confirms your king." And people danced the hymns
acclaiming Atreus.

The gods' golden hearths opened wide, and all,
all the town was alight as fire
on every altar rose to a bright blaze.   740
And listen—the Muses' servant,
a flute, lifts its clear, lovely trill.
And songs of the golden ram lit
sweet desires. Then Thyestes
played his trick. He lured his brother's
wife into his bed and in the heat
of secret love persuaded her
to steal the ram from Atreus.
And he howled to the people:
"I am your king, for I have in *my* keeping   750
the ram with the golden fleece."

Then thunder boomed, then Zeus
reversed the stars' radiant sweep
and the dazzling sunlight
and morning's white face, and the sun
for the first time drove up in the west
while lightning flamed and seared earth,
but storm clouds flew north, hoarding
their rain, and robbed of sweet water,
the green oases, even that of Libyan Zeus,   760
became lifeless desert.

I cannot know the truth
of this tale, but the reason, they say,
the sun's golden face changed its course
and brought such misfortune to men
was heavenly judgment pronounced
against crimes that mortals commit.
And stories that strike fear in mankind
remind us to worship the gods.
But you, sister of famous brothers—you forgot.   770
You murdered your husband.

Offstage, cries are heard.

CHORUS LEADER (*speaking*) EA! EA!
Do you hear the howls? Do I imagine them—
shouts like an earthquake's thunder?
Sounds ride on the wind.
My lady! Electra! Come out, come out!

ELECTRA *runs, sword in hand, from the farmhouse.*

ELECTRA What's happening? The contest is over?

CHORUS LEADER I don't know. I heard the howls of death.

ELECTRA I heard them, too. They came from far away.

CHORUS LEADER Far away, yes, but plain to hear.   780

ELECTRA Did an enemy howl, or a friend?

CHORUS LEADER I don't know. Such a muddle of cries!

ELECTRA They plunge the sword in my heart. Why wait?

CHORUS LEADER Stop! Wait till you know what fortune brings.

ELECTRA No. We're beaten. Otherwise, wouldn't there be some news?

CHORUS LEADER News will come. It's no small matter to kill a king.

The MESSENGER *enters.*

MESSENGER Now let winning light up your faces.
I bring you word that Orestes has won.
Agamemnon's murderer Aigisthos
sprawls on the ground. Give thanks to the gods.   790

ELECTRA Who are you? How can you make me believe you?

MESSENGER Don't you know your brother's servant?

ELECTRA Welcome! All I could see was my own fear.
Now I recognize you.
My father's murderer is truly dead?

MESSENGER He's dead. So you'll believe me, I repeat it.

ELECTRA O gods, O Justice, you watched and waited.
At last you come.

(to the MESSENGER*)*

How *did* Aigisthos die?
What weapon, what kind of wound?   800

MESSENGER Soon after leaving your house, we marched
on a road built wide enough for two chariots abreast

till we found the new lord of Argos.
He was walking through a stream-watered garden
picking fresh myrtle to wreathe his head.
He sees us and calls, "Hello, strangers. Who are you?
Where are you going? What is your country?"
Orestes calls back, "Thessalians. Heading
for the river at Olympia and a sacrifice to Zeus."
Hearing that, Aigisthos says,   810
"Now you must be my guests and join me in the feast.
It happens I'm sacrificing a calf
to the Nymphs. Put off your journey till dawn—
delay makes no difference—and enter my house."
As he speaks, he takes our hands
tugging us forward. "You must not say no."
And when we're inside, he orders a slave
to fetch water quickly so that his guests
may stand at the altar with clean hands.
But Orestes tells him, "We have already bathed   820
in living water to make ourselves pure for the gods.
If you insist that strangers share the rites with citizens,
we are ready, my lord. We shall not refuse."

All conversation ended then.
The slaves guarding that high and mighty master
laid down their spears and put their hands to work.
Some carried bowls outside to catch the victim's blood,
some brought baskets, others built the fire and set cauldrons
straight around the altar-hearth. Their noise filled the house.
And taking barley grains, your mother's husband   830
cast them on the altar as he prayed;
"Nymphs who hallow these rocks, again I honor you
with sacrifice so that my wife and I shall prosper
as we do now, and that my enemies, as now, will fail."
Enemies—you and Orestes! But my own lord
prayed without a sound for something else—
to seize his home and heritage.
                              Aigisthos took
the ritual knife from its basket, cut the calf's forelock
and placed it with his right hand on the sacred fire,   840

and then, the calf on a slave's shoulders, its neck pulled back,
he cuts its throat and says this to your brother,
"Thessalians claim the skills of gentlemen—how neatly
they can dismember a bull, how quickly
break the wildest horse. My guest, the sword is yours.
Show me the substance behind Thessalian talk."

Orestes takes up a newly sharpened blade,
flings back his cloak to free his arms for work,
dismisses the waiting slaves, and chooses
Pylades as acolyte. Taking the calf   850
by a hoof, he lays the white flesh bare.
Groin to throat and back again, he stripped off the hide
faster than a runner can round two laps,
and he slit the belly open. Then Aigisthos
took the innards to read what they foretold.
Part of the liver was missing; portal vein
and gall bladder both had an ominous look.
Aigisthos grows rigid, and my lord asks,
"Why so dispirited?"

                              "Stranger, treachery   860
stalks me from abroad by the man I most hate,
Agamemnon's son, the kingdom's enemy and mine."
And Orestes replies, "Can a king fear
a fugitive? No, it's time to feast.
Let someone take this knife and bring me
a cleaver. I'll break the rib cage."
And he cracks the bone. Aigisthos wanted
to inspect the heart and lungs. As he stooped low,
your brother, rising to his fullest height,
drove the cleaver in Aigisthos' neck and split   870
his backbone. And his whole body thrashed, up, down,
flung by convulsions. He died hard.
The slaves, wide-eyed, grabbed up their spears,
many to battle a mere two. But sheer gut-courage
let Pylades and Orestes stand firm, weapons
ready. Then Orestes says, "I come here
bent on no harm to the state or those who follow me.
I, Orestes, have avenged my father's

murder. Long ago you served him faithfully.
No need to kill his son."   880
        When they heard that,
they lowered their spears, and he was recognized
by one old man who'd long served the court.
Right there, cheering him, crying in triumph,
they put a crown on your brother's head. And he comes
bringing you a head—not the Gorgon's
but his whom you hate, Aigisthos. Yes, blood for blood,
his bitter loan came due. He paid with death.

                  The MESSENGER *exits.*

CHORUS (*singing and dancing*)
    Dance with us, dance, O Electra, step light.
    Bound like a fawn   890
    soaring toward heaven, shining with joy.
    He wins a crown
    finer by far than Olympia's prize.
    Your brother wins! Come
        weave, as I dance,
            your garlands of victory song.

ELECTRA (*speaking*) O light! O sun wheeling brilliant above me!
    O Earth and Night whose darkness was all I saw,
    now my eyes are open and free—
    my father's murderer lies on the ground.   900
    I must find, bring out whatever ribbons, beads
    the house still holds to grace a head,
    to crown my brother who brings victory home.

            ELECTRA *exits into the farmhouse.*

      ORESTES, PYLADES, *and their attendants enter carrying*
                AIGISTHOS' *body and head.*

CHORUS (*singing and dancing*)
    Make him a wreath that could grace a god's head.
    Our voices will dance,
    our dancing feet echo heaven's delight.

A king we may love
because of his just rule shall rule us again.
Injustice lies dead! Come
    sing the sweet music,   910
        cry out *joy, joy, he has won!*

> ELECTRA, *carrying two wreaths, enters from the*
> *farmhouse.*

ELECTRA (*crowning* ORESTES *as she speaks*)
Victory becomes a son whose father
battled Troy and brought home victory. Orestes,
accept these braided ribbons as your crown,
for you return not from running some bloodless
footrace but from killing the enemy,
Aigisthos, who destroyed your father and mine.

> (*crowning* PYLADES)

And you, obedient to the lessons of your most
pious father—you fought beside him. Pylades,
accept this crown, for you shared in the contest   920
equally. Always may I see you fortune-blessed.

ORESTES The gods, Electra—think first of them as the cause
of our good fortune. Then, only then, praise me,
mere servant to fortune and the gods.
Let deeds, not words, tell you of Aigisthos'
killing. Nothing proves it more clearly
than what we deliver.

> (*holding up* AIGISTHOS' *head*)

I give you his head.

Do as you wish—toss it to the dogs, set it out
as carrion for the air's children,   930
impale it on a stake. Now the man
once called your lord and master is your slave.

ELECTRA Shame calls for silence, but I long to speak out.

ORESTES Why not? Now you have nothing to fear.

ELECTRA Except censure for speaking ill of the dead.

ORESTES No one would blame you.

ELECTRA Our city is squeamish. It dotes on casting blame.

ORESTES My sister, speak as you will, for you and I, both
        hating him implacably, have done this together.

          ORESTES *hands* AIGISTHOS' *head to* ELECTRA.

ELECTRA (*holding and addressing the head*) So be it.   940
        Where to begin to catalogue your wrongs?
        Where end? And how fill in the parts between?
        Each day before dawn I never once stopped
        rehearsing what I would have told you to your face
        if only I'd been free from fear that lasted
        much too long. Now we *are* free. And I present you
        with the words that should have reached your living ears.

          (*putting down the head so that it faces her*)

        You ruined me, for no just reason orphaned
        my brother and me of the father we loved.
        And you shamed yourself, killing my mother's husband   950
        who led the Greeks to Troy while you—you shirked the war.
        You came to such a point of stupid brutishness
        that you dared hope, after fouling my father's bed,
        that my mother would prove a virtuous woman.
        But he who beds another's wife in secret
        should be aware, when marriage springs its trap,
        that she shall not restore for him
        the chastity she has already flouted.
        Your life spread pain, though you thought it hurt no one.
        You saw the shamefulness of godless marriage, yes,   960
        and knew my mother had wed an impious man.

But both of you were tainted then—you shouldering
her destiny and she, your wickedness.
You must have heard the talk that buzzed through Argos:
"Oh look. He lets her have her way in everything."

Sheer disgrace—to see not husband but wife
dominate a household! And this I also find
abhorrent—male children called in public
not by their father's name but by the mother's.
The man who marries to advance himself remains   970
a nothing, for his wife still has the final word.
You didn't know that fact. Ignorance fooled you
into boasting of the power great wealth gave you.
It's no more than a fleeting companion.
Only human character stands firm
and lasts forever, surmounting every trouble,
while wealth unjustly gained by public mischief
flowers for a short time, then takes wing.

And your way with women—too crass for innocent
lips. I'll merely hint at what I know.   980
How you strutted and preened, living in a king's house,
showing off your well-made body. But I want no
girl-faced husband. Give me a man,
for *his* sons make courageous soldiers
while pretty boys can only decorate the dance.

(*taking up* AIGISTHOS' *head and pitching it toward his
                                                    body*)

Be damned! I regret you cannot know how you have
paid at last a just price. You who work evil
may start the race on a sure foot, but never think
you've outrun justice and won before the final turn
is rounded and you sprint down life's last lap.   990

CHORUS LEADER   The dreadful things he did call for the dreadful
death you gave him. Justice has great strength.

ELECTRA Strength indeed. Now to dispose of the body, consign it
to the dark so that my mother, when she comes
for sacrifice, does not see the corpse.

ORESTES' *attendants, carrying* AIGISTHOS' *remains, exeunt
into the farmhouse.*

ELECTRA *turns to follow them.*

ORESTES Stop! Enough! We need to talk more.

ELECTRA About what? Are soldiers coming to help him?

ORESTES Not soldiers, but the mother who gave me birth.

ELECTRA She's carried to our net, then, in glittering style—
riding in a chariot, wearing splendid robes of state.   1000

ORESTES What shall we do? Kill our own mother?

ELECTRA Now that you see her, do you feel pity?

ORESTES Pity—
she brought me up, she bore me. How can I kill her?

ELECTRA The way she slaughtered your father and mine.

ORESTES Phoibos, your oracle was brutal!

ELECTRA If even Apollo's judgment fails, is anyone wise?

ORESTES Kill my mother—his voice should not have told me that.

ELECTRA How can it harm you to avenge our father?

ORESTES For killing her, I'll stand trial—I, pure till then.   1010

ELECTRA Not honoring a father—that's sacrilege!

ORESTES I know. But my mother's murder—how must I pay?

ELECTRA Would you choose someone else to avenge *your* father?

ORESTES God, did some demon of vengeance speak in your voice?

ELECTRA At Delphi? From the sacred tripod? No.

ORESTES I'll never believe the prophecy rings true.

ELECTRA Let no coward's thoughts topple your manhood,
but bring to this task the same guile our mother used
to kill her lord and husband with Aigisthos' help.

ORESTES It shall be done. I start on a course I dread.   1020
I'll do things I dread. If that please the gods,
so be it. For me this sport is bitter, not sweet.

> ORESTES *exits into the farmhouse.*

> CLYTEMNESTRA, *accompanied by her Trojan slave
> women, enters in a regally caparisoned horse-drawn
> wagon.*

CHORUS (*severally*)—My lady, queen of Argos.

—Daughter of Tyndareos.

—Sister of Zeus' sons, Castor and Polydeukes,
twin stars lighting a new blaze in heaven
and honored as saviors of men
who sail the storm-tossed waves.

—You merit reverence for equaling
The gods themselves in wealth and boundless joy.   1030

—Good fortune in such fine balance
deserves to be treated with respect.

—My lady queen.

CLYTEMNESTRA Step down, Trojan women. Here, take my hand.
Help me put my feet on firm ground.

(*to* ELECTRA)

The temples of the gods have been adorned
with plunder from Troy. As a small but fine reward
for my house, I've chosen living spoils, these women—
petty recompense for a daughter lost.

ELECTRA I, too, am a slave cast out from home   1040
and heritage, consigned to this hovel. So
may I not, Mother, take your royal hand?

CLYTEMNESTRA (*dismounting*)
My slaves are here to spare you work on my account.

ELECTRA Why spare me, held captive far from home?
When I was seized, seized from my home as they were,
I became one of them, fatherless, orphaned.

CLYTEMNESTRA That, I assure you, was your father's doing. He
should not have schemed as he did against his dear ones.
I also say that when a woman forms a wrong opinion,
her tongue turns bitter. In your situation,   1050
one can't fault you. But when the facts are learned,
if you find me worth loathing, then
to hate is right. If not, why do we need to hate?

Tyndareos gave me to your father not
that I should die, nor the children I bore.
But your father, promising my daughter marriage
to Achilles, lured her to Aulis where his ships were
held in irons, and there, racking her on the altar,
he slashed my Iphigenia's white throat.
And if, to avert the city's fall or help   1060
his own family or save other children, he'd killed one
for the sake of many, his act would be excusable.
But as it was, when Helen went mad with lust,

61

Menelaos did nothing to control his faithless wife
and punish her adultery. Then, to counter
such inaction, your father killed my child.
Just for these things—though I was sorely wronged—
I would not have turned savage nor killed my husband.
But then he came home, a raving, god-smitten girl
on his arm, in his bed. Thus did one house   1070
suffer occupation by two brides.

Yes, women can be foolish. I won't deny it.
But granting this, whenever a husband strays
and abandons his marriage bed, the woman wants
to imitate his lead and find her own friend.
Yet censure strikes hard at women, while men,
the true agents of trouble, hear no reproach.
Now, if Menelaos had been swept off in secret,
should I have killed Orestes to save
my sister's husband? And how would your father   1080
have borne his son's death? Should a killer
not be executed? Was I to keep suffering?

I did kill him. Taking the only possible path,
I joined his enemies. Would any of his friends
have aided me in his destruction?
Rebut me, if you must. You are quite free
to tell me that your father died unjustly.

CHORUS LEADER The reasons are just, but *this* justice is ugly.
A woman knows, if she has common sense,
that she defers in all things to her husband.   1090
Else, I cannot count her as a proper wife.

ELECTRA Let me remind you, Mother, that you concluded
your defense with words permitting me frankness.

CLYTEMNESTRA Be frank, child. I won't retract that permission.

ELECTRA But, Mother, will you use what you hear to hurt me?

CLYTEMNESTRA I'll hurt you only with sweet understanding.

ELECTRA Then I have leave to speak. To begin with, Mother,
I wish your understanding were more balanced.
Indeed, the outward beauty you and Helen share
brings well-earned praise, but inside both you sisters are   1100
rotten with lust, unworthy of your brother Castor.
She was ruined by consenting to her own rape,
and you destroyed the best, the finest man in Greece,
offering a child's death as your excuse
for killing your husband. But I know you better.

Long before your daughter's sacrifice had been decreed,
but not long after your lord husband sailed for Troy,
you smiled at the mirror teasing your golden hair.
But when a woman whose man is elsewhere struts out
in festive garb, she can be written off as a slut.   1110
A woman should never show the streets her painted face
unless she goes prowling with mischief in mind.
And I know that you alone, of all the Greeks,
tingled with pleasure when the odds favored Troy,
but when Troy's luck turned bad, your eyes gathered clouds,
for you did not desire Agamemnon's safe return.
Yet, you had a fine, fair chance to show restraint.
Your husband was not a man worse than Aigisthos
but a man whom Greece herself chose commander-in-chief.
And when your sister Helen did such fatal harm,   1120
you could have taken on great praise. Vice
gives its lesson as virtue's mirror-image.

But if, as you state, my father killed your daughter,
how have my brother and I done you wrong?
Why, when you'd killed him, were we not deeded
our heritage? Because you used what was not yours
as dowry to pay your bedmate's keep.
Your present husband is not exiled on your son's behalf,
nor has he died for me, though mine is a living
death worse than my killed sister's. And if blood   1130

calls for blood in the name of Justice, I will kill you—
I and your son Orestes—to avenge our father.

(*stepping back*)

If death was just there, here it is also just.
[The man's a fool who, dazzled by her wealth and rank,
marries a worthless schemer. A pauper's bed
that honors chastity is softer than a king's.

CHORUS LEADER Marriage is a woman's gamble. I've seen
the dice fall to bring good luck and bad.]

CLYTEMNESTRA Daughter, by nature you've always loved your father,
and it happens that some children prefer the male parent 1140
while some hold greater fondness for the mother.
I shall excuse you, for I do not find
much reason in my own acts for rejoicing.
Oh how my best intentions went astray when I
drove more passion than I meant against my husband.

ELECTRA Too late to lament. There's no cure now.
My father is dead, dead. Why not call home
the wanderer, your exiled son?

CLYTEMNESTRA I've been afraid to. I look to my good, not his.
They say he's angry at the murder of his father.   1150

ELECTRA Why turn your husband savage against us?

CLYTEMNESTRA It's his way, just as you were born willful.

ELECTRA I'm in pain. But I'll bring my anger to an end.

CLYTEMNESTRA And then he'll no longer be hard on you.

ELECTRA He dreams of greatness while he sprawls in my house.

CLYTEMNESTRA You see? It's you who add new tinder to the quarrel.

ELECTRA I'm *silent*, for I fear him as I do fear him.

CLYTEMNESTRA Stop this talk! Child, why do you want me here?

ELECTRA You heard, I think, that I was brought to bed.
Make the sacrifice for me—I don't know how—   1160
the one required on a child's tenth day.
I'm a new mother with no experience.

CLYTEMNESTRA That's work for the midwife who delivered you.

ELECTRA I delivered myself. I gave birth alone.

CLYTEMNESTRA You live here without friends and neighbors?

ELECTRA A poor working man—no one wants him for a friend.

CLYTEMNESTRA And look at you, unkempt and clad in tatters!
Is this the way you've rested from childbirth?
I'll help. Because the child completes its tenth day,
I'll make the sacrifice. For you, I'll do this favor   1170
before I meet my husband at his own sacrifice
in honor of the Nymphs.

(*to her attendants*)

Stable the horses
and fodder them. And when I have finished
with this little sacrifice, be ready,
for husbands also need their favors.

CLYTEMNESTRA'S *attendants exeunt with the horses.*

ELECTRA   (*motioning* CLYTEMNESTRA *to precede her into the*
                                                         farmhouse)
Welcome to my humble house. But take care, please,
not to smudge your finery with clinging soot.
You shall indeed make the sacrifice
as must be done to satisfy the powers of heaven.   1180

65

(*addressing* CLYTEMNESTRA'S *back as she walks to the farmhouse*)

The basket waits, and the new-whetted knife that killed
the bull. You'll fall beside him when you take your blow.
And you shall be bride again in death's house to him
you lay with while he lived. I will render you this favor,
and you render me just payment for my father.

ELECTRA *follows* CLYTEMNESTRA *into the farmhouse.*

CHORUS (*singing and dancing*)
Exchange for evils! Oh how the winds
of the house turn around. Once my true king
was struck down as he bathed
and massive roof timbers and walls built of marble
all echoed, repeating his deathwails, "You   1190
ingrate! Savage! Woman, why kill me? Dear country—
ten springtimes gone,
at last I've come home."

Just payment reclaims the reckless one
who strayed from her bed not once but again,
when at last he came home
to his city where towers built by giants reach into heaven.
And her hand lifted the weapon, and her hand
chopped the axe down. She killed you, O husband
most grievously wronged   1200
by a faithless wife.
Just like some angry mountain lioness
that leaves her thicket-guarded den, she stalked and struck.

CLYTEMNESTRA (*inside the farmhouse*).
Children! Dear god, I'm your mother! Don't kill me.

CHORUS LEADER (*speaking*) Do you hear—"My god, don't kill me"?

CLYTEMNESTRA NO! NOT ME! NO-O-O-O!

CHORUS LEADER No! Not her! No! Killed by her own children.

CHORUS (*chanting*) God deals just payment as fortune requires.
Savage your death, poor creature, but godless
the death you devised.   1210

CHORUS LEADER (*speaking*)
But they're leaving the house, walking our way,
splashed by their mother's fresh blood.
                                        I want to run
from such unhappy proof of sacrifice.
No family and its many generations
have been more their own victim.

> ELECTRA, ORESTES, *and* PYLADES *enter from the
> farmhouse, followed by attendants carrying the
> bodies of* CLYTEMNESTRA *and* AIGISTHOS.

> *The lines from here until* CASTOR'S *opening speech are
> chanted.*

ORESTES IO,
Earth and Zeus who sees everything
human, look now on the blood
that defiles me—two bodies   1220
struck to the ground by my hand
as poor reparation
for wrongs I have suffered.

ELECTRA This rush of tears—oh brother, mine the guilt and shame.
On fire, the daughter dared rage at the mother
who gave her birth.

CHORUS Oh fate, your fate, Mother,
when you birthed pain the world
won't forget or forgive and, worse,
were killed by your children's hands.   1230
But, blood for blood, you paid the just price.

ORESTES IO,

Apollo, your voice hymned a justice
I could not see clear, but all too clear
the anguish you caused, the bloodhaunted,
homeless future you've doled out.
What nation will have me?
What host, what god-fearing person
will look in the face of a man
who killed his own mother?   1240

ELECTRA And where, oh where shall I go? What dancing be mine?
What marriage? What husband will lead me,
a bride, to his bed?

CHORUS Again, again your mind
has changed course with the wind.
For you think now of godly things
ignored when you worked dreadful
deeds on your brother against his will.

ORESTES Did you see how terror made her rip open
her robes, exposing her breasts against bloodshed?   1250
How slowly the naked limbs that bore me
sagged to the ground. And I melted away.

CHORUS You walked through anguish, I know,
when you heard the mother who bore you
singing her own dirge.

ORESTES She wailed it, she screamed, she reached up placing
soft begging hands on my cheeks, "My son, my own son!"
and pressed her palms tight on my face
so pity would loosen my grip on the knife.

CHORUS Poor woman. How could you bear   1260
the sight of the mother you murdered
breathing her last breath?

ORESTES I cast my cloak over my eyes.
                              And then I began

the ritual act, loosing
the knife in my mother's neck.

ELECTRA But calling the stroke, my hand on yours, I took
the knife and guided it home. Of most
dreadful suffering, I am the cause.

ORESTES Cover my mother's body with robes,   1270
                                    and cleanse her, close
the wounds of sacrifice.
You gave birth to your own death.

> ORESTES *takes off his cloak and, with* ELECTRA'S *help,
> uses it to cover* CLYTEMNESTRA'S *body.*

ELECTRA Bear witness for one who is loved and not loved:
we cast the cloak gently around her,
an end of great woe for our house.

> *As the* CHORUS *chants the next lines,* CASTOR *and*
> POLYDEUKES *appear on the roof of the farmhouse.*

CHORUS (*severally*)—But look, up there on the rooftop,
a shimmer of lights.

                        —Who are they,
spirits or gods? No mortal foot walks   1280
the pathway of air.

                        —Why do they show themselves
brightly to human eyes?

CASTOR Agamemnon's son, pay heed. As brothers
to your mother, as twin sons of Zeus, we,
Castor and Polydeukes, claim your attention.
As soon as we had calmed high waves for passing ships,
we came here, for we had perceived
the sacrifice you made—our sister, your mother.
She has her just deserts but by your unjust act.   1290

Apollo, Apollo—but he is my lord. I will
keep silence. He is wise forever, though his oracle
spoke brutal words. We are bound to acquiesce.
And you must do now as Fate and Zeus ordain.

First, give Pylades Electra as his bride.
Then, leave Argos. You who killed your mother
may not enter your inheritance, this city.
The terror you called forth, the hounding goddesses of doom,
shall hunt you, driving you here, there, homeless and mad.
But when you stagger into Athens, embrace   1300
the image of Pallas. She shall then lift
her Gorgon shield above your head to keep the spitting
fury of those hideous snakes from touching you.
Nearby you shall find Ares' hill where gods themselves
first cast the votes on a matter of blood when rage
brought Ares' always savage temper to a flash
and he killed the son of the Sea-God for raping
his daughter. Since then, the votes of the court command
utmost respect; its decisions stand firm.
On that spot, pursued, you must be tried for murder,   1310
but votes cast evenly shall save you from being
put to death. Apollo shall take your guilt back on himself
because his oracle foretold your mother's murder.
In the future this shall be law: that the accused
always win acquittal on an even vote.
The baying goddesses shall vanish, thwarted,
when earth beside the hill splits in a holy gape
where men shall afterwards tremble, listening to oracles.
But you must go to live by Arkadia's wild river
near the shrine haunted by Zeus of the Wolves   1320
and there found a city that bears your name.

This is your lot. For Aigisthos, the gods ordain
that citizens shall bury him in native earth.
And your mother shall be honored with a funeral
by Menelaos, now in homeport on return from Troy;
by Helen, too. Leaving her safe retreat, Helen
comes from Egypt. She never went to Troy.

Zeus—yes, Zeus—intending war and slaughtered men
sent only Helen's image to that battleground.
And Pylades—let him receive this maiden-wife   1330
and take her to his home. Let him also lead
your pretended brother-in-law to his city
and there give him wealth beyond his dreams.

As for you, cross the Isthmus and make your way
to Athens' templed hill that gleams with heaven's blessings.
When you have paid as Fate decrees for murder,
heaven shall bless you by releasing you from pain.

The lines from here until ELECTRA *and* PYLADES *exeunt*
are chanted.

ORESTES   O sons of Zeus, does heaven grant
          mortal voices the right to address you?

CASTOR   You have the right. The blood of sacrifice   1340
          does not defile you.

ELECTRA   And I may speak to Tyndareos' sons?

CASTOR   You may. I will refer the murder
          back to Apollo.

ORESTES   Why, as gods and brothers to her
          who was slain, did you not
          keep Death-Spirits away?

CASTOR   Fate and the unwise cry of Apollo
          fulfilled necessity's binding demand.

ELECTRA   But when did Apollo—when did his voice   1350
          ever ordain that *I* kill my mother?

CASTOR   Deeds in common, destinies in common:
          mother and father,
          one ancestral curse destroyed them both.

ORESTES   My sister, whom it took too long to find,
          too soon I am robbed of your love,
          and I shall abandon you, you leave me.

CASTOR   A husband is hers, a noble house.
          The girl suffers nothing save leaving
          her country forever.   1360

ELECTRA   What greater sorrow than being forced
          to leave behind my native earth?

ORESTES   But I, my heritage forever lost,
          must wander till I pay the price
          for a mother's blood.

CASTOR   Take heart. You shall reach
          Athena's city. Exercise patience.

ELECTRA   Hold me close, brother, let me hold you.
          Oh how I love you!
          One from the other, both from our home,   1370
          we're torn—cursed by a mother's murder—apart.

ORESTES   Hurry, come hold me, though I am dead.
          Shed tears on my body as on my grave.

                        ELECTRA *and* ORESTES *embrace.*

CASTOR   Pain, such pain in your words that even
          gods hear its anguish.
          I and my heavenly kind know
          pity for men who must suffer and die.

ORESTES   Never again shall I see you.

ELECTRA   Nor I see myself in your eyes.

ORESTES   This, the last time I'll talk with you ever.   1380

ELECTRA   O my homeland, goodbye.
           Goodbye to you, women of home.

ORESTES   Most loyal of sisters, do you leave now?

ELECTRA   I leave with tears blurring all that I see.

ORESTES   Pylades, go. I wish you all joy
           in Electra your bride.

                          ELECTRA *and* PYLADES *exeunt.*

CASTOR (*speaking*)
           Marriage awaits them. But you, run! The hounds
           snap fierce at your heels. Turn toward Athens.
           I hear them pelting hard on you, I see
           black flesh and snake-hands coiling   1390
           round a fruit of agonizing pain.

                          ORESTES, *panicked, exits.*

           Ships are breaking in high seas off Sicily.
           Our immediate presence is required. But first,
           let me tell you we speed through wide air
           not to rescue those whom murder pollutes
           but those who hold precious in life all things
           godly and just. Such are the people
           we save when we hear of their peril.
           Let none of you, then, commit an injustice
           or go aboard ship with perjured men.   1400
           As a god, I give warning to you who must die.

                          CASTOR *and* POLYDEUKES *exeunt.*

CHORUS   I wish you joy. To spend life's fleeting days
          mid joy that never meets an evil hour
          is to be blessed beyond compare.

                          The CHORUS *exits slowly.*

NOTES

1–171 / 1–139 *Prologue* In Aristotle's definition (*Poetics* 52b19), everything that comes before the entry of the Chorus, here, with a formal complexity characteristic of Euripides, including an expository monologue, spoken dialogue, a second monologue, and a lyric monody (solo song).

1–54 / 1–53 *Age-old valley... he's the fool* The prologue begins with well-known material: Agamemnon's victory at Troy, his murder by Clytemnestra his wife and her lover Aigisthos, the latter's illegitimate rule, the sending away of the child Orestes (here smuggled out by an old retainer) to Strophios, king of Phokis. The new, surprising additions concern Electra. In this version she is "married" to the Farmer, but their marriage has not been consummated. This makes Electra a dangerous, liminal figure, between virgin and wife.

9–10 / 9–10 *he was killed... Aigisthos* Reports differ on how this was done, and by whom. In Homer, Agamemnon is trapped and killed by Aigisthos, with Clytemnestra's help; in Aeschylus, by Clytemnestra, backed by Aigisthos; in Euripides, by Aigisthos, driven by Clytemnestra (though at 1198–99 / 1159–60 the Chorus has her kill Agamemnon herself, with an axe, not the usual sword). By their suggestive word order lines 9–10 / 9–10 make it clear that Clytemnestra's cunning (*dolōi*) is the active force behind the murder, Aigisthos' hand her instrument. Here, as elsewhere, Aigisthos is referred to as "Thyestes' son" in the Greek, recalling family guilt and revenge (see the Introduction).

15–18 / 15–18 *the baby Orestes... protection* A mere babe when Agamemnon left for Troy, Orestes is now a strapping youth of eighteen or nineteen. Electra is somewhat older. In Sophocles' version, she had mothered the child Orestes and had herself arranged to have him sent away from Argos.

Who, to Euripides' mind, would have taken that initiative? Agamemnon's old retainer? Or, just possibly, Clytemnestra?

25–28 / 25–28 *Yet, when he planned... Aigisthos' hand* The innovation is significant. Clytemnestra, though raw-minded, yet prevents Aigisthos from killing her daughter. She is capable of pity, and of remorse.

29 / 29 *Clytemnestra had excuses* These were, first, Agamemnon's sacrifice of their daughter Iphigenia, so the ships could sail from Aulis to Troy; second, and less cogent, his bringing home the Trojan prophetess Cassandra as his mistress.

43 / 42 *Aigisthos would have paid the penalty* The word *dikē* is central. We translate it variously by vengeance, justice, a just price, judgment, and just payment.

61 / 60 *Tyndareos' daughter* This refers to Clytemnestra, daughter of Leda and Tyndareos, but it could equally refer to her half-sister Helen, Zeus' daughter in fact, Tyndareos' daughter by courtesy. Euripides often connects the sisters as bearers of ruin.

63 / 61 *home and heritage* We use this phrase to translate *oikos* (house, home, family), as here, and *domos patrōios* (ancestral house) elsewhere.

91 / 87–88 *He ordered me home* This is implied in the Greek but not precisely stated. In Aeschylus, Orestes says more about Apollo's bidding and the dire threats accompanying it should Orestes fail to avenge his father. In Sophocles the oracle's advice is ambiguous and perhaps deceptive.

110–12 / 107–9 *Look, here comes... somebody's slave* These lines supply retroactive stage directions. Electra's cropped hair, her ragged clothes, and the water-jar she carries mark her clearly (and misleadingly) as a slave.

115–71 / 112–66 *Speed your step... lie in her bed* Electra's sung lament will stir the audience's sympathy and will make a strong impression on the listening Orestes. She *has* suffered, she *has* many reasons for her continued mourning, and any hints that her grief is excessive, or that she is alienated from society, are subtle as yet.

142–43 / 139–40 ELECTRA *takes the water-jar* She might have called an attendant to take it. More likely, she self-consciously directs her own actions.

172–222 / 167–212 *Parodos* These are young, unmarried women who live in the uplands, remote from town, eager for gossip and for special occasions like Hera's festival. Their bright clothing, cheerfulness, and sociability make a powerful contrast with Electra's appearance, mourning, and isolation.

179 / 173–74 *at Hera's temple* Hera was goddess of marriage as well as patron of Argos. The Heraia festival, celebrated at her temple between Argos and Mycenae, included athletic contests and military displays; its high point was probably a representation of the sacred marriage of Hera and Zeus.

223–447 / 213–431 *First episode*

225–301 / 215–89 ORESTES, PYLADES A scene of only partial recognition. Electra, afraid at first of bandits, is delighted to find that the "stranger" brings word from Orestes; but the "stranger," apart from revealing that Orestes lives, evades Electra's direct questions and redirects her thoughts to her own situation of pain, grief, and indignity, which she exaggerates for the benefit of the "absent" Orestes. The latter tries rather lamely to conceal his strong emotion—and strong self-concern.

231 / 221 *Apollo* Electra may turn to an actual statue of Apollo before her cottage. If such exists, it will remind us of Apollo's presence behind the scenes, sanctioning (rightly or wrongly) the forthcoming murders.

270 / 260 *Only Orestes has that right* If a woman's father was dead or missing, she would normally be given in marriage by her new *kyrios* (legal guardian), the nearest male relative.

283 / 272 *Are they your friends* As often happens in Euripides' plays, the Chorus will keep silent in order to help the main character(s). In so doing, the Chorus becomes an accomplice to the revenge.

292 / 281 *from my mother's throat* Forms of the verb *sphattō* (to cut the throat) are ordinarily used of animal sacrifice. In *Electra* they are applied often, and significantly, to the killing of human victims.

324–25 / 312–13 *and stand ashamed before Castor ... my own kind* Castor and Polydeukes, the Dioskouroi, were sons of Zeus and Leda, brothers of Helen, half-brothers of Clytemnestra, uncles of Electra and Orestes. Together with a few other privileged demigods, including Heracles and Dionysos, they were admitted to Olympos. A probably later variant makes Castor mortal and Polydeukes immortal; the twins share their fate, spending six months in Hades, six on Olympos. It seems that, in the old days, Electra was courted by Castor and might have expected to marry him.

373 / 360 [*Take in their gear.*] The line has been thought spurious, but needlessly: the Farmer is not dirt poor, and he would naturally have slaves. With self-mocking humor he refers to his "attendants," and to the "gates" of his

domain. (We take *tōnde* to refer to Orestes and Pylades [these people's baggage]; it is possible, however, that the Farmer addresses *their* attendants, including a servant who will reappear as messenger, line 787 / 761.)

381–404 / 367–90 *There's no precise mark . . . courage* Orestes' rather lengthy remarks on nobility reflect contemporary discussions at Athens: Is nobility (*eugeneia*) inherited or learned? How best can it be fostered? And (Orestes' main concern) how can inner nobility be discerned as against mere outward semblances? Compare the interest of Boccaccio and Chaucer in discussions of what constitutes true *gentilezza* or *gentilesse*.

387–93 / 373–79 *How does one find . . . speculation* These seven lines are bracketed by Diggle as possible interpolations. We argue that the truisms (1) are in character for Orestes, (2) cover his hesitation, and (3) challenge the audience to form its own judgment—about the "noble" Orestes, among others.

400–404 / 386–90 [*Such people bring credit . . . courage*] These lines, also bracketed by Diggle, seem less relevant, and more far-fetched, than lines 387–93 / 373–79, but they bear ironically on the evaluation of Orestes, who is characterized at least metaphorically as a successful athlete.

448–502 / 432–86 *First stasimon* While time, by the usual convention, goes forward in the outer world during the singing and dancing of this choral ode, the Chorus moves backward, singing (1) how Achilles came to Troy, (2) how (before that) he received his divinely made arms, and (3) how (before that) he was brought up by the good centaur Chiron.

468–95 / 452–78 *And I heard . . . black dust* The audience will recall Homer's description in *Iliad* 18 of the great shield made for Achilles by Hephaistos, with its typical, contrasting scenes of war and peace. The figures on Euripides' armor are fearful and portentous, intended to dazzle the eyes of the Trojans and especially those of Hector, the Trojan champion (who would be killed by Achilles). They include: (1) Perseus slaying the Gorgon, with Hermes' help; (2) the murderous Sphinx, here not overcome, and (3) Bellerophon riding the winged horse Pegasos, to attack the monstrous Chimaera. The first group foreshadows, and is foil to, Orestes' killing of Clytemnestra. Compare Aeschylus' *Libation Bearers* (832–37), where the Chorus urges Orestes (who is inside) to "take up the heart of Perseus" in his breast and to "kill the evil Gorgon by spreading a cloak" before his eyes so he won't be turned to stone. It is all right to look as he kills Aigisthos. Euripides will develop this comparison, with bitter irony.

503–723 / 487–698 *Second episode*, with a brief choral interjection at **607–19 / 585–95**.

503 / 487 The Old Man had been Agamemnon's *tropheus* (compare **17 / 16**, **425 / 409**) and *paidagōgos*, not just a tutor in the modern sense, but a male nursemaid, companion, and guide.

529–31 / 513–15 *And there on the altar . . . someone's head* The recognition-signs here rejected by Electra are taken from Aeschylus' *Libation Bearers* (164–234), where Electra discovers (1) a lock of hair at the tomb, like hers, that Orestes might have laid there—or sent; (2) footprints matching hers—as she demonstrates by experiment. When Orestes reveals himself, after that, he adds (3) a piece of Electra's weaving that he had kept with him all those years. Full recognition quickly ensues.

570–71 / 553–54 *To which of your friends . . . belong* Orestes assumes, with typical snobbery, that the Old Man is a slave. Compare his quick assumption earlier that Electra must be married to some low ditchdigger or cowherd.

591 / 573 *The scar over his eyebrow* This is evidently Euripides' invention. It is played off against the scar of Odysseus that Eurykleia, the old nurse, recognizes when she is bathing "the stranger" in *Odyssey* 19—but Odysseus forces her to keep silence, and Athena diverts Penelope's mind and vision elsewhere so that she fails, at least consciously, to perceive her husband's presence, and the expected recognition is delayed. The Homeric scar, inflicted by a wild boar, was emblematic of Odysseus' initiation into heroic manhood. In Euripides' play, Orestes' scar (Why didn't Electra notice it earlier?) belongs to a less heroic world. (In Sophocles' *Electra*, Orestes more appropriately displays their father's signet ring.)

638 / 614 *I've come for just this crown* This is one of many allusions to the great Games of Hellas, where victors were crowned with wreaths. In a happier world Orestes would have been a star athlete, not a matricide. Killing is played off against sport. Later on, Aigisthos will be fooled by Orestes' pretense of being a Thessalian gentleman en route to Olympia. In Sophocles' *Electra*, Aigisthos and Clytemnestra are fooled by the story that Orestes was accidentally killed in a chariot race at Delphi.

649 / 625 *Preparing a feast* The Nymphs were protectors of family life. One might make sacrifices to them in gratitude for existing children or in the hope of children yet to come.

671 / 647 *I myself will arrange* Or, reading *exaitēsomai*, "I will ask the privilege of my mother's murder" (Denniston). A quick, confident, cold-blooded assertion—either way.

674 / 650 *As you wish* If the Old Man spoke this line, as seems probable, then line 675 / 651 ("Go to Clytemnestra") becomes unnecessary. If Orestes spoke it, then Electra's turning to the Old Man, giving blunt directions and ignoring Orestes until line 692 / 668, is all the more striking.

678 / 654 *postpartum rites* This refers to the purification ceremony by which the mother was reintegrated into normal society after childbirth. The naming of the child took place on the same tenth day.

682 / 658 *She'll come* Electra's tone is cold, sarcastic. She believes that Clytemnestra, once having heard of the newborn child, will come out of curiosity and concern, perhaps wanting to ascertain that it is truly lowborn.

694–706 / 670–83 The order of speakers in this prayer is uncertain. Following Denniston's lead, we give line 698 / 674 to Electra, who would appropriately invoke the goddess Hera; but we also give her line 704 / 680, for dramatic symmetry.

702 / 678 (*kneeling and beating on the ground*) The stage directions are inferred from the text, not supplied by it. For a Greek audience, they would help recall the great invocation scene in Aeschylus' *Libation Bearers*.

707–20 / 682–95 *You, forever wronged... waiting* Our arrangement of lines 707–20 / 682–95, following Diggle, leaves many problems inadequately solved. It may be preferable, as David Kovacs suggests, (1) to restore line 708 / 684 to Electra, who cuts ceremony short with her usual abruptness; (2) to bracket lines 714–18 / 688–92, not 711–15 / 685–89, as an otiose attempt to explain and expand upon 712–13 / 686–87, and (3) to restore line 709 / 693 to its place after 718 / 692 but divide it between Orestes ("I get it") and Electra, who speaks first to Orestes ("Be the man ...") and then to the Chorus.

724–71 / 699–746 *Second stasimon* Once again the choral ode covers the passing of time while the murder of Aigisthos is being carried out. It refers, somewhat one-sidedly, to Thyestes' adultery with Aerope, wife of his brother Atreus, and her conveying to him the Golden Lamb, emblem of divinely ordained kingship; there is no mention of Atreus' horrible vengeance ("Thyestes' Feast"), an even more likely cause of the heavenly portents.

752–61 / 726–36 *Then thunder boomed... lifeless desert* In other versions, the sun reversed his course only temporarily, whether from horror or to confirm Atreus' rightful kingship. The present, apparently unique version makes him change his course to drive westward, as he has done *ever since*.

Oddly enough, this change is accompanied by another reversal, of north (to be wet) and south (dry).

768–69 / 743–45 *And stories that strike fear...the gods* The young women of the Chorus, who have grown somewhat sophisticated since the last choral ode, hint at an "opiate of the people" theory that was held by, among others, the oligarch Kritias (c. 460–403 B.C.) In this view, religion was invented by a few clever people to enforce a general fear of unseen transgressions.

772–888 / 747–858 *Third episode*

772 / 747 *EA! EA!* These inarticulate cries are transliterated from the Greek.

787 / 761 *Now let winning* The messenger proclaims victory, as in battle or an athletic contest, for the "maidens of Mycenae" through their champion Orestes (*kallinikoi* 787 / 761, picked up at 894 / 865, 911 / 886). Other athletic comparisons are given at 852–53 / 824–25, 901–3 / 862–65, 912–21 / 880–85, and 987–90 / 954–56.

799 / 772–73 *How did Aigisthos die?* In Greek he is "Thyestes' son," recalling the ancient feud. There is also a play on *Thyestes* and *thyein* (to sacrifice).

820–21 / 793–94 *But Orestes tells him...for the gods* To avoid possible contamination of the sacrifice, the stranger is invited to wash his hands; but Orestes refuses, "presumably because that would make him a full participant in the religious ceremony and involve him in sacrilege" (Denniston). His subsequent behavior shows fewer scruples.

827–72 / 800–843 *Some carried bowls...died hard* Euripides describes ritual sacrifice both as it should be and as, in this instance, it is perverted into murder.

855 / 826 *took the innards* Aigisthos practices haruspicy (the inspection of an animal's entrails for good or bad signs), and he discovers warning of a truly approaching danger. Orestes reassures him, with splendid irony.

885 / 854 *they put a crown* This is the victory garland (*stephanos*) for the head of a military or athletic victor. Electra will shortly crown the heads of Orestes and Pylades (901–3 / 870–72, 912–21 / 880–89)—and insult the head of the dead Aigisthos.

889–911 / 859–79 *Kommos* (lyric dialogue between Chorus and speaker) in place of a stasimon.

890–1185 / 880–1146 *Fourth episode*, with a brief choral interjection at 1023–33 / 988–97.

928 / 895 *I give you his head* Or, literally, "I bring you the dead man himself." Euripides gives hints, perhaps (especially at 885–87 / 855–57), but no clear stage directions here; we take full responsibility for separating Aigisthos' head from the rest of his body, despite the strong arguments of David Kovacs (*Classical Philology* 82 [1987]: 139–41).

935 / 902 *Except censure* Speaking ill of the dead ran contrary to strongly held Greek custom. Electra's insults to Aigisthos' corpse are represented as *hybris*, on a par with Aigisthos' insults, reported earlier by Electra, to Agamemnon's corpse and tomb.

941–90 / 907–56 *Where to begin . . . life's last lap* Electra's insults tumble out without plan or structure, conveying the vehemence of her loathing for the dead Aigisthos.

966–69 / 932–35 *Sheer disgrace . . . the mother's* Although Greek households were male-centered, a wife's high birth and rich dowry could give her more than usual authority. Electra's antifeminist comments are especially inappropriate in the mouth of this domineering daughter of a domineering mother.

996–1022 / 962–87 *Stop! Enough! . . . not sweet* The tension of the following scene, in which Electra pushes Orestes to be bloody, bold, and resolute, is enhanced by the already visible and audible approach of Clytemnestra with her entourage. Notice the great emphasis, by turn, on the words "mother" and "father."

1019 / 984 *with Aigisthos' help* We read *Aigisthou meta* (with Aigisthos: Wilamowitz) or, still better, *Aigisthou cheri* (by Aigisthos' hand: Parmentier; and compare 10 / 10, 16 / 17). Orestes should kill Clytemnestra by a trick, as she killed Agamemnon, using Aigisthos as a helper or instrument— which is, ironically, how Electra is using Orestes now.

1029–32 / 994–97 *You merit reverence . . . respect* The Chorus praises Clytemnestra in exaggerated terms that should elicit the gods' resentment (*phthonos*). This closely recalls the scene in Aeschylus' *Agamemnon* where Clytemnestra pressed Agamemnon to tread on the red carpet of precious cloths.

1047–87 / 1011–50 *That, I assure you* Clytemnestra's remarks open what becomes virtually a defendant's plea in a court trial; we know that she has already been condemned without a hearing and that the executioner is waiting within. Trial scenes of this kind (*agōnes*) were common in Euripides' plays, exciting for the audience and a means of exploring, though not solving, complex issues of moral choice and responsibility. Generally, as here, the second speaker successfully refutes the first.

250 / 1015 *In your situation* Other readings and interpretations of this line are possible: (1) In our situation, this is understandable (reading, *hēmin, ou kakōs*); (2) In my view, this is not well done (*hēmin, ou kalōs*). In either case, Clytemnestra argues that, once the facts are known, the prejudice against her must disappear.

269 / 1032 *a raving god-smitten girl* This is Cassandra, Apollo's prophetess, who foretold Troy's fall but never was believed. Agamemnon brought her back to Argos as his mistress.

121–22 / 1084–85 *vice gives its lesson … mirror-image* Electra means that, for good people, the wicked behavior of others gives negative examples of what they should avoid. There is also a typically Euripidean suggestion that the example of vice is infectious, a powerful miseducation.

134–38 / 1097–1101 *The man's a fool … good luck and bad* These lines have been deleted by some editors as anticlimactic and even silly, but they serve an important dramatic purpose. Electra has come very near the brink of telling the truth, frightening her mother away. Now she steps back, into commonplaces (angry speeches frequently end with such generalizations), and the Chorus quickly seconds her move.

145 / 1110 *against my husband* Or, alternatively, "drove my husband [= Aigisthos] to anger," a reflection that Electra may pick up sarcastically at line 1151 / 1116.

157 / 1122 *I do fear him* The irony is strong, and Electra again runs the risk of frightening her mother away.

167–68 / 1107–8 *And look at you … childbirth* With Diggle, we accept Weil's transposition of these lines to this place. Clytemnestra seems to see her daughter for the first time: a typical occurrence in this play of moral blindness.

186–283 / 1147–237 *Kommos*, in place of a final stasimon, presenting the climatic action (and reaction of the agents) in an emotionally intensified form.

197 / 1159 *towers built by giants* The great Mycenaean walls, of Cyclopean masonry, were supposedly built by the Kyklopes, huge one-eyed giants.

217 / 1177 *IO* Another direct transliteration, pronounced "EE-OH."

256–58 / 1214–17 *she reached up … on my face* This is the gesture of not only a mother but also a suppliant, regularly honored by the gods.

1276 / 1232 *an end of great woe* The Greek text of this line (following Diggle, we give this to Orestes) is equally ambiguous: woe "has ended" or "has come into its fullness" with Clytemnestra's death.

1276–77 / 1232–33 These final lines of the *kommos* prepare us for the arrival of Castor *and* Polydeukes. In addition to their family connection (see note on **324–25 / 312–13**), the Dioskouroi sometimes appear as bright stars or flames on ships' rigging, a sign of hope and salvation.

1284–404 / 1238–369 *Exodos*

1298–321 / 1252–75 *The terror you called forth…bears your name* The Furies will pursue Orestes to Athens, where he will be tried before the divinely established court of the Areopagos and acquitted. So much is reassuringly Aeschylean. But notice that (1) the court is not established for Orestes' sake—or the rule that "equal votes spell acquittal"; (2) the Furies will not be reconciled, this time, by Athena's gentle persuasion (in Euripides' *Iphigenia in Tauris* [968–82], only half the Furies are reconciled, and half continue to pursue Orestes); and (3) Orestes will not reenter his city as its rightful heir and ruler but will found Oresteion, a savage, remote village in Arkadia.

1304 / 1258 *Ares' hill* Halirrhothios, the son of Poseidon, raped Ares' daughter Alkippe; Ares killed him in anger, was tried for murder by a divinely instituted court, and was acquitted. Thus the Areopagos (Ares' hill) lends its name to the ancient and once-powerful Athenian court that, in Euripides' time, still tried homicide cases.

1327 / 1281 *She never went to Troy* In the lovely, unorthodox version told by the sixth-century lyric poet Stesichoros and used by Euripides himself in his *Helen* of 412 B.C., Helen was innocent; she remained in, or was sent to, Egypt; and the Trojan war was fought for her image. On the one hand, this means forgiveness for Helen and perhaps, by implication, for all of us. On the other hand, the mystery of evil, of suffering, is referred back to Zeus.

1338–54 / 1292–307 *O sons of Zeus…destroyed them both* For the choice and order of speakers here (Orestes and Electra, not the Chorus, speaking with the Dioskouroi), we follow the manuscript readings, defended by David Kovacs (*Classical Quarterly* 35 [1985]: 310–14). If Kovacs' reading of lines **1340–41 / 1294** is correct, the Dioskouroi are behaving like very liberal justices, indeed, for Castor asserts that Orestes and Electra are not polluted.

392–93 / 1347–48 *Ships are breaking . . . required* Castor's mention of their hurrying to the Sicilian Sea has often been taken as an allusion to the Sicilian Expedition of 415–413 B.C., and specifically to Demosthenes' relief expedition in the spring of 413. But this seems overprecise. It is enough that Euripides alludes to perils of nature and history to which cities, not just individuals, must be exposed.

IPHIGENIA IN TAURIS

Translated by

RICHMOND LATTIMORE

INTRODUCTION

I

Iphigenia in Tauris was probably presented in 414 B.C. It is almost certainly later than the *Trojan Women* (415 B.C.) and earlier than *Helen* (412 B.C.). The drama in theme and structure is entirely different from the *Trojan Women* and still more strikingly similar to *Helen*. This fact has been pointed out before, but the more one studies the two plays the more similarities appear. Without claiming that the list is exhaustive, I would offer the following table:

Iphigeneia	*Helen*
The heroine has been divinely transported to the ends of the earth (the land of the Taurians on the Black Sea) and thus rescued from danger (death).	The heroine has been divinely transported to the ends of the earth (Egypt) and thus rescued from danger (abduction and rape).
The heroine opens the play by telling her story in a monologue of sixty-six lines.	The heroine opens the play by telling her story in a monologue of sixty-seven lines.
The heroine is maintained in honorable captivity by the local barbarian prince, Thoas. Thoas loves Iphigeneia? Thus Goethe in his version, but, despite 1190 / 1213, I doubt this.	The heroine is maintained in honorable captivity by the local barbarian prince, Theoklymenos, who loves Helen and seeks to marry her.

The heroine is attended by a Chorus of homesick Greek women, who are captive slaves.

The heroine presumes, on very slight evidence, that her long-lost brother is dead, just before he appears.

The heroine with the Chorus mourns the death of her brother.

The heroine is told of the fall of Troy and the fates of various Achaians.

Brother and sister recognize each other.

Brother and sister plan their escape. After two futile suggestions by the hero (one of which is the killing of the king), the heroine propounds the successful plot.

The escape plot uses the pretext of a religious ceremony, thus playing on the piety of the barbarian king, who grants the Greeks an escort.

The messenger gives the king an account of the flight in ninety-three lines.

The king's men have suspected a trick but did not dare to act until almost too late.

Pursuit is ultimately halted by a divine epiphany. The king's *rage* is ended and the Chorus is saved.

The heroine is attended by a Chorus of homesick Greek women, who are captive slaves.

The heroine presumes, on very slight evidence, that her long-lost husband is dead, just before he appears.

The heroine with the Chorus mourns the death of her husband.

The heroine is told of the fall of Troy and the fates of various Achaians.

Husband and wife recognize each other.

Husband and wife plan their escape. After two futile suggestions by the hero (one of which is the killing of the king), the heroine propounds the successful plot.

The escape plot uses the pretext of a religious ceremony, thus playing on the piety of the barbarian king, who grants the Greeks an escort.

The messenger gives the king an account of the flight in ninety-three lines.

The king's men have suspected a trick but did not dare to act until too late.

The escape is ultimately expounded by a divine epiphany. The king's rage is ended and his sister is saved.

In addition to these parallels, each play contains one stasimon, or choral ode, which has little or nothing to do with the action of the drama. These odes are divine myths, sacred stories of the gods as interludes in the adventures of heroes. In *Iphigenia in Tauris* (1211–56 / 1234–83) we hear of the wrath of earth against Apollo when he usurped the oracle at Delphi; in *Helen* (1301–68), of the wrath of Demeter when her daughter was ravished.

There are, of course, many noteworthy differences between the two plays. The recognition scenes, for example, are in themselves quite differently contrived. Greek plays have been shown frequently to conform, in their several portions, to certain structural conventions; that is, there are repeated forms for (especially) prologue, theophany or *deus ex machina*, messenger scene or catastrophe, dirge. These two plays, beyond other extant tragedies, conform in pattern through their entire action.

Iphigenia in Tauris, like *Helen*, retells the *end* of a long tale of tribulation and loss, through final discovery and reunion, and points to a fortunate future for a loving pair. It is a well-made, conventional play whose author is well aware of the demands of plot. And in simple terms, it moves from bad to good rather than, like *Oedipus*, good to bad or, better, bad to worse. Such features have suggested to modern critics that our play, along with *Helen*, *Ion*, and many lost dramas especially by Euripides, belongs with comedy rather than tragedy, and we hear such terms as "romantic comedy" or "tragicomedy." It is necessary to recognize that the term "tragedy" is commonly applied in modern criticism in a sense quite different from its original sense. While no critic would soberly deny that Sophocles' *Philoktetes* is a genuine tragedy, happy ending and all, we do persistently associate the term with downfall, death, disaster. Such associations have been so sanctioned by usage since the Middle Ages that they cannot be ignored. At the same time, we should realize that to call *Iphigenia in Tauris* "not a tragedy at all" (thus Platnauer, my debt to whom is acknowledged below) would have been virtually nonsensical to Euripides, Aristotle, and Athens. The occasion and sanctions of performance, the use of heroic legend, the tragic diction and meters, the tragic actors, costumes, and every circumstance defined it as tragedy, and the happy ending made no difference. By these genuine standards, *Iphigenia in Tauris* is just as much a tragedy as *Antigone*, just as surely as *Tosca* and *The Marriage of Figaro* are both operas.

II

Perhaps "romantic tragedy" is a better term (though it might remind one of *Romeo and Juliet*). I have tried elsewhere to show some essential distinctions between the happy-ending plays of Euripides and the romantic comedy of Menanader and his successors, which does in great part derive from them. But we are concerned here with the difference between *Iphigenia in Tauris*, *Helen*, and perhaps *Ion* on the one hand, and *Medea*, *Hippolytos*, and *Herakles* on the other. For despite all the foregoing, there are vital differences, not only in story type but in dramatic quality and characterization.

What manner of dramatic person do we find in Iphigeneia, Orestes, and their lesser supporting characters? Character is expressed in action and has to do with the nature of the story. In this play, the emphasis is on what happens, and how, rather than why. Things have happened and do happen to Iphigeneia and Orestes, but their histories do not spring inevitably from anything inherent in their own natures. They are more like sets of responses than dynamic characters with insistent wills. Iphigeneia responds to events as would a good normal young woman to whom astonishing things have happened. Orestes has murdered, and is prepared to murder again if necessary, but he is not murderous; the murder is part of the whole series of events through which he has been pushed about. Brother and sister come of a house that has suffered under a curse, despite its glories, through the brilliant but bloody and corrupt saga of Pelops and Hippodameia, Atreus and Thyestes, Agamemnon and Clytemnestra. All this is recognized and alluded to, but it does not haunt the present action as in Aeschylus the present actors are haunted by a sick and sickening past. That is not the business of this play, for these people are to be the survivors escaping from adventure into respectability, which is what they desire. Iphigeneia once wanted Achilles; she will get a lifetime office attached once more to a shrine; but she will be content. The emotion is there, but it is homesickness and longing for family reunions.

Recognition and escape, action, plot, are dominant in this play. Some sacrifices are made and one can sometimes see the machinery at work. Here is an example: After the ecstasies over recognition, Pylades (880 / 902) points out that escape is now the priority. Orestes agrees. But Iphigeneia insists on extracting some further information about the family. She is entitled to know about this before we are through with her, and here is the only place the action's economy will allow it. But when the murder of Clytemnestra comes up and Iphigeneia asks about her motives, Orestes curtly cuts her off, and she meekly agrees. She is not really so meek, and shall she go through the rest of her life not knowing what Clytemnestra was about? Certainly not. But if Orestes went into that, it would not so much delay the pace of the action as alter the tone of the play, which is not about the sins of the house but about the reunion and escape of its survivors. It is very neat to make Orestes appeal to the standard of what an unmarried, still-young lady ought or ought not to be told about.

Consider also the messenger's recounting the escape to the ship. The messenger's speech is by now a standard feature of tragedy. It gives the poet a chance to indulge his powers in straight narration—for the messenger himself is usually little more than an announcer—and was doubtless awaited with eagerness by the audience. Without it, the story of this escape would be woefully incomplete. But the messenger scene can also, sometimes, strain a too literal credulity. In *Medea* and *Ion* the messenger begins with something like "Run for your life," and then proceeds to a deliberately detailed narrative. Here, the natural impulse of Thoas would be to rush to the scene. So he and the messenger assure each other that escape is impossible and there is no real need for haste; and the king, and we, can listen to the story.

Such considerations may seem prosaic when applied to a beautiful poetic play; but in truth this drama is not one of the deep ones, nor is it personal, or intense. The dominant emotions are homesickness and family feeling, The Euripidean drive for escape is there, but this time it is not escape from love, sex, self, or life, but from disliked foreign climes to Greece, symbolized in the rescue of Artemis herself from her outlandish cult and her removal to civilized Attica. But the feeling of homesickness is most poignantly expressed by the captive women in the loveliest choral ode in the play (1067–128 / 1089–152). Behind their presence on stage one can see the Greek women from stormed cities actually sold as slaves into barbary. It is only here, through them, I think, that the time of war in which this drama was written makes itself felt. The horror of destructive war cannot be escaped in the *Trojan Women*, presented, probably, only one year earlier. In *Iphigenia in Tauris* the women of the Chorus will, by Athena's orders, be restored to their homes. The Trojan Women, like the real women of Melos, had no homes to go to.

But our play is not, like the *Trojan Women*, an artistic expression of protest. We do not find here resentment against things as they are, or angry criticism of the gods. The gods figure mainly as manipulators. The play begins with one miracle, and ends with another; they are not miracles which Euripides, or most of his audience, was likely to believe in. Apollo has pushed Orestes here and there. When his benevolence, or competence, is challenged, this is not so much Euripides challenging divinity as a dramatic trope: the true helper thought to be false just before his truth is vindicated. Apollo seems to me to be a credible object of religious feeling only in the little amoral hymn about the baby god (1211–56 / 1234–83). The Artemis who is a piece of consecrated wood is also an object of religious feeling, though her priestess uses her sanctity in the most cynical kind of strategy. She has to be rescued and transported by human hands with the help of another goddess; but she still retains more divinity than the story-contrivance goddess who snatched Iphigeneia away from Aulis. Iphigeneia dislikes her Taurian rites; but her criticism of illogical aspects of this cult, while standard Euripides, is aimed at human practice rather than at divinities as such. The *deus ex machina* in the conclusion facilitates the completion of the plot, and ties up most of the loose ends. It also establishes a cult, which Euripides might well have respected; and Athena, as well as being a story-goddess, represents Athens. Euripides had his complaints about Athens and his complaints about religion, but this happy-ending tragedy—and that is not a contradiction in terms—was not the proper medium for their expression. The gods are used here in uncontroversial terms.

III

Iphigeneia is not in Homer, unless she is the same as the Iphianassa named in Book IX of the *Iliad* (but Sophocles in his *Elektra* distinguishes them). At any rate, in Homer nobody sacrifices or attempts to sacrifice any daughter of Agamemnon. The slaughter of Iphigeneia is a constant theme in tragedy, but no extant tragedy recounts that slaughter. The post-Homeric epic *Kypria*[1] told how, when Iphigeneia was about to be sacrificed at Aulis, Artemis snatched her away, substituting a fawn in her place, and immortalized her among the Taurians. The rescue is also attested in a rather recently published fragment of Hesiod.[2] Hesiod calls her Iphimede, but obviously means the same heroine, since he records that the Achaians sacrificed only the image of the girl (as Paris married Helen's image only). Iphimede herself was rescued and immortalized by Artemis, like her aunt, Phylonoë, according to the same fragment. These are the earliest sources we have for Iphigeneia. On the other hand, Pindar, in his Pythian XI (either 474 or 454 B.C.), implies that Iphigeneia really was slaughtered. Aeschylus in *Agamemnon* breaks off his moving and magnificent description of the sacrifice just before the blow falls.

---

1. Conveniently found in *Hesiod, the Homeric Hymns, and Homerica*, ed. H. G. Evelyn-White, 2d ed. (Loeb Series) (London and Cambridge, Mass., 1936).
2. *Fragmenta Hesiodea*, ed. R. Merkelbach and M. L. West (Oxford, 1967).

The genuine ending of Euripides' own *Iphigenia at Aulis* is lost; but there is evidence that in this play, too, the divine rescue took place. Sophocles, it seems, and certainly one later tragic poet had Iphigeneia survive and be found by Orestes. Thus the version in which Iphigeneia is saved is well attested, even prevalent. But all her people, as in this play, believe that she has been slaughtered; though it is difficult to reconstruct the feelings of spectators at the sacrifice at Aulis when they saw the slain fawn on the altar. Pindar and the dramatists state or suggest that her sacrifice was a motive for Clytemnestra's murder of Agamemnon. If the mother was made to believe that the sacrifice was really consummated, the poet does not have to go into the question of rescue. He can eat his cake and have it, depending on which end of the story he is telling.

This Introduction began with a study of the analogies between Iphigeneia and Helen. There is one more point of resemblance. Helen was worshiped as a goddess in Sparta and Iphigeneia was immortalized and closely associated with Artemis. Herodotos in his *History* says that the goddess to whom the Taurians offered human sacrifice was, according to the Taurians themselves, Iphigeneia the daughter of Agamemnon. Both Iphigeneia and Helen doubled as heroines and goddesses.

IV

This translation is based on the Greek text of Gilbert Murray as published in Oxford Classical Texts, second edition, 1913. I have consulted the excellent commentary of Maurice Platnauer in his edition of the play (Oxford, 1938) at every step, and am immensely indebted. My errors will be my own. The text as it has come down to us is full of difficulties and corruptions. At times I have simply had to adopt a makeshift interpretation which seemed to make some kind of sense.

RICHMOND LATTIMORE

IPHIGENIA IN TAURIS

Translated by

RICHMOND LATTIMORE

CHARACTERS

IPHIGENEIA   daughter of Agamemnon, priestess of Artemis in the land of the
            Taurians

ORESTES   brother of Iphigeneia

PYLADES   son of Strophies, Orestes' cousin and close friend

THOAS   king of the Taurians

HERDSMAN

MESSENGER   one of Thoas' guards

CHORUS   of fifteen Greek women, captive slaves of Thoas

ATHENA   the goddess

            Girls, attendants of Iphigeneia
            Guards, in charge of Orestes and Pylades
            Attendants of Thoas

Line numbers in the right-hand margin of the text refer to the English
translation only, and the Notes beginning at page 153 are keyed to
these lines. The bracketed line numbers in the running heads refer to
the Greek text.

Before the door of the temple of Artemis, in the Taurian country. Enter IPHIGENEIA, *alone, to speak the prologue.*

IPHIGENEIA Pelops, the son of Tantalos, came to Pisa once
with his swift chariot, married Oinomaos' daughter,
who bore him Atreus. Atreus had sons. They were
Menelaos and Agamemnon. I am Agamemnon's child.
I am Iphigeneia, Clytemnestra's daughter.
And where Euripos strait with pulsing gusts of wind
tosses the blue sea-water and reverses it,
my father thought he sacrificed me to Artemis
because of Helen, in the famous Aulis bay.
For at that place lord Agamemnon had assembled   10
the expedition of a thousand Hellenes' ships.
He wished the crown of victory over Ilion
for the Achaians, and to avenge the marriage of Helen
outraged by violence, and to comfort Menelaos.
But hard winds were against him, and he could not sail.
He turned to divination. Kalchas said to him:
"Agamemnon, lord over this Greek armament,
you cannot clear your ship from shore till Artemis
has taken Iphigeneia, your daughter, sacrificed
by you. You vowed to offer up the loveliest thing   20
the year gave birth to, to the goddess who brings light.
Your consort Clytemnestra bore a child in your house."
(By this he meant that I was the year's loveliest gift.)
"You must offer her up." They took me from my mother
        then.
Odysseus lied, and said I was to marry Achilles.
I came to Aulis, wretched I. I was caught and held
above the death-pyre, and the sword was ready to kill.
But Artemis stole me away, and gave to the Achaians
a fawn in my place, and carried me through the bright air

99

to this land of the Taurians, and settled me here.   30
Here the lord of the country, the barbarian
Thoas, rules his barbarians. His name means swift.
He is wing-footed, and his speed makes good the name.
He has established me as priestess in this shrine.
There are rituals here; the goddess Artemis is pleased
with them: a holy service: only the name is good.
I must not tell the details, for I fear the god,
but I sacrifice, by custom known before my time
in the state, any Greek man who comes upon this shore.
I dedicate them: the real killing is left to others,   40
and done in secret in the temple of this god.
      But this past night brought with it dreams both strange
        and new.
I will tell them to the air. It may bring some relief.
I thought within my dream I had escaped this land
and lived in Argos. There I slept among my girls.
And then the earth was shaken like a stormy sea,
but I escaped and stood outside and watched the cornice
of the house fall apart, and all the covering roof
was tumbled from its high position to the ground.
One single pillar, as it seemed to me, was left   50
in my father's house, and from its capital the blond
hair streamed, and it took human voice and spoke. Then I,
faithful to my own deadly duty done to strangers,
sprinkled him with the water that prepares for death,
myself in tears. I reconstruct my vision thus.
Orestes, whom I dedicated, is now dead,
for the male children are the pillars of the house,
but those on whom my lustral waters fall must die.
I cannot make the rest of the family fit this dream.
Strophios had no children when I faced my death.   60
I wish, then, to attend the absent, give my brother
his last rites. So much I can do for him—with help
from my attendants, those Greek women given me
by the king. Where are they? For some reason or another
they have not yet arrived. I will retire to the house,
this temple of the goddess which is now my home.   *Exit*

Enter ORESTES *and* PYLADES.

ORESTES Look around. Be careful. Somebody may be on the road.

PYLADES So I do. I am looking. My eyes go everywhere.

ORESTES Pylades, do you think this is the temple
of that goddess for whom we sailed from Argos, and came
                  here?   70

PYLADES I think so, Orestes. You must think so, too.

ORESTES And this is the altar, dripping with Hellenic blood?

PYLADES At least the top of it is brown with bloodstains.

ORESTES And hanging under the edge itself, do you see the spoils?

PYLADES Yes, skulls of slaughtered strangers, as an offering.
But it is best to take a good look all around.

ORESTES Phoibos, what trap is this? Where have you brought me now
by prophecies? I have avenged my father's blood.
I killed my mother. Relays of vindictive Furies
have driven me in flight, an exile out of my land,   80
and many are the reversing courses I have run.
I came to you and asked you how to reach the end
and respite from my headlong madness and the pain
and weariness of wandering all the length of Greece.
You told me to come here, into the Taurian land,
where Artemis, your sister, has her altar, here
to seize that image of the goddess, which they say
fell once upon this very temple from the sky.
When I have captured it, by cleverness or luck,
and won the perilous quest, I must deliver it   90
to Attic soil. Nothing was ordered beyond that.
But I shall have rest from labors when this task is done.
It was through your persuasive words that I came here

to this unknown unfriendly country.
                                        Pylades,
you are my helper in this work. I ask for counsel.
What shall we do? You see the surrounding walls, how high
they are. Can we go straight up on the temple stair
to the door? How can we do this and remain unseen?
Can we with crowbars force apart the brazen doors?
We know of no crowbars. Furthermore, if we are caught   100
forcing the doors open, contriving entrances,
then we shall die. Sooner than die, let us escape
aboard that ship in which we made our voyage here.

PYLADES Flight is unendurable. It is not our way.
         We must not spoil the force of the god's utterance.
         But let us leave the temple now, and hide ourselves
         in caves carved out with water by the darkening sea,
         away from the ship, for fear that someone may spy the hull
         and tell the king; for then we should be caught by force.
         But after sunset, when the face of night comes on,   110
         then we must practice all our ingenuity
         and dare to steal the wooden image from the shrine.
         See there between the triglyphs, there is an empty space
         where one could slip inside. It is the brave who dare
         adventures. Cowards never amount to anything.

ORESTES It shall not be that we have come this long sea way
         and then, short of our destination, turned for home.
         You are right, then, and to be obeyed. We must withdraw
         and find some place in this land where we can hide
                  ourselves.
         The god's cause shall not be so ended that his word   120
         is being spent upon futility. We must be bold,
         for hardship offers no excuse when men are young.

                   Exeunt. Enter the CHORUS *and* IPHIGENEIA.

CHORUS   Silence, oh silence,
         all who dwell by the Clashing Rocks

on the unfriendly sea.
Daughter of Leto,
Diktynna of the wild mountains,
to your court, to the golden
wall of the columned temple,
I come with devout and maidenly step,   130
slave to the devout key-bearer,
exiled from the walls and towers of Greece,
from forest range and grassland,
exiled from Europe
and the mansion house of my fathers.
I am here. What is new? What care is yours,
O daughter of Agamemnon
who came against the fortress of Troy
with his famous fleet,
the thousand ships   140
and thousands and thousands of armed men?

IPHIGENEIA O my attendant women,
hard mourning melodies are my task,
discordant singing of sorrows,
lyreless complaints
the tears of pity.
Disaster has fallen upon me.
I mourn the death of my brother.
Such was the vision I saw,
a dream in my sleep   150
in the dark of the night now ended.
Ruin, I am ruined.
The house of my father is gone;
its seed is perished.
Alas, the sorrows of Argos.
O divine spirit,
you robbed me of my sole brother, sent him
to Hades; for him I prepare
the bowl of libations poured for the perished
to splash on earth's surface: 160
streams of milk from the mountain cattle,

wine, the liquid of Bacchus,
the artful work of the tawny bees:
charms for the dead established by use.

Give me the all-gold vessel
and the libations for Hades.

O scion of Agamemnon, beneath
the ground, I give you this, as to one dead.
Accept. I shall not bring my tears
nor my blond hair to your tomb.   170
I have been exiled far from the land
which is yours and mine, and where I am thought
to have been killed, to lie buried.

CHORUS   I will sing you an answering song,
            the Asian strain, the barbarian dirge,
            mistress, the melody used
            in lamentation,
            dirges for the dead, the song that is sung
            by Hades, no peal of triumph.
            Alas for the house of Atreus and his line.   180
            The light of their scepters is gone
            from the house of your fathers.
            There was a reign of prospering kings
            in Argos once
            and trouble on trouble assailed them.
            There was the charioteer hurled out
            by Pelops once from his flying chariot,
            and the sacred gleam of the sun forsook
            his former place. A succession of pains
            befell the house because of the golden lamb,   190
            murder on murder, grief on grief.
            Thus for those of the Tantalid line
            who were killed before, retribution comes
            on the house, and the spirit inflicts on you
            what should not be.

IPHIGENEIA My fortune has been misfortune
since the bridal night of my mother
when I was conceived; from the outset
the divine fates who were present
at my birth have schooled me in hardship.   200
My mother, sad daughter of Leda,
was courted among the Hellenes.
I was her first child born in her chambers.
For sacrifice and for slaughter
unhallowed, for the disgrace of my father
she bore and raised me.
In a chariot drawn by horses
they brought me to the sands of Aulis,
a bride cursed in her bridal
for Achilles, son of the Nereid.   210
Now, an alien by the unfriendly sea,
without marriage or child, without city or friend,
I am housed in an arid country.
I do not dance for Argive Hera,
nor on the murmuring loom
work out with my shuttle the pictured form
of Titans and Pallas Athena;
but with bloody and harsh music
I work bloody despair of strangers
whose cries are pitiful   220
as are pitiful the tears they shed.
But now I forget my pity for these,
and bewail the dead man in Argos,
my brother, whom I left as a child at the breast,
still a baby, growing and flourishing,
in his mother's arms, held fast to her breast,
and prince of Argos, Orestes.

CHORUS I see a herdsman coming in our direction.
He comes from the sea shore, with something to report.

Enter the HERDSMAN.

HERDSMAN Daughter of Agamemnon and of Clytemnestra   230
          I bring you news of strange happenings. Hear my story.

IPHIGENEIA What is startling about the story you have to tell?

HERDSMAN Two young men have slipped through the dark and
                clashing rocks
          in their ship, and made their way to our country. They will be
          a sacrifice and a burnt offering that will please
          the goddess Artemis. Make ready then the water
          and other preparations. You cannot act too soon.

IPHIGENEIA Where are they from? What country's costume do they
                wear?

HERDSMAN They are Greeks, but that is all I know about them.

IPHIGENEIA You did not hear either of the strangers use a name?   240

HERDSMAN I heard one of them call the other Pylades.

IPHIGENEIA What then was the name of this stranger's companion?

HERDSMAN Nobody knows that. We heard nothing.

IPHIGENEIA How did you happen to see them and to capture them?

HERDSMAN By the sea side, at the beach of the unfriendly strait . . .

IPHIGENEIA (interrupting) What have oxherds to do with the sea?

HERDSMAN We had gone down to bathe our cattle in the water.

IPHIGENEIA Come back to my first question, how you captured them
          and by what means, since this is what I wish to hear.
          They have been long in coming. Never yet has blood   250
          of Greeks been shed upon the altar of the goddess.

HERDSMAN When we had brought our forest-feeding cattle down
          into the sea that flows between the Clashing Rocks,
          there was a cave in the cliffs that had been hollowed
          by the breaking of much surf, where purple-fishers camp.
          In there one herdsman of our company espied
          a pair of young men. He came back to us again
          walking on tiptoe very carefully, and said:
          "There are some gods sitting in there. Will you not go
          and look?" One of our number then, a pious man,   260
          looked in the cave, then raised his arms in the air and
                    prayed:
          "Son of Leukothea of the sea, savior of ships,
          Palaimon, lord, be gracious, and be gracious, too,
          if you are the Dioscuri who are seated there,
          nurslings dear to Nereus, who is the father
          of Nereids, all fifty in their lovely choir."
          But there was another, a rough man, lawless and rude,
          who laughed at prayers, said they were shipwrecked
                    mariners
          who had taken refuge in the cave, fearing our custom,
          having been told of how we sacrifice outlanders.   270
          This man was right, most of us thought, and we resolved
          to seize and offer them to the god, as is our rule.
                    Meanwhile, one of the strangers came out of the cave
          and stood there, shaking his head up and down, trembling
          to the fingertips, and screamed aloud, caught in some fit
          of madness, and cried out, the way a hunter cries:
          "Pylades, there, did you see her? There's another one,
          a serpent of the god of death, who tries to kill me,
          and arms against me all the vipers of her hair.
          Another, blasting fire and murder from her clothes,   280
          swoops over me on beating wings. She holds my mother
          in her arms, to drop her on me like a weight of stone.
          Oh, she will kill me. Where shall I run?" There was nothing
                    there
          to be seen that looked like any such creatures. He mistook
          the voices of the lowing cattle and barking dogs,
          and thought they reproduced the clamor of the Furies.

107

We drew together in a group, and held our place,
silent and wondering; but then he drew his sword
and like a lion sprang into the midst of the cows
and laid about him with the steel, struck flank and rib,   290
thinking so to beat off the divine Furies' attack.
He made the surface of the sea bloom bright with blood.
At this, all of us, when we saw our pastured herds
were being felled, wasted and ruined, rushed to arms
and blew the sea-horns to arouse the neighborhood.
We thought that we mere herdsmen were too weak to fight
these foreign men who were so young and strongly built.
We grew into a multitude, though it took time.
Now the young man, after his fit was gone, fell down
with the foam running down his chin. We, seeing him   300
felled and at our mercy, then did all we could
to stone and pelt him, but the other foreigner
wiped the foam from his face, guarded the prostrate man,
and held his handsome woven robe in front of him,
dodging the dangerous missiles that we threw at both
and doing everything he could to help his friend.
And now, restored to sanity, the fallen man
sprang up, and saw the tide of war that threatened them
and the advancing ruin that was all but there.
He groaned; but we did not give up our shower of stones   310
and kept attacking, now from this side, now from that,
until we heard the dread cry of encouragement:
"Pylades, we must die, but if we must die then
with all honor. Out with your sword and follow me."
We, when we saw the onset of two waving swords,
ran back, and filled the stony gullies with our numbers,
but where some fled, others would then attack in turn
and throw at them; then if they turned and stabbed at these,
those who had run away before would now throw stones.
But it was unbelievable. So many threw,   320
but none could hit the destined victims of the god.
At last we beat them, not by courage or by strength,
but we surrounded them and with a shower of stones

knocked the swords from their hands, and they, for sheer
       fatigue,
sank to the ground. So we conveyed them to the king
of the country. He looked at them and sent them to you
with all speed, for consecration and for sacrifice.
Young mistress, you were praying that such foreigners
be yours to offer up. If you can waste this kind of stranger
in numbers, Hellas thus shall give you satisfaction   330
for their attempt to murder you in Aulis once.

CHORUS This was a strange tale of the mad man, who lived once
in Hellas, and has come to our unfriendly sea.

IPHIGENEIA Very well. Go fetch the strangers then, and bring them
      to me.
I shall see to the sacraments that take place here.
O wretched heart of mine, you were considerate
toward strangers formerly, and always pitied them.
The tie of kinship could be measured by your tears
whenever it was Greeks who came into your hands.
But now, by reason of my dream, which has made me fierce   340
because I think Orestes sees daylight no more,
you who arrive from this time forth will find me harsh.
For here, friends, is a truth which I have just now learned.
When people are unfortunate, their suffering
makes them no kinder to those even less fortunate.
But no wind sent from Zeus has ever come to us,
nor any vessel through the Clashing Rocks, that brought
me Helen, the one who ruined me, nor Menelaos.
Had they been in my power, I could have punished them,
making this place an Aulis like that other Aulis   350
where, like a young calf, I was seized by the Danaans
as a victim, and the sacrificer was my father.
I never can forget the sorrows of that time,
how many times I tried to clutch my father's chin
or throw my arms around his knees and cling to them.
Thus I would babble: "Father, this is my marriage time,

but you have made it into a thing of shame. While you
are killing me, my mother and the Argive women
are singing marriage songs, and all the house is full
of flute music, while I am being killed by you.   360
Achilles is then no son of Peleus. He is Death.
I am his bride. You tempted, and escorted me
treacherously by chariot to a bloody marriage."
I had kept my face and eyes behind my delicate veil.
I could not bring myself to throw my arms around
my brother, who is dead now, nor to kiss the lips
of my sister. I was bashful, being on the way
to Peleus' house, but I was saving many kisses
for the time when I would visit Argos once again.
Now, poor Orestes, if you are dead, from what high hopes   370
your father had and from what splendors are you fallen.

      But the goddess is too subtle. I do not approve.
When she considers any mortal stained with blood,
if only from childbirth or from contact with a corpse,
she keeps him from her altars, thinking him unclean,
while she herself is pleased with human sacrifice.
It is impossible that Leto, bride of Zeus,
produced so unfeeling a child. I myself think
the tale of how Tantalos entertained the gods
by feeding them his son is not to be believed.   380
I also think these people, being murderous,
put off the blame for their own vice upon the gods.
I do not think any divinity is bad.

CHORUS   Dark oh dark
      meeting-place of two seas
      where Io driven and flying came
      from Argos to the Euxine
      and made the change
      from Europe over to Asia.
      But who are these? Was it from the reedy sweet stream   390
      of Eurotas they left behind
      or the hallowed waters of Dirke
      when they came to this inhospitable land
      where the altars and porticoed

temple of the bright maiden
are stained with the blood of humans?

Or did they sail
with double beat of the fir-wood
oars across the surge of the sea,
riding with sails wind-driven   400
upon a distant quest
to increase their halls' treasures?
For hope is fond, and, to people's misfortune,
insatiable for the persons
who bring back the rich cargoes,
wanderers over the sea to the cities and the outlanders.
All with one single
purpose; sometimes their judgment of profit
fails; sometimes it attains.

How did they pass the Clashing Rocks,   410
how pass the sleepless strands
of Phineus' harpies,
running across
the foam to the far beach
of Amphitrite,
where the chorus of fifty girls,
the Nereids, step and weave their dance
circles? How did they pass
as the cradled oars
sang at the stern before airs   420
that filled the sail,
blowing from the south
or winds from the west
to the land where the birds gather,
the white strand where Achilles
runs his shining races
along the unfriendly sea?

If only my mistress' prayers
could come true, and Helen,
Leda's darling daughter,   430

could come here
on her way from Troy, and with deadly
lustral water poured on her hair
die with her throat cut
by the hand of our mistress,
and pay the penalty she deserves.
But the sweetest news I could hear
would be that some seafarer
from Greece had arrived
to put an end to the pain   440
of my sad slavery.
For in my dreams I would be
in my house and my father's city,
to enjoy the delight of our songs,
a grace shared by all of us.

> ORESTES *and* PYLADES *are brought in by temple*
> *attendants.*

But here, with their hands bound, leaning
on each other, are the two young men, a fresh
sacrifice to the goddess. Hush, dear friends,
for these are a choice offering
from Greece who come to our temple.   450
The oxherd man
told us, then, no false story.
Goddess, if you are pleased with the way
of this city, accept the sacrifice;
but our custom in Greece
declares that it is not holy.

IPHIGENEIA So.
My first consideration must be for the goddess
and how to please her. Now untie the strangers' hands.
They are sacred victims and must be no longer bound.   460
Go into the temple and have everything in order
which is needed and customary for our present business.

> *Attendants go into the temple.* IPHIGENEIA *contemplates*
> ORESTES *and* PYLADES.

Who was the mother who gave you birth? Who was your
    father?
Who is your sister? Did you ever have a sister?
What a pair of young brothers she has lost in you
and will be brotherless. Who knows which ones will suffer
this kind of loss? The progress of the gods' designs
goes through the dark. Our own misfortunes are unknown.
Fortune twists everything, so it is hard to see.

Where do you come from, O unhappy travelers?   470
You have sailed a great distance in order to reach this land,
and, far from home, must spend eternity below.

ORESTES Why, mistress, whoever you are, these words of pity,
    thus adding to the pain we must look forward to?
    I find no wisdom in one who, about to kill,
    tries to combat the fear of death by sympathy,
    nor one who comforts a person on the brink of death
    but gives no hope of rescue. Out of a single evil
    he makes two, by being silly, while the victim
    dies anyway. We should take fortune as it comes.   480
    Stop being sorry for us. We well understand
    the kind of sacrifice that is conducted here.

IPHIGENEIA Which of you two is the one who was addressed by name
    as Pylades? This is the first thing I would know.

ORESTES He is. Do you get any pleasure from learning that?

IPHIGENEIA Of which city in Greece is he a citizen?

ORESTES What good would it do you, mistress, if we told you that?

IPHIGENEIA Are you brothers, then, born of a single mother?

ORESTES Brothers in love we are, but not brothers by birth.

IPHIGENEIA What was the name that your father bestowed on you?   490

ORESTES The right name to call me would be Unlucky Man.

IPHIGENEIA That is not what I mean. Give that name to your fate.

ORESTES If we die nameless, no one can insult our names.

IPHIGENEIA But why do you begrudge me? Are you then so proud?

ORESTES It will be my body, not my name, you sacrifice.

IPHIGENEIA Will you not even tell me what your city is?

ORESTES It will do no good to answer. I am going to die.

IPHIGENEIA But what prevents you from doing me this favor?

ORESTES I claim glorious Argos for my fatherland.

IPHIGENEIA In the gods' name, is that true, my friend? Were you
         born there?   500

ORESTES I am from Mycenae, which was once a prospering city.

IPHIGENEIA Are you an exile from your land, or what has happened?

ORESTES I am an involuntary voluntary exile.

IPHIGENEIA Now will you tell me one more thing I wish to know?

ORESTES I suppose so. My misfortune gives me plenty of time.

IPHIGENEIA But your arrival from Argos is a welcome thing.

ORESTES I do not welcome it, but you may, if you like.

IPHIGENEIA Perhaps you know of Troy, which is spoken of everywhere.

ORESTES I wish I had never even dreamed of its existence.

IPHIGENEIA They say the spear has captured it and the town is gone.   510

ORESTES That is the truth, and what they told you was accurate.

IPHIGENEIA Has Helen come back to the house of Menelaos?

ORESTES She has. It was bad news for one of my family.

IPHIGENEIA Where is she? I also owe her no good will.

ORESTES She is in Sparta, living with her former husband.

IPHIGENEIA Hateful to all the Greeks and not to me alone.

ORESTES I, too, have been affected because she ran away.

IPHIGENEIA Did the Achaians reach home, as the rumor goes?

ORESTES You are asking me to tell you everything at once.

IPHIGENEIA Before you die, I would like to hear everything.   520

ORESTES Ask then, since that is what you want, and I will answer.

IPHIGENEIA Did a certain prophet called Kalchas ever come back from
           Troy?

ORESTES The report in Mycenae was that he is dead.

IPHIGENEIA Thanks be to Artemis. What of Odysseus, Laertes' son?

ORESTES The story was that he was alive, but not returned.

IPHIGENEIA A curse on him. I hope he dies and never comes home.

ORESTES Curse him no more. His fortunes are in a sorry state.

IPHIGENEIA Achilles, son of Nereid Thetis—is he alive?

115

ORESTES No. His marriage at Aulis was an empty thing.

IPHIGENEIA It was betrayal. Those who suffered from it know.   530

ORESTES Who are you? You ask so knowingly about Greece.

IPHIGENEIA I am from there. I was lost when still a child.

ORESTES Naturally, then, you wish to know what happened there.

IPHIGENEIA What of the general whom they call "the fortunate man?"

ORESTES Who? The general I am thinking of was not fortunate.

IPHIGENEIA There was one called Agamemnon, son of Atreus.

ORESTES I do not know, mistress. Please leave that subject alone.

IPHIGENEIA I implore you by the gods, tell me, just to please me.

ORESTES The unhappy man is dead. His death ruined another.

IPHIGENEIA Dead? How could that have happened? How I grieve for
            him.   540

ORESTES Why this lament? Was he somehow related to you?

IPHIGENEIA I grieve over his former great prosperity.

ORESTES He died in a terrible fashion, murdered by his wife.

IPHIGENEIA I weep for her, who killed him, and for him, who died.

ORESTES Stop now, and do not ask me any more about it.

IPHIGENEIA Only this: is the murdered man's wife living still?

ORESTES She is not; and her murderer is her own son.

IPHIGENEIA The house is all in ruins. How could he do it? Why?

ORESTES To take revenge upon her for his father's death.

IPHIGENEIA Ah.   550
        How just, how evil was this righteous punishment.

ORESTES Though he is just, he gets no favor from the gods.

IPHIGENEIA Are other children of Agamemnon still in the house?

ORESTES He left one daughter, Elektra, a girl still young.

IPHIGENEIA What do you hear of the daughter who was sacrificed?

ORESTES Only that she is dead and sees the light no more.

IPHIGENEIA She suffered much. Her father, who killed her, suffered, too.

ORESTES Her death was a graceless grace for a bad woman's sake.

IPHIGENEIA The son of that man killed in Argos—does he live?

ORESTES He lives, a wretched man, nowhere and everywhere.   560

IPHIGENEIA False dreams, farewell; you never meant anything after all.

ORESTES Nor are the gods, who are considered wise by men,
        any more to be trusted than the flying dreams.
        There is much confusion in the workings of the gods
        as there is among mortals: only one thing hurts,
        when one who has good sense has listened to the words
        of prophets and is ruined, as the wise men know.

CHORUS Alas, but what of us then and our own parents?
        Are they alive or not? Who will ever tell us?

IPHIGENEIA Listen to me, for I have come upon a plan   570
            which will be to your advantage, friends, but also help
            my cause. All enterprises have the most success
            when all who are involved have common interest.
            If I could save you, would you be willing to take a message
            to Argos and deliver it to my family there:
            a letter, that is, which a prisoner wrote for me?
            He was sorry for me, and he did not think my hand
            was murderous, but knew that victims of the goddess
            must die, because the goddess holds that custom good.
            I had no messenger who could go back for me   580
            to Argos and, if he survived, carry my letter,
            and deliver it to someone in my family there.
            You, therefore—if, as it now seems you do not hate me,
            and since you know Mycenae, and those whom I want—
            save your own life, with a reward that is not mean.
            Be rescued just for carrying a little note.
                    But this man, since the state enforces it, must be
            kept back and sacrificed to the divinity.

ORESTES   All you have said was good, mistress, except one thing.
            His sacrifice would be a burden on my soul.   590
            I am the man in charge of this shipload of grief;
            he sails along out of sympathy for my troubles.
            Thus, to do you a favor and myself escape
            from danger is unfair, if it costs him his life.
            Let it be done this way. Give the tablet to him.
            He will take it to Argos, so you will be satisfied.
            Let anyone, who wants to, kill me. It is shameful
            when a man drops his friendship because times are bad
            and saves himself. This man is truly dear to me.
            I value his life no less than I do my own.   600

IPHIGENEIA O brave spirit! You must be born of noble stock,
            and are a true friend to your friends. Oh, how I hope
            that the one male survivor of my family
            is such as you are. Yes, friends, since I also am not
            without a brother—only that I never see him.

Since you so wish it, we shall send the other man
to take the letter for me, while you die. It seems
evident that his safety is your great concern.

ORESTES Who will endure the horror of sacrificing me?

IPHIGENEIA I. For this goddess, this is my service to perform.   610

ORESTES A grim and thankless office for a girl to have.

IPHIGENEIA I am constrained to do it, and must keep the law.

ORESTES You are a woman. Can you kill men with a sword?

IPHIGENEIA No. I will sprinkle lustral water on your hair.

ORESTES Who is the slaughterer, if I may ask that question?

IPHIGENEIA There are people in the temple who attend to this.

ORESTES And what shall be my burial, when I am dead?

IPHIGENEIA A sacred fire inside, and a great cleft in the rock.

ORESTES Oh, how I wish my sister's hand could tend my body.

IPHIGENEIA Poor man, whoever you may be, that was a vain wish,   620
since she is settled far from any barbaric shore.
But still, since it is true that you are Argive born,
I shall omit no grace that I can give to you.
I shall lay many ornaments upon your bier,
and make your body soft with yellow olive oil,
and cast upon your pyre the flower-fragrant pride
of honey that the brown bee makes among the hills.
But I go now to fetch the tablet from the shrine
of the goddess. Only do not hate me for my duty.
Guard them, attendants. Do not use the manacles.   630
Perhaps I shall give that one whom I love the most

of my loved ones in Argos news beyond his hopes;
this letter, telling him that those thought dead are still
alive, will give the glad news, and he will believe.

CHORUS I grieve for you, devoted
to this bloody lustral spray.

ORESTES No cause for grief, friends; but I thank you for the thought.

CHORUS (to PYLADES) We are happy in your blest fortune,
young man, that you yet will tread
the soil of your native land.   640

PYLADES Friends would not want this, if it means that friends must
         die.

CHORUS Oh, the errand is grim.
You also are brought to grief.
Which lot of the two is worse?
My heart still hesitates over the doubtful choice
to mourn you, who must die, or you, who must survive.

ORESTES Pylades, in God's name, are you struck by what strikes me?

PYLADES I do not know. You ask me what I cannot answer.

ORESTES Who is this girl? How like a very Greek she spoke
and questioned us about the wars at Ilion,   650
the homecoming of the Achaians, Kalchas skilled
in augury, and named Achilles, how she sorrowed
over unhappy Agamemnon, questioned me
about his wife and children. Yes, this stranger is
Argive by birth, from there. She would not otherwise
be sending a letter there, would not have questioned me
as if the Argive fortune were her fortune, too.

PYLADES You are a little beyond me, and I would agree
with what you said first, except for one thing: all men know

the sorrows of kings, when they have had to do with them. 660
But I was going in my mind over something else.

ORESTES What is it? Share it with me. Thus you can think better.

PYLADES I would be shamed to see the daylight while you die.
I shared your voyage. I must also share your death.
I shall be established as a weakling and a coward
in Argos, also in the Phocians' land of valleys.
The multitude—the multitude is bad—will think
that I betrayed you to come home alone alive,
or even killed you, seeing the weakness of your house,
and devised murder for the sake of your kingly power,   670
being wed to your sister, who holds the inheritance.
All this I fear and hold shameful; it cannot be
otherwise; I must draw my last breath when you do,
be sacrificed with you and have my body burned
because I feared reproach and proved I was your friend.

ORESTES Hush. Speak no blasphemy. I must bear my own troubles,
but still not bear them double when they could be single.
All that which you call painful, and which will bring
                reproach,
remains for me, if I kill you after you shared
my sufferings. It is not really bad for me   680
to end my life, since the gods make it what it is.
You are a happy man, you hold a house that's clean,
not sick, like mine; my house is cursed and evil-starred.
If you survive, and beget children from my sister
whom I have given you to have and hold as wife,
our name might be continued, and my father's house
not be obliterated with no children born.
Go on your way, and live, and hold your father's house.
But when you come to Hellas and horse-breeding Argos,
I lay this charge upon you. Give me your right hand.   690
Heap up a burial mound and monument to me,
and let my sister give the grave her tears and hair.
Announce that I have perished by the hand of a woman

from Argos, dedicated to the altar of death.
Never forsake my sister, just because you see
that you are marrying into a family with no head.
Goodbye. You are the dearest friend that I have found,
my fellow huntsman, raised to manhood at my side,
who bore with me the many burdens of my grief.

    Phoibos is a diviner, but he lied to me.   700
He applied his arts and drove me to the farthest point
from Greece, for shame over the prophecies he spoke.
I gave him everything I had, followed his word
and killed my mother. Now I am myself destroyed.

PYLADES Your grave shall be given you, and I will not betray
your sister's bed, unhappy friend, since you must be
my friend among the dead, not one who sees the light.
But the god's prophecy to you has not yet come
to nothing, even though you stand so close to death.
Still it is true, it is, that extreme suffering   710
provides extreme reversals, when the luck is changed.

ORESTES No more! The words of Phoibos are no use to me.
Here is the lady; she is coming from the temple.

IPHIGENEIA (*to the attendants*) Withdraw, all of you. Go to those who
               are entrusted
with the sacrificing, and make ready all within.
(To ORESTES and PYLADES) Here is the letter-tablet with its
               many folds,
my friends. But there is something more I wish to say.
Hear me. A man is not the same man in distress
and when, with fear past, he is once more confident.
I am afraid that he who is to take the letter   720
to Argos, once he finds himself in his own land,
may never think again about my messages.

ORESTES What do you wish, then? What do you find difficult?

IPHIGENEIA He must give me an oath that he will carry this letter
to Argos, and take it to my loved ones, as I wish.

ORESTES Then will you give him in return the self-same oath?

IPHIGENEIA Yes, tell me. What must I not do? What must I do?

ORESTES Release him free and living from this barbarous land.

IPHIGENEIA Fair enough. How else could he be my messenger?

ORESTES Yes, but will the lord of the land agree to that?   730

IPHIGENEIA He will. I will persuade him
and I myself will see your friend aboard his ship.

ORESTES (to PYLADES) Swear, Pylades. (*To* IPHIGENEIA) Dictate the
oath religion asks.

IPHIGENEIA Then he must say: "I will give this to those you love."

PYLADES I will duly present this note to those you love.

IPHIGENEIA And I will get you safely away past the Black Rocks.

PYLADES Which of the gods do you name as witness to your oath?

IPHIGENEIA Artemis, in whose temple I officiate.

PYLADES And I invoke the lord of the sky, Zeus the august.

IPHIGENEIA What would you suffer, if you wrong me and fail your oath? 740

PYLADES Never reach home. And you, if you do not rescue me?

IPHIGENEIA Never set foot on Argos as long as I live.

PYLADES But note this other point, which we have overpassed.

IPHIGENEIA We shall make some addition, if the point is good.

123

PYLADES   Then grant me this exception, if the ship goes down,
and if this letter, with the cargo, disappears
into the sea, and I can only save myself,
that this oath will no longer be binding on me.

IPHIGENEIA   Here's what I will do. There are many possibilities.
I will inform you verbally of the whole message   750
contained and written down inside the folded tablet.
That is secure. If you can carry the letter through,
the silent writing then will tell its own message;
but if the written letter is lost in the sea,
you will save my message, if you only save yourself.

PYLADES   That was well said, both for your own sake and for mine.
Name me the person in Argos to whom I should give
this letter, and the message I should repeat from you.

IPHIGENEIA   Then say this to Orestes, Agamemnon's son:
"Iphigeneia, sacrificed at Aulis, sends   760
this message. She is alive, although thought dead at home."

ORESTES   Where is she? Did she die? Did she come back to life?

IPHIGENEIA   I am Iphigeneia. Do not break my thread.
"Bring me to Argos, O my brother, before I die.
Release me from barbarian country and the god's
sacrifices, in which my rites mean strangers' deaths."

ORESTES   Pylades, what shall I say? Where do we find ourselves?

IPHIGENEIA   "Or I shall be a spirit who will haunt your house,
Orestes." I repeat the name, so you will know it.

PYLADES   O gods.   770

IPHIGENEIA   Why do you summon the gods? This case is mine.

PYLADES   No matter. Continue. I was thinking of something else.
Presently I will return to the question of these marvels.

IPHIGENEIA Tell him that I was saved by the goddess Artemis
who substituted the fawn my father sacrificed,
supposing that with the sharp sword he struck me home.
She settled me in this country. Those are your instructions.
This is the message written in the closed tablets.

PYLADES How easy are the oaths that you have bound me in
and sworn me to most fairly. I will not wait long,   780
but I shall validate the oath I swore to you.
        Behold, Orestes! I deliver here to you
the letter that was given me by your sister's hand.

ORESTES And I accept, but will postpone reading the letter
to seize a joy expressed in action, not in words.
Oh, dearest sister, though astonished, I will still
embrace you in these arms that scarcely dare believe,
and, told of wonders, rush to take delight with you.

        He attempts to embrace IPHIGENEIA, *who resists him.*

CHORUS Sir, you do wrong! This is the priestess of the god
whose clothing, never to be defiled, your arms profane.   790

ORESTES O sister, my own sister from a single sire,
daughter of Agamemnon, do not turn from me.
You have me here, your brother, as you never hoped.

IPHIGENEIA I have you for my brother? Stop it, will you not?
Argos contains him now and Nauplia is his place.

ORESTES O cruel one, your brother is not in those parts.

IPHIGENEIA The Spartan, daughter of Tyndareos, gave you birth?

ORESTES To Agamemnon, Pelops' grandson. I am his.

IPHIGENEIA Tell me then, do you have some evidence of this?

ORESTES I do. Ask me some question about my father's house.   800

IPHIGENEIA Rather, you should speak first and I shall be the judge.

ORESTES Very well. Here first is something that Elektra told.
You know the rivalry of Atreus and Thyestes?

IPHIGENEIA I have heard. There was a quarrel over the golden lamb.

ORESTES You know you wove a pretty pattern of the scene?

IPHIGENEIA Oh, good! You reach very close to my memory.

ORESTES It had an image of the sun changing its course?

IPHIGENEIA I wove that picture also with my dainty threads.

ORESTES Your mother gave you lustral water, to take to Aulis?

IPHIGENEIA I remember. No happy marriage has made me forget.   810

ORESTES What then? Did you cut your hair and give it to your
mother?

IPHIGENEIA My cenotaph, for memory of my lost body.

ORESTES Now I will give you evidence of what I saw:
the ancient spear of Pelops in our father's house.
Wielding it in his hands he killed Oinomaos,
and won Hippodameia, the Pisatid girl.
This was hidden away in your own maiden room.

IPHIGENEIA (embracing him) O dearest, dearest. That is my only name
for you.
I hold you now, grown to manhood as you are,
but far from Argos, my dear.   820

ORESTES And I hold you, the one who was thought dead.
Tears, in mourning and joy combined,
drench your eyes and mine.

IPHIGENEIA This is the child
            I left still in his nurse's arms,
            a baby still in the house.
            Oh, happiness greater than words can tell,
            my soul, what shall I say?
            This passes wonder and speech.

ORESTES I hope our life together still will be so good.   830

IPHIGENEIA A strange thing, friends, the joy I have won.
            I fear he might slip away out of my hands
            winging into the air.
            O Cyclopean hearth, beloved
            Mycenae, my country,
            I thank you for his life, I thank you for his nurture,
            because you raised this brother
            to light our house.

ORESTES We are fortunate in our birth, my sister, but our life
         has been unhappy, with disasters in its course.   840

IPHIGENEIA I know it, wretched I, I remember
            my harsh father's knife against my throat.

ORESTES Oh, I can see you, though I was not even there.

IPHIGENEIA Never a bride, my brother, to Achilles,
            when I was led to his shelter and that
            false promise of marriage.
            Beside the altar there were tears and wailing for me.
            The lustral water was there.

ORESTES I, too, groan because our father was so hard-hearted.

IPHIGENEIA The father I was given was no father,   850
            and suffering follows suffering still.
            Some divinity sends it.

ORESTES But if, O wretched one, you had killed your brother?

IPHIGENEIA Oh terrible, terrible that daring
I had then, my brother; by so little
did you escape an impious death at my hands
which would have torn you.
But now, what will be the end of it all?
What chance will come my way?
What route can I find   860
to send you away from the city, away from slaughter
back to your Argive home
before the sword draws your blood?
O hard-pressed soul, this is your task,
to find some means.
Shall it be by land, not by ship?
But, trusting to flying feet,
you will find your death, going through barbarous tribes
and roads that are no roads; but through the narrow strait
by the black rock is a far way   870
for sea-borne escape.
Wretched, wretched am I.
What god or mortal man
or creature of mystery
can find an impossible way
for the two last children of Atreus
to escape from evil?

CHORUS As witness, not from hearsay, I will testify
to these events, marvels and past the power of words.

PYLADES When those beloved come into the presence of those they
              love,   880
Orestes, it is proper to embrace; but now
you must leave commiserations and return to facts,

so we may seize on safety, gloriously named,
and take ourselves away from this barbarian land.

For prudent men, when they are not yet free from fortune,
seize further joys by seizing opportunity.

ORESTES Well said; and yet I think that fortune has in mind
to help us in this matter; yet when one is keen,
divinity can be expected to gain strength.

IPHIGENEIA You must not keep me from my question, nor prevent   890
my asking you about Elektra, and what fate
is hers, since you and she are all I have to love.

ORESTES (*indicating* PYLADES) With this man she enjoys a happy
married life.

IPHIGENEIA Where then does this man come from, and whose son is he?

ORESTES His father is the famous Strophios of Phocis.

IPHIGENEIA He is son of Atreus' daughter, and a relative?

ORESTES He is our cousin, and he is my one true friend.

IPHIGENEIA He was not born yet, when our father sought to kill me.

ORESTES He was not born. Strophios was childless a long time.

IPHIGENEIA I give you greeting, Pylades, husband of my sister.   900

ORESTES He is not only my kinsman, but my rescuer.

IPHIGENEIA How could you dare that awful thing done to our mother?

ORESTES To avenge my father; let us speak of it no more.

IPHIGENEIA But what reason did she have for killing her husband?

ORESTES   Let my mother be; it is not proper for you to hear.

IPHIGENEIA   I obey. Does Argos look to you for leadership?

ORESTES   To Menelaos. I am exiled from my country.

IPHIGENEIA   But could our uncle so outrage our weakened house?

ORESTES   Not he. The Furies' terror drove me from the land.

IPHIGENEIA   This was the seizure they reported from the beach?   910

ORESTES   My wretchedness was seen, and not for the first time.

IPHIGENEIA   I understand; they harry you, for our mother's sake.

ORESTES   The bit is bloody that they force into my mouth.

IPHIGENEIA   Why have you had to cross the sea and walk this shore?

ORESTES   Prophetic orders from Apollo made me come.

IPHIGENEIA   Why? Can you tell me, or is it a holy secret?

ORESTES   I can tell you. Here is how my many toils began.
          After my quarrel with my mother forced my act—
          I will not speak of that—the onslaught of the Furies
          drove me in flight, until Apollo Loxias   920
          guided my feet to Athens, so as there to give
          due satisfaction to the nameless goddesses.
          A sacred judgment takes place there, which Zeus ordained
          for Ares, when his hands were stained with guilty blood.
          When I came there, nobody in the city
          would take me in; they thought the gods all hated me.
          Then some took pity on me. These arranged for me
          a table to myself, though they were in the house,
          and their silence made me one unspoken to

so I should be no part of their feast, nor of their drinking.   930
They filled an individual vessel for each man
with equal stints of wine, and so enjoyed themselves.
Since I did not presume to argue with my hosts,
I suffered in silence and pretended not to notice,
while mourning that I was my mother's murderer.
I hear that the Athenians have based a custom
on my misfortunes, and the usage still obtains
with Pallas' people to observe the feast of pots.
When I came to the Areopagos, I stood
for trial, taking my place on one of the platforms,   940
while the leader of the Furies took the other stone.
I spoke to accusations over my mother's blood,
but Phoibos spoke on my behalf and rescued me,
and Pallas' arm counted an equal tale of votes.
Thus I emerged the winner from my murder trial.
Those Furies who were satisfied with judgment given
established a sanctuary at the place of trial.
But those who were not satisfied with the decree
kept driving me in chases that allowed no rest
until I came again to Apollo's holy ledge,   950
and, prone before his sanctuary, faint and starved,
swore then and there to die and break away my life
if Phoibos, who destroyed me, would not save me now.
Then from his golden tripod Phoibos spoke aloud
and sent me to this country, to reclaim the image
that fell from heaven, and settle it on Attic soil.
Then help me win that rescue which he has defined
for me. If we can seize the image of the goddess,
I shall be freed from madness, and in my oared ship
will take you to Mycenae, where your home will be.   960
But, O beloved sister, O my dearest one,
rescue your father's house and save me; all I have
is lost, and all the house of the Pelopidai,
unless we win the heavenly image of the god.

CHORUS   Some deadly divine anger has boiled up against
the seed of Tantalos and drives it on, through pain.

IPHIGENEIA   Even before you came I had always been eager
             to be in Argos and, dear brother, to see you:
             I wish what you wish: to release you from your trials,
             and to restore our father's weakened house. I hold   970
             no grudge, though he tried to kill me. This is what I wish.
             For so my hand would not be guilty of your death,
             and I would save our house. But I am afraid. How can I
             escape the goddess and this tyrant, when he finds
             the marble base is empty and the image gone?
             Must I not then be killed? What could be my defense?
             But if it all can be done in one single act,
             if you can take both me and the image to the trim
             ship, then the chance makes it an honorable risk.
             If my part in this venture fails, then I must die;   980
             but you, if you succeed in your part, might get home.
             I do not try to avoid this, even if I must die
             when once I have saved you. No. When the man of the
                           household dies
             his loss is mourned. A woman does not count for much.

ORESTES   I will not be the murderer both of my mother
             and you. Her blood suffices. I would share your will
             and try to live, but die together if we die.
             If I myself can go there, I will take you home
             as well; or else I must remain and die with you.
             But hear my thought. If all this were against the will   990
             of Artemis, how could Apollo have ordained
             that I should take her image to Athena's ship?
             That I should see your face? Combining all these thoughts,
             I have good hope that we shall have our homecoming.

IPHIGENEIA   How then can we contrive so that we do not die
             and get what we desire? For this is the weakness
             in our plans for homecoming, though the will is there.

ORESTES   Could there be any way for us to kill the king?

IPHIGENEIA   A terrible thought, for visitors to kill their host.

ORESTES Still, if it will save you and me, it should be dared.   1000

IPHIGENEIA I cannot do it, although I admire your zeal.

ORESTES What if you hid me secretly inside the shrine?

IPHIGENEIA So we should wait for dark to come, and then escape?

ORESTES Yes, since night is for thieves and daylight for the truth.

IPHIGENEIA But there are temple guards. We cannot hide from them.

ORESTES Alas, then, we are ruined. How can we escape?

IPHIGENEIA I have a new thought, and it might be the way out.

ORESTES What kind of thought? Share it with me, so I may know.

IPHIGENEIA I shall make artful use of your infirmities.

ORESTES Women are terribly clever in inventing schemes.   1010

IPHIGENEIA I will say you came from Argos as a matricide.

ORESTES Yes, use my sorrows, if you can turn them to our good.

IPHIGENEIA Thus, I shall say, we must not offer you to the goddess.

ORESTES What reason will you give? I think perhaps I see.

IPHIGENEIA That you are unclean. I'll make their piety serve their fear.

ORESTES But how, with all this, is the goddess-image stolen?

IPHIGENEIA I shall want to wash you clean in the waves of the sea.

ORESTES This leaves the image, which we sailed for, in the shrine.

133

IPHIGENEIA I will say, since you touched it, I must wash that too.

ORESTES Where in the sea? Do you mean where it joins a bay?   1020

IPHIGENEIA Right where your ship is tethered by its strands of rope.

ORESTES Will you or someone else carry the image down?

IPHIGENEIA I must. I alone am allowed to handle it.

ORESTES And what part shall our Pylades be given in this?

IPHIGENEIA We'll say his hands are stained with the same blood as yours.

ORESTES You plan this with or without the knowledge of the king?

IPHIGENEIA I must speak and persuade him, for I cannot hide.

ORESTES And then our ship is ready, and its oars are swift.

IPHIGENEIA Yes. Success in what follows must be in your hands.

ORESTES We need one more thing. These women must help keep   1030
the secret. Plead with them and find some words to win
their hearts. A woman has the power to work on pity.
The rest, perhaps—oh, may everything come out well!

IPHIGENEIA O dearest women, now I turn my eyes to you.
My fate is in your hands, whether I shall succeed
or come to nothing, lose the land where I was born,
and my dear brother, and my dearest sister, too.
Let this be the beginning of my argument:
we are all women. We are loyal to each other,
surest protectors of all the interests we all share.   1040
Keep the secret of what we do, help us achieve
escape. Honor to her whose lips deserve their trust.
You see how we three, dearest friends, have all one chance
together, to come home again, or else to die.

If I am saved, I will save you, so that you share
my luck, and come to Hellas. You by your right hand
I supplicate, and you and you, you by your dear
cheek, by your knees, by all that's dearest in your homes,
mother and father, children of those who are mothers.
What is your answer? Who consents? Who will not?   1050
Speak. Who will do this? For if you refuse my plea,
then I am lost, and my unhappy brother, too.

CHORUS   Dear mistress, do not fear, but only save yourself.
          I will keep silence about everything you do.
          May great Zeus be my witness—and do all you say.

IPHIGENEIA May you never be sorry you said this, but be blessed.
          (*To* ORESTES *and* PYLADES) It is time for you, and you, to go
                    inside the shrine.
          The master of this country will come presently
          to see if the strangers have been duly sacrified.

                    ORESTES *and* PYLADES *enter the temple.*

          Artemis, queen, who saved me once at Aulis bay   1060
          from my own father's terrible and murderous hand,
          save me now also, and these men; or else the world
          will never trust Apollo again, all through your fault.
          Consent with grace to abandon this barbaric land
          for Athens; here is no fit place for you to live
          when you could have a city which the gods approve.

                    IPHIGENEIA *enters the temple.*

CHORUS   Bird, sea bird by the rocky cliff,
          halcyon of the waters,
          yours is a song of sorrow.
          cry the gifted can understand,   1070
          mourning even in song your lost husband.
          I match your complaint with my own,
          I, a bird, too, but wingless,
          longing for gatherings of the Greeks,

135

longing for Artemis, bringer of birth,
who beside the Cynthian hill
dwells, and the slim-tressed palm tree,
sweet branching of laurel,
sacred growth of the olive gray,
friend to Leto in childbirth,   1080
by the pool with its spiral stream
where the swan, the singer of songs,
ministers to the Muses.

Many then were the streams of tears
down my cheeks coursing
when the towers of my city fell,
when I went away in the ship,
among the enemy's rowers and their spearmen.
I was traded dearly for gold
and came to a barbarous homeland.   1090
Here I serve Agamemnon's child,
priestess-maiden, who serves in turn
the goddess who slew the deer. She tends
sacrifices, but not of sheep.
I envy that sad life
that was grim throughout, for one grows used
to force, and can endure it.
It is the change that ruins.
Misfortune following happiness
comes as a crushing burden.   1100

You, our lady, the Argive ship
will carry home to Argos
as the wax-bound pipe of reed,
gift of Pan who ranges the hills,
whistles the oars onward,
and prophetic Apollo, making
music from his seven-stringed lyre,
brings you, singing, with fair landfall
to the shining country of Athens.
While I stay behind forsaken   1110

you will go with the splashing oars
as, at the bow, stays hold the straining
sail that bellies over the bowsprit
on the speeding vessel.

But I would follow the shining course
where the sun-flame goes with his horses,
and over the chambers of my own house
I would fold my wings on my back
and still them from their beating:
join the groups where once, as a girl   1120
and part of the marriage festival,
I danced away from my mother dear
to join the companies of my friends,
the contest of beauties,
rivalries of our glorious hair,
light-footed, and cast over my curls
and around my cheeks, shielding them from sunlight,
my bright and shimmering veil.

                                    Enter THOAS, *attended.*

THOAS Where is the keeper of this temple, the Greek woman?
      Has she yet dedicated the strangers? Do their bodies   1130
      shine with fire in the holy inner sanctuary?

CHORUS Here she is lord. She will give you a full account.

                    Enter IPHIGENEIA *from the temple, with the wooden
                              image of Artemis in her arms.*

THOAS What is this?
      Why, daughter of Agamemnon, have you carried off
      the image from the fixed and holy pedestal?

IPHIGENEIA Do not step forward, lord! Keep your distance from it.

THOAS Iphigeneia, what has happened in the temple?

IPHIGENEIA I spit it out. Hear me, O spirit of religion!

THOAS What does this strange preamble mean? Tell me, more
clearly.

IPHIGENEIA Lord, the victims you captured for me are unclean. 1140

THOAS What made this clear to you, or do you only guess?

IPHIGENEIA The goddess-image turned about and faced away.

THOAS All by herself, or did an earthquake turn her about?

IPHIGENEIA All by herself; and closed the lids over her eyes.

THOAS What was the cause? You mean, it was the strangers' guilt?

IPHIGENEIA That, nothing else, for they have done an awful thing.

THOAS Did they kill someone here on our barbarian shore?

IPHIGENEIA They came already guilty of murder at home.

THOAS Whom did they kill? I find myself longing to know.

IPHIGENEIA They killed their mother. Both their sword-hands shared
the act. 1150

THOAS Apollo! None of our barbarians could have done it.

IPHIGENEIA They were pursued and driven out from all Hellas.

THOAS They are the cause, then, for your carrying out the image?

IPHIGENEIA Yes, into holy daylight, to allay the taint.

THOAS By what means did you learn about the strangers' guilt?

IPHIGENEIA I questioned them, after the image turned away.

THOAS Greece made you clever, so you understood this well.

IPHIGENEIA They thought they had a bait that would attract my mind.

THOAS They thought good news from Argos would endear your
heart?

IPHIGENEIA They said Orestes, my sole brother, prospered well.   1160

THOAS They hoped that you would save them; joyful at the news.

IPHIGENEIA They said my father was alive and prospering.

THOAS You took the goddess' side, though, as you ought to do?

IPHIGENEIA Yes, since I hate all Greece, the Greece that ruined me.

THOAS Tell me then, what must we do about these strangers?

IPHIGENEIA We must respect the law as it has been laid down.

THOAS We use your lustral waters, then? We use your sword?

IPHIGENEIA But first I wish to purify and make them clean.

THOAS In running springs, or in the waters of the sea?

IPHIGENEIA The sea washes away the ills of humankind.   1170

THOAS Thus they would fall as holier offerings to the god.

IPHIGENEIA And thus also it would be the better for me.

THOAS Do not the waves wash up about the very shrine?

IPHIGENEIA We need privacy. We have other tasks as well.

THOAS Take them where you will. I want no forbidden sight.

IPHIGENEIA I must also make clean the image of the goddess.

THOAS Yes, if the stain of mother-blood has sullied her.

IPHIGENEIA I would not otherwise have moved her from her base.

THOAS Your piety and forethought are commendable.

IPHIGENEIA Do you know then what I wish?

THOAS   It rests with you to give the
                                                    word.   1180

IPHIGENEIA Put these foreigners in chains.

THOAS   If they escaped, where could
                                                    they go?

IPHIGENEIA Greeks are never to be trusted.

THOAS   Go, you servants, get the chains.

IPHIGENEIA Have them also bring the strangers out to us.

THOAS   It shall be done.

IPHIGENEIA But put coverings on their heads.

THOAS   To keep pollution from the
                                                    sun.

IPHIGENEIA Send some of your henchmen with me.

THOAS   These shall be your
                                                    followers.

IPHIGENEIA Send one also who shall tell the city.

THOAS   What then shall he say?

IPHIGENEIA Tell all to remain indoors.

THOAS   For fear they meet the murderers?

IPHIGENEIA Yes, for such things are infectious.

THOAS *(to an attendant)*   Go and tell them, as she
                                              said.

IPHIGENEIA None must look upon them.

THOAS   How you labor for our city's
                                         good.

IPHIGENEIA Yes, and for my friends who most deserve it.

THOAS   That was meant
                                                   for me!   1190

IPHIGENEIA (And for all.)

THOAS   So all the Taurians admire and love you, as
                         they should.

IPHIGENEIA Yes, remaining here before the temple of the goddess . . .

THOAS   Yes, what then?

IPHIGENEIA Cleanse the place with fire.

THOAS   So you may find it pure when
                                   you come back.

IPHIGENEIA When the strangers come out from the temple . . .

THOAS   Then
                                                 what must I do?

IPHIGENEIA Hold your robe before your eyes.

THOAS   For fear pollution fall
                                            on me.

IPHIGENEIA If I seem to take too long a time . . .

THOAS   What limit should
                                            I set?

IPHIGENEIA Do not wonder.

THOAS   Go, and serve the goddess well. Your time
                          is yours.

IPHIGENEIA May this ritual only come out as I wish!

THOAS   Your prayers are
                                            mine.

IPHIGENEIA Now I see the strangers coming from the shrine. I see as well
                    holy properties of the goddess, young lambs, so that, blood
                              by blood,   1200
                    I can wash away the stain; I see the lighted torches, all
                    that I ordered for the cleansing of the strangers and the god.
                    Now I warn the citizens: avoid infection and stand clear,
                    all who come to serve the temple, clean of hands before the
                              gods,
                    all who come to join in marriage, or relief in giving birth:
                    stand back all; take flight; begone, lest this pollution fall on
                              you.
                    Maiden queen, daughter of Zeus and Leto: if I wash the
                              blood
                    from these, and offer them where I ought to, you shall live in
                              a clean house,

142

and we shall be high in fortune. Of the rest I do not speak,
only, goddess, tell the gods and you, for you know more than
       we.   1210

All leave except the CHORUS *and the (silent) attendants.*

CHORUS Beautiful was the child
        Leto bore in the grain-giving valley on Delos,
        A god with golden hair,
        skilled in the lyre, and with him the sister who glories
        in marksmanship with the bow. His mother
        carried him from the island ridge,
        leaving the storied place of birth,
        to the mountain, Parnassos,
        celebrant of Dionysos,
        place of the streaming torrents.   1220
        There a great snake, spangled
        of back, bright of eye,
        coiled in the dark shadow
        of laurel leafage,
        a monster out of primeval earth, controlled
        the chthonic oracle.
        You, Phoibos, still only a child
        in your mother's arms leaping,
        you killed it, and mounted the sacred oracle.
        You sit on the golden tripod, on the throne that never is false, 1230
        dealing out the prophetic answers to mortals
        from the inner chamber, neighbors to Kastalian springs,
                keeping
        your house at the world's center.

        When Apollo, going to Pytho,
        had driven Themis, daughter of Earth, from that sacred
        oracular place, then Earth
        produced the Dreams, nocturnal apparitions,
        and these to mortal multitudes divined
        things primeval, things of the time of telling,
        and what she would bring to pass,   1240

by incubation in sleep under the dark ground.
Earth, angry in her daughter's cause,
took from Phoibos his privilege.
But Lord Apollo ran on swift
feet to Olympos,
clung with his infant hand
to the throne of Zeus, pleading
that the grudge of the earth goddess be taken away
from the Pythian temple.
Zeus laughed, because his child   1250
had come in haste for the spoils with their golden treasures,
and shook his curls to affirm surcease of the night voices,
took away truth from what was shown men in night
                    visions,
restored to Apollo his privileges,
and to mortals at the throne thronged with strangers gave
                    confidence
in his oracular poems.

> Enter MESSENGER, *who addresses at first not the*
> CHORUS, *but persons supposed to be behind the closed*
> *doors of the temple.*

MESSENGER   You temple guards and ministers who tend the altar,
            where is the lord of the land, Thoas, now to be found?
            Open the strongly nailed-together temple gates
            and summon from its fastnesses this country's king.   1260

CHORUS   What is it? May I ask this uninvited question?

MESSENGER   Those two young men have got loose, and are on their way,
            and Agamemnon's daughter plotted the escape.
            They are in flight from our country, and they have possession
            of the holy image, in the hull of a Greek ship.

CHORUS   Your story is incredible. But the man you seek,
         the king of the country, left the temple in great haste.

MESSENGER Where did he go? He must be told of these events.

CHORUS We do not know. But go and see if you can find him,
and when you do, then you can tell him all your story.   1270

MESSENGER See, how untrustworthy is all the breed of women.
You, too, have had some part in this conspiracy.

CHORUS You are mad. What has the strangers' escape to do with us?
Better make for the palace gates, and lose no time.

MESSENGER No, not until the spokesman here gives me an answer,
and tells me whether or not the king is in the shrine.
Ho, you inside the temple, open up the doors,
and tell your master that I stand within the gates
burdened with bad news which I must announce to him.

THOAS *(appearing as the doors open)* Who makes this outcry at
the temple of the goddess   1280
and batters at the doors and can be heard inside?

MESSENGER Why did these women try to keep me off, and tell me
that you were gone? You were in the building all the time.

THOAS What could they have expected to gain by telling you that?

MESSENGER I will tell you later about them, but hear from me
what is immediate. The young woman who was here,
Iphigeneia, who served the altar: she is gone
out of the country with these strangers, and has taken
the holy goddess-image. It was a treacherous plot.

THOAS What are you saying? What could have inspired her to
this?   1290

MESSENGER Her purpose puzzles you. It was to save Orestes.

145

THOAS Whom do you mean? Her brother, of the Tyndarid line?

MESSENGER Yes, and the very man who was to be sacrificed.

THOAS Astonishing event! How else could I describe it?

MESSENGER Do not bother your mind with that, but hear my story;
           when you have heard and studied the facts, then you can
                     plan
           the best way of pursuit to run the strangers down.

THOAS Well argued. Tell your story. They have no short course
       to run, before they can escape my force of arms.

MESSENGER When we had reached the sea shore, where Orestes' ship 1300
           lay moored within its hiding-place, then we, the ones
           you sent to guard the foreigners and hold their chains,
           were nodded to by Agamemnon's daughter, and told
           to stand off out of the way, since she was occupied
           with mysteries of flame and lustral sacrifice.
           She herself held the bonds behind the strangers' backs
           and went away. All this was matter for suspicion,
           but had to be accepted by your servants, lord.
           At last, so we might think something was being done,
           she raised the cry, and sang incomprehensible   1310
           songs of magic, as if she were washing bloodstains away.
           But when we felt we had been sitting there too long,
           a fear came into our minds; the strangers might have
                     got free,
           murdered the priestess, and made off, and sailed away.
           Still, fear of what we must not look at kept us sitting
           in silence, till at last everyone there agreed
           that we must go and find them, though it was forbidden.
               And there we saw the hull of a Hellenic ship,
           winged with oars, which were dipped in the water, ready
                     to go,
           and fifty sailors at the benches with their oars.   1320
           We saw the young men, liberated from their bonds,

and there were sailors, standing at the stern of the ship,
who hastily pulled up the cables with their hands.
Others with poles held fast the prow, others drew up
the anchor to the cathead, others let down ladders
into the sea, for those three Greeks to come aboard.
      We cast out all consideration when we saw
the treacherous games they played, laid hands on the Greek
            girl,
and seized the cables. We reached through the rudder-ports
and tried to drag the steering oars from the stout ship.   1330
And words came out: "What do you mean, to steal and
            carry
our images and priestesses out of the country?
You are depriving us of her. What is your name?"
He said: "If you must know, I am Orestes, son
of Agamemnon, and her brother. Thus I take
my sister to that home from which she once was lost."
In spite of this we kept our hold on the Greek girl
and tried to force her to come back to you with us.
Hence came these terrible bruises you see on my face,
since neither they nor we had steel weapons to use,   1340
but there were fist-fights, in which we were sorely battered.
Also, these two young men used their feet in the fighting
and drove them home to ribs and stomach; thus, if one
of us closed with them, he was knocked helpless at once.
Wearing the marks their fists had left upon our faces,
we fled back to the sea cliffs, some with bloody wounds
upon their heads, while others had been hit in the eyes.
There, standing on the high ground, we thought to fight
            with them
to better advantage, and we pelted them with stones;
still, archers stationed on the stern deck held us off   1350
with showers of arrows, driving us still further back.
Meanwhile, a difficult surf was washing the ship ashore,
and there was danger that anyone might be submerged.
Orestes caught his sister up on his left shoulder,
waded into the sea, and sprang upon the ladder,
and set her down aboard the well-constructed ship,
together with the thing that fell from the sky, the image

of Artemis. From amidships, someone cried aloud:
"You mariners of Greece, seize your oars in your hands,
whiten the water. We have all that for whose sake   1360
we ever came to this inhospitable sea
and passed within the entrance of the Clashing Rocks."
    The sailors, answering him with a hearty roar,
lashed at the water. While the ship was still inside
the bay, she went straight on, but when she passed the
                mouth,
she came to grips with the rough sea, and had to fight,
for the hard wind fell on her in a sudden squall
and took her sails aback. The men still struggled on,
bracing their heels to fight it, but the contrary sea
forced the ship back again toward land. Then
                Agamemnon's   1370
daughter stood up and prayed, saying: "O Leto's child,
bring me, your priestess, safely back again to Greece
from this barbaric country, and forgive my theft.
You, Artemis, love your own brother; thus I, too,
think it is right that I should love my family."
    The sailors blessed the girl's prayer with a
                cheerful song,
and with their sleeves rolled up and arms bared all their
                length
plied their oars to the rhythm of the coxswain's chant;
but, little by little, the ship was forced back to the rocks.
Then some of us ran into the sea and waded out,   1380
and others made fast looping ropes to hold them with,
and I was sent away, to come direct to you
and tell you, lord, about what has been happening there.
But go there, taking bonds and halters in your hands.
Unless all wind suddenly vanishes on the sea,
the foreigners have no hope of escaping us.
Holy Poseidon watches over Ilion still,
lord of the sea, ever opposed to Pelops' line,
and he, it seems, will give up Agamemnon's son
a prisoner to your hands and to your citizens';   1390
with him his sister, whose ingratitude is proved
toward Artemis; who rescued her; whom she betrayed.

CHORUS Oh, poor Iphigeneia; with your brother, you
        shall be brought back into our master's hands, and die.

THOAS Oh all you citizens of our barbarian land,
        haste, will you not? And put the harness on your horses,
        gallop along the shore and meet them as they land
        from their Greek ship, and with the help of Artemis
        and your good speed, you will hunt out these godless men.
        Sailors, drag your swift-rowing ships down to the sea.   1400
        So we shall ride them down by water and by land,
        and after we have caught them we shall throw them down
        the steep cliff, or impale their bodies on sharp spikes.
        As for you women implicated in this plot,
        at some time later, when I find leisure to spare,
        I'll punish you, but now the urgent task at hand
        has occupied us, and we have no time to rest.

                    ATHENA *appears aloft, above the temple.*

ATHENA King Thoas: What pursuit is this? Where do you mean
        to carry it? Listen to what Athena says.
        Call off your streaming soldiery. Stop the pursuit.   1410
        By destiny and the decrees of Loxias
        Orestes came here, fleeing from the Furies' rage,
        to find his sister and to take her home to Argos,
        and carry the sacred image to my own country,
        for thus they shall be quitted of the present pains.
        This is my speech, Thoas, to you. You mean to kill
        Orestes when you catch him on the stormy shore;
        but even now Poseidon, to please me, has made
        the heaving waters calm, so that his ship can sail.
            And now, Orestes, study my commands to you,   1420
        for you, though far away, can hear the goddess speak.
        Proceed, taking the statue with you, and your sister.
        But when you come to Athens the divinely built,
        you will find there is a place in Attica, the last
        before the border, across from the Karystian mount;
        a sacred place, which is called Halai by my people.

There found a temple (and install the image there),
named from the Tauric country and your wanderings,
when you labored hard, ranging through the land of Greece,
stung by the Furies. People for the rest of time   1430
shall sing her praise as Artemis Tauropolos.
Establish there this custom: at the festival,
to atone for your uncompleted sacrifice,
let a sword be held to a man's throat, and blood be drawn,
for religion's sake, so that the goddess may have her rights.
Iphigeneia, on the sacred terraced ground
of Brauron, you must keep the keys for Artemis.
There, when you die, you shall be buried. They shall bring
to you in dedication the fine-woven clothes
which wives, who die in the pangs of childbirth, leave behind 1440
in their houses.
                         Thoas, now I charge you to release
these Greek women from your country and send them
                         home,
because of their good will.
                                   Orestes, once before
I saved you on the Areopagos, with my
judgment of even votes. The custom now shall be
acquittal of the accused whenever the score is tied.
Now, son of Agamemnon, sail, convey your sister
away from this country.
                              And you, Thoas, cease to rage.

THOAS   Goddess Athena, when the gods speak to a man
         and he will not believe them, then he is a fool.   1450
         I am not angry with Orestes and his sister
         though he has taken the image. What honor is there
         in setting ourselves against the gods, who have the power?
         Let them go to your country, let them take the image
         and there establish it with all good auspices.
         So also I shall send these women back to Greece
         and happiness. Such is your will and your command.
         I shall disband the force I raised against the Greeks,
         and my ships, goddess, in accordance with your will.

ATHENA Good. You, and the gods also, yield to what must be.   1460
        Then go, you winds, and waft the son of Agamemnon
        to Athens. I myself shall go along with you
        and guard the holy image of Artemis, my sister.

CHORUS Go, fortunate, numbered among the saved,
        in good fortune, go.
        O Pallas Athena, worshipful
        among immortals and mortals, too,
        we shall do all you would have us do,
        for what we have heard is full of joy
        and beyond all hope.   1470
        O Victory, great and august, control,
        if you will, my life,
        and continue to crown me with garlands.

NOTES

A NOTE ON PRODUCTION
The cast: The rules for the highly competitive tragic productions allowed each dramatist only three actors for spoken parts, in addition to the Chorus. They were called in order of importance *protagonist, deuteragonist,* and *tritagonist.* There was also an allowance of nonspeaking parts; we do not know how many. The distribution of parts for this play would certainly have given Iphigeneia to the protagonist and Orestes to the deuteragonist; the total distribution was probably somewhat as follows:

Protagonist: Iphigeneia, Athena
Deuteragonist: Orestes, Herdsman, Messenger
Tritagonist: Pylades, Thoas

When Orestes and Pylades are brought into the presence of Thoas, Thoas and Pylades are on together. But Pylades (like Orestes) has his head covered! In any case, of course, the actors changed their identity by changing not only their costumes but also their masks.

The scene: The shrine, or temple, of Artemis stands on a slightly raised platform, and is approached by a wide flight of steps. It has a single door. The roof is gabled, with an open space at the peak. In front of the temple is an altar, blood-stained and hung with human skulls. At the foot of the steps is a round level space, the orchestra. Paved walks to left and right lead out of the theater. These, plus the temple door, are the only entrances. Stage right, to the audience's left, is understood by convention to lead to and from the country and the sea; stage left, audience right, to and from the town. All entrances and exits, except in and out of the temple, are made by means of these entrances, which means that to reach the level of the temple the persons must mount the steps. Iphigeneia remains on the temple level throughout until she comes down to lead her procession off. The Chorus remains on the lower level throughout.

A NOTE ON THE PARTS OF TRAGEDY

The conventional terms are derived from Aristotle: *Prologue*: everything which precedes the entrance of the Chorus. *Parodos*: the entrance lines of the Chorus. *Episode*: all that takes place between two choral songs. *Stasimon*: all choral songs except the *parodos* and *kommos* (a section partly in lyric meters in which one or more of the actors and the Chorus take part; sometimes substituted for *stasimon*). *Exodos*: everything which follows the last stasimon.

Thus the "acts" of the play are *prologue*, the *episodes*, and *exodos*. In Aristotelian terms, the prologue to our play would include the dialogue between Orestes and Pylades (**67–122** / 67–122). But the term is often applied to the monologue with which Euripides regularly opened his plays, where the speaker identifies himself or herself and brings the story up to date, as Iphigeneia does in **1–66** / 1–66. Aristophanes ridiculed Euripides for his prologues, considering them factual, genealogical, and pedestrian.

1–122 / 1–122 *Prologue*

1–5 / 1–5 A brief outline of the family tree, in part:

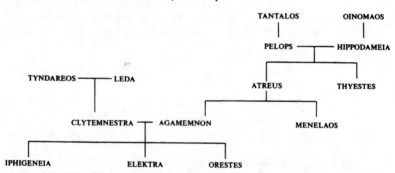

2 / 2 *with his swift chariot* Pelops won Hippodameia by defeating her father in a chariot race (actually, a pursuit). Oinomaos (see Glossary) was killed, with the aid of his daughter and Myrtilos, his treacherous charioteer. This and other crimes and betrayals in the family history are ignored in this account; but see **186–95** / 192–202 and note.

15–25 / 15–25 Kalchas, the diviner of Agamemnon, is always made responsible for the advice to sacrifice Iphigeneia; and Odysseus is always made the agent of the treacherous plot. Iphigeneia speaks of both with hatred (**522–26** / 531–35), as do other persons in the plays of Euripides, who disliked both soothsayers and clever politicians.

20 / 21 *the loveliest thing* Elsewhere, Agamemnon is made to enrage Artemis by claiming to surpass her in archery. In this version, the vow must have been made in the year Iphigeneia was born, and remained unfulfilled until she was of marriageable age—fourteen or fifteen years at least. Do we have a trace of a version in which an infant Iphigeneia was sacrificed?

21 / 21 *goddess who brings light* If this means Artemis as moon-goddess, it is the earliest case of this identification known to me. Normally, Selene, not Artemis, is the moon, just as Helios, not Apollo, is the sun. It is interesting that Euripides, in his fragmentary *Phaëthon*, seems to offer the earliest attested identification of Apollo and the sun. *Phaëthon* was probably written at about the same time as *Iphigenia in Tauris*.

30 / 30 *to this land of the Taurians* There never was any country, real or mythical, called Tauris. The general acceptance of the title *Iphigenia in Tauris* is due to a combination of accidents. Greek works have been conventionally described by Latin titles, Latin being the universal language of western scholars. In Latin, *Iphigenia in Tauris* is perfectly correct; but what it means is "Iphigeneia among the *Tauri*," that is, Taurians. The analogy of the correct title, *Iphigenia at Aulis*, which almost rhymes with our title, has further encouraged its acceptance.

31 / 31 *the barbarian* The Greeks called all non-Greeks barbarian. They also, quaintly, make barbarians call themselves barbarians (for instance, 1395 / 1422). Possibly the terms should always be capitalized.

42–60 / 42–60 The dream is false, or misinterpreted. In the hymn about Apollo, dreams, once genuinely prophetic, were deprived of their truthfulness by Zeus (1253 / 1278–79).

60 / 60 *Strophios had no children* Strophios married Anaxibia, sister of Agamemnon; any child of his would be a first cousin (see 895–900 / 917–22). If Pylades had not yet been born when Iphigeneia was "sacrificed," he would have to be at least fourteen years younger than she, though married to her full sister. I find this a little awkward, but Euripides insists on it. It enables him to have the Herdsman's use of "Pylades" (241 / 249, 277 / 285, 313 / 321, 484 / 493) mean nothing to Iphigeneia while it does mean something to us, audience or readers: a kind of irony, which plays to the audience at the expense of the dramatic character.

112 / 111–12 *the wooden image* We are to think of it as small, light, thus easily portable.

123–227 / 123–235 *Parodos including kommos*

155

123 / 123 *Silence, oh silence* They expect a religious ceremony, during the course of which no one must speak, for fear of evil omens. These lines are addressed to any of the populace who may be within hearing (compare **1395 / 1422**). The Chorus then addresses Artemis, by one of her foreign names, and finally, Iphigeneia.

124 / 124–25 *Clashing Rocks* These are referred to again and again in the play. They are also sometimes called the Black Rocks (**736 / 746**) without any apparent distinction. As generally told in legend, they stood at the entrance to the Black Sea. They had moved together and crushed ships trying to pass, until the *Argo* got through on its way to the Golden Fleece and, in so doing, miraculously put an end to that miracle. Sometimes in this play Euripides seems to locate them in their traditional place. Sometimes, as here, he writes as if they were very close to the scene of action. There were two Bosporuses, one at the entrance to the Black Sea, one near the Taurian land, often confused. Principally, Euripides may be using these rocks simply as a badge to label the whole Black Sea region.

159–73 / 159–77 The libations are the best she can do. If she could be at his tomb, she could offer a lock of her hair.

175 / 180 *the Asian strain, the barbarian dirge* Why Asian, why barbarian? The women are Greek, and dirges are Greek; there is one in almost every tragedy. Perhaps this only means that Greeks considered barbarians to be more emotional than Greeks.

180–95 / 186–202 Lament for the house of Atreus. After Pelops defeated Oinomaos with the help of Myrtilos, the charioteer (see **1–5 / 1–5** and note), Pelops hurled Myrtilos to death from his chariot. But the MS. reading is uncertain, and the chariot referred to may be the chariot of the sun.

The golden lamb symbolized the kingship of Argos or Mycenae. Atreus and Thyestes quarreled over it. Theyestes, with the help of Aërope, the unfaithful wife of Atreus, obtained possession of the lamb; Atreus in revenge tricked Thyestes into eating his own children. In horror at these acts, the Sun, who had formerly risen in the west and set in the east, reversed his course. These events are only a part of the lurid history of the house of Tantalos, and are touched on here with a relatively light hand (compare Aeschylus in *Agamemnon*). This is one of those grand and awful family sagas whose material is the very stuff of tragedy. Other great tragic houses are those of Laios in Thebes, of Amphiaraos and Alkmaion in Argos, and of Oineus in Aitolia.

196–227 / 203–35 Lament by Iphigeneia for Iphigeneia herself, not her house.

209 / 216 *a bride cursed* A princess would expect to marry, and she expected Achilles, the most brilliant of all.

214 / 221 *I do not dance* A princess even if not married would take part in the decorous pastimes of Greek girls, not the outlandish pastimes of the Taurians.

228–383 / 236–391 *First episode*

241 / 249 *Pylades* See note on 60 / 60.

246 / 254 *What have oxherds to do with the sea?* The aristocratic heroes and heroines of tragedy are sometimes curt with rustics and underlings (Hippolytos in *Hippolytos*; Hektor in *Rhesos*; Elektra in Euripides, *Elektra*).

250–51 / 258–59 *Never yet...upon the altar* There is a real problem here and it connects with another problem. What duties have been performed by Iphigeneia since her arrival in the Taurian land, and on whom has she performed them? Here she states positively that no Greeks have been sacrificed yet. Elsewhere she certainly implies that they have; otherwise 38–41 / 38–41 is meaningless. The altar has been stained with Greek blood (72–75 / 72–75). Iphigeneia has always pitied any Greeks who came her way (336–39 / 344–47); this makes no sense if no Greeks have come, or if those who have have been spared. See also 269 / 277. Furthermore, the kind Greek who wrote her letter for her (574–79 / 582–87) did not deliver it and would, in the context, certainly have been put to death.

Some editors have dealt with the problem by deleting these lines as spurious. We are left with a choice. We must assume an idiotic interpolator, or else a careless author. Idiotic interpolators have no doubt existed, though perhaps not in quite such numbers as some editors of Greek texts would have us believe. But a careless author seems the more likely when we face the connected problem and ask ourselves what part Iphigeneia played in the sacrifices. She is made to tell us twice, explicitly, that she merely consecrates the victims, who are then dispatched by male executioners (38–41 / 38–41, 614–16 / 622–24; at 714 / 725 she addresses such people). But "he did not think my *hand* / was murderous" (577 / 585–86) suggests an Iphigeneia who wielded a weapon, and the wish expressed in 434 / 444–45 implies this. 856–57 / 871–72 is more explicit: "death at my hands / which would have torn you." Then finally there is Thoas to Iphigeneia with "your sword" (1167 / 1190). Here are too many contradictions to be removed by emendation or excision. I can only suppose something like this. At one point in composition Euripides entertained the concept of an Iphigeneia who actually wielded a knife against her brother, just as her father had wielded a knife against her.

Then, committed to mere consecration, he failed to remove all traces of the other version. Or vice versa. Similarly, he might have delayed his decision as to whether or not Orestes and Pylades were the first Greeks to be brought to sacrifice.

262–66 / 270–74 Ino, daughter of Kadmos and wife of Athamas, leapt into the sea with her son, Learchos, in her arms. They turned into sea deities named Leukothea and Palaimon. "Nurslings dear to Nereus" suggests Achilles, son of the Nereid, thus grandson of Nereus. The Dioscuri are the Heavenly Twins. (See Glossary.) Throughout this narrative we are made to feel the physical superiority of the Greek heroes to the Taurian herdsmen.

267 / 275 *a rough man* A similar wise guy who had been in the city incites the herdsmen to violence in the Bacchae.

282 / 290 Reading *achthos* (Greverus, Platnauer) for *ochthon* (MMS., Murray).

283 / 292 *There was nothing there* Aeschylus in the Eumenides used the Furies as his Chorus. In this play also at 939–49 / 961–71 a physical presence of the Furies is implied.

338–49 / 346–57 One may doubt whether Iphigeneia is meant to be as fierce as she says she is. She is full of sympathy for the two young men as soon as she confronts them. But in tragedy all virtuous women hate Helen, and the Chorus echoes her sentiments about this (428–36 / 438–46).

361 / 369 The theme of Death and the Maiden. Hades is a ravisher.

378–80 / 386–88 The crudities of accepted myth. Tantalos was said to have cut up his son, Pelops, and offered him to the gods, who, however, restored him to life.

384–456 / 392–466 *First stasimon*

384–90 / 392–99 The meeting-place of two seas is usually taken as the Bosporus, joining the Sea of Marmora to the Black Sea. Here Io, in the form of a cow, crossed over and made her way ultimately to Egypt. The story is told by Aeschylus in the *Suppliants* and *Prometheus*. In the poets, however, whose great strength is not geography, this Bosporus is often confused with the Cimmerian (Crimean) Bosporus; near the land of the Taurians, and both in turn are confused with the Black or Clashing Rocks. (See note on 124 / 124–25.)

387 / 394–95 *Euxine* This name for the Black Sea properly means "hospitable" (a propitiatory name to ingratiate a surly body of water). Sometimes it

seems in this play to be called *axenos*, "inhospitable," but the readings are not always certain.

390–92 / 399–401 That is, they are Greeks, but what Greek place is their home? Sparta (its river is the Eurotas) or Thebes (its river is Dirke)?

397–409 / 407–20 Only desperate need or lust for money would induce sane men to go on long sea voyages. This is the unromantic thought expressed here; it goes back to Hesiod and Solon.

410–27 / 421–38 These lines describe the coast between the entrance to the Black Sea and the land of the Taurians. For Phineus and the Nereids, see Glossary.

425 / 436 *the white strand* The myth was that Achilles after death was transported to the island of Leuke opposite the mouth of the Danube, where, fleet footed, he continued to race. Herodotos, writing serious geography, speaks of a "Race course of Achilles" on the mainland. The Chorus in its ode refers to Achilles as a known hero of myth, although the Chorus presumably does not know yet that he is dead (**528–29 / 537–38**).

428–36 / 438–46 See the note on **338–49 / 346–57**.

457–634 / 467–643 *Second episode*

493 / 502 It would be undramatic if Orestes gave away his name too soon. No enemy can exult over his death if no one knows who has died. Hence Orestes' testy responses to what he considers misplaced and useless sympathy.

499 / 508 *Argos* Here Orestes says he is from Argos, at **501 / 510** that he is from Mycenae, as if they were synonymous. See ARGOS in Glossary. At **795 / 804** Iphigeneia names both Argos and Nauplia.

503 / 512 *involuntary voluntary* The "sophistic cleverness" of Euripides. Voluntary because his city had not exiled him; involuntary, because the Furies drove him, and he had not wished to leave his city.

513 / 522 *bad news for one of my family* The troubles of the whole family, in this generation, originated in the flight, or (to be Euripidean) voluntary rape, of Helen. Thus the reference could be either to Orestes himself or, if the dead can be brought in, Agamemnon, or even Iphigeneia. Note that Euripides here ignores the version of Helen's disappearance which he adopted in *Helen* and introduced at the end of *Elektra*.

522–27 / 531–36 Kalchas and Odysseus. See note on **15–25 / 15–25**.

529 / 538 *His marriage at Aulis* A strange answer for Orestes to give to Iphigeneia's question, and in fact a *non sequitur.* The marriage was a swindle, but would Achilles be any the more alive if he had married Iphigeneia? But these lines are composed as if mostly from the heroine's point of view. To her he is above all else the falsely promised bridegroom.

534–35 / 543–44 The word, *eudaimon,* used by both speakers, could mean either "great and powerful" or "ultimately fortunate." But Euripides is very likely thinking of *Iliad* III. 182, where Priam says: "O son of Atreus, blessed, child of fortune and favor."

544 / 553 Reading *thanōn* (variant MS. reading) rather than *ktanōn* (Murray, with MS. authority).

554 / 563 *one daughter, Elektra, a girl still young* The names and number of Agamemnon's daughters vary considerably in epic and tragedy. The strange thing here is that Orestes speaks as if his sister were unmarried (the word used, *parthenos,* usually means "virgin"). But she already is married to Pylades, as Orestes says later, 893 / 915. Another contradiction? Rather, the detail of explaining about Pylades, who is silently present, would complicate the progress of this question-and-answer.

561–67 / 569–75 Later, in the mythic hymn about Apollo, we shall be told that dreams are indeed false prophets, but Apollo a true one.

570–88 / 578–96 The rule must be understood to be that, out of any group of more than one, one person must be sacrificed. Iphigeneia, presumably, is illiterate.

635–46 / 644–57 Short *kommos,* which occupies the place where we would normally find a stasimon.

647–1066 / 658–1088 *Third episode*

664 / 675 *I must also share your death* Perhaps it would not be reasonable to expect Pylades to offer to die instead of Orestes; but that would be a more useful offer than this one, to die with him.

700–704 / 711–15, 712 / 723 Since Apollo is very soon going to be vindicated, this baiting of him is not so much Euripidean challenge of the gods as dramatic tact. See Introduction II.

756 / 766 Reading *tōn te sōn* (Haupt, approved by Platnauer, adopted by Murray in his translation though not in his text) for *tōn theōn* (MSS.).

769 / 779 I give all the line to Iphigeneia, with Platnauer. The MSS. are confused about attribution.

779 / 788 Beginning the famous recognition scene. A later dramatist, Polyeidos (as we learn from Aristotle), made the key line Orestes' remark: "So I was fated to be sacrificed, like my sister." She would then recognize him. Aristotle (*Poetics*) mentions this later variant with approval; but the handing over of the letter before our eyes is a sure dramatic touch.

782–801 / 791–810 It is normal in the scene of recognition of the long-lost loved one to have the recognized character reluctant and skeptical.

795 / 804 See the note on 499 / 508.

803 / 812, 807 / 816 See the note on 180–95 / 186–202.

817 / 826 *in your own . . . room* No young male, if not one of the household, would have been allowed in her bedchamber.

880–86 / 902–8 Strange as it seems by later standards, these are the last lines Pylades speaks; but he must stand by, wordless, for almost two hundred more lines.

898 / 920 See 60 / 60 and note there.

902–5 / 924–27 Neat and very cool. See Introduction.

917–64 / 939–86 This is a considerable narrative speech, to be undramatically delivered at a time when the audience, like Pylades, might have been chafing to hear plans for a quick, efficient escape. I take it that Euripides felt it necessary to detail the compromise by which he stitched together the version that had Orestes acquitted and set free at Athens (Aeschylus) and the one that made him have to go and rescue Artemis (and, as it turned out, his sister) from the Taurians. Like the jurors, the Furies themselves were divided (946–56 / 968–82).

924 / 945 *for Ares* Hence the name Areopagos ("hill of Ares"). Ares had murdered Halirrhothios, son of Poseidon.

925–26 / 947–48 *nobody in the city* What follows is a good example of the etiological myth, a story told to explain a fact or custom. If a man, however morally innocent, were guilty of bloodshed or corruption, none, for fear of pollution, could share hearth or board with him. The hospitable Athenians, so as to entertain Orestes without suffering themselves, decreed that every man should eat by himself; as, at the Feast of the Pots in historical times, they continued to do.

940 / 961–62 At Athens, the accused and accuser faced each other standing on two rocks, the stone of Hybris (outrageous violence) and that of Anaideia (relentlessness); or, to simplify it, crime and punishment.

983–84 / 1005–6 *When the man … count for much* In *Iphigenia at Aulis* the heroine
puts this Athenian sentiment even more forcibly: better for one man to
live than ten thousand women. But Orestes, at least, will not even
consider it.

999 / 1021 *kill their host* Not much of a host to Orestes and Pylades; but she,
too, would be implicated in such a murder, and Thoas has been kind
to her.

1010 / 1032 *terribly clever* Certainly in the corresponding scene in *Helen* the heroine is
sharper than Menelaos; and one could make a good case for contending
that Euripides really thought women were cleverer and quicker than
men. But the compliment is as much left-handed as right-handed; the
term I have so translated indicates unwilling admiration of something
sinister.

1012 / 1034 In the corresponding scene in *Helen*, 1050–52, the hero also consents
to something unpleasant, if it will serve the purpose; namely, the ill-
omened pretense that he is dead.

1045 / 1068 *I will save you* How she intends to set about doing this is not clear. It takes
a divine appearance and command to save these women.

1049 / 1071 *children of those who are mothers* According to Platnauer, most editors
have rejected the line, on the ground that the Chorus is composed of
virgins (the "maidenly step" of 130 / 130). That seems hardly enough
evidence; the same word (*parthenos*) is used of Elektra, who is married
(see note on 554 / 563). At 1120–28 / 1143–51 the Chorus members speak
of the experience of a young girl, but are remembering the past, perhaps
remote as well as immediate.

1067–128 / 1089–152 *Second stasimon* This well-known ode became much beloved by
English-speaking readers through Gilbert Murray's now unfashionable
but still beautiful rendering. Unfortunately the text of the second half is
in very bad shape, and the meaning some of the time quite uncertain.

1068 / 1090 *halcyon* The bird is Alkyone, wife of Keyx, who mourned for her lost
husband until she turned into a bird; some say kingfisher, but this is
doubtful. So the Chorus, too, mourns its lost country.

1074–80 / 1096–1102 But why, particularly and exclusively, Delos, place of the
Cynthian hill, where Leto gave birth to Apollo and Artemis? Delos
had been a festal gathering-place of the Ionians; but the association
here seems to be with the birthplace of Artemis, goddess of childbirth.

1082 / 1104 *the swan* Apollo's bird, whose final song is fabulous.

1084–90 / 1106–12 The women remember when their city fell and they were taken prisoner and sold as slaves; something which happened to Greek women at the hands of Greeks several times during the late phase of Euripides' career, most notoriously at the capture of Melos by the Athenians in 416 B.C.

1097 / 1119 Reading *kamnei* (John Milton according, according to Platnauer) for *kamneis* (older MSS., Murray).

1101–5 / 1123–27 The women wistfully contrast their fate with that of the fugitives. But whom do they mean by "you"? One would expect them to address Iphigeneia, and the mention of the Argive ship suggests that "home" is Argos. But at the end (1109 / 1131) the destination is Athens, as if for Artemis. The destination of Iphigeneia at this point is Argos, and she is going home. Further, the term *potnia*, "my lady," used at the beginning, is mostly reserved for goddesses; and to have two gods in person lending their music to time the rowers is more suitable for the transportation of a goddess than the stealthy flight of a human heroine. There probably is a real confusion here, arising perhaps from the latent relationship, even identity, of heroine and goddess (see note on 1424–41 / 1450–67). I have left it vague.

1112 / 1134–36 Readings and sense are confused and doubtful.

1115–20 / 1138–43 Not in the halcyon theme at the beginning of this ode—for there the women lament with or like the halcyon—but here, do they wish for wings that would carry them across the world and—who knows—back into girlhood again?

1124 / 1147 *contest of beauties* Beauty contests for real girls, not just trios of goddesses, are attested by Alkaios and others. But here, I think, the girls merely rival each other in beauty.

1129–210 / 1153–233 *Fourth episode*

1138 / 1161 *I spit it out* That is, I want nothing to do with it. Word for action.

1151 / 1174 *None of our barbarians* In *Medea*, Jason says of Medea's murders: "No Greek woman would have done it."

1167 / 1190 *your sword* See the note on 250 / 258.

1190–91 / 1213–14 See Introduction I. The fatuity of the poor gulled pious barbarian outwitted by a Greek woman, clever on both counts, is evident in every line. I do not believe Thoas is in love with the unmarriageable priestess; rather, he is pleased with her gratitude and proud of her friendship.

1191 / 1214 Three syllables missing. Thoas' answer almost calls for something like this.

1195 / 1218 *your eyes* Pollution infected the eye of the beholder as it infected the sun, the eye of the world (1185 / 1207).

1211–56 / 1234–83 *Third stasimon* A hymn to Apollo. The contents in brief are: Leto carried her infant son from Delos to his other, prophetic, home at Pytho (Delphi) on the lower slopes of Mount Parnassos. There was already an oracle there, in charge of Themis, daughter of Earth, and guarded by a great snake, the original Python, a son of Earth. When the snake was slain and Themis driven from the throne of prophecy, Earth took it away again and established Dreams as prophetic agents. But the still-infant Apollo ran with his claims to Zeus, his father, who, amused by his child's truly Olympian rapacity, restored the rights to him.

1218–19 / 1243–44 *Parnassos, celebrant of Dionysos* Delphi (Pytho) on the lower slopes belonged to Apollo, but the great mountain itself to Dionysos, whose revels were held higher up. So the mountain itself was celebrant at these sacred revels. Mountains in central Greece and Boeotia, such as Parnassos, Helikon, and Kithairon, were regarded, especially in Boeotian thought, as personalities.

1227 / 1249 The baby killing the monstrous snake recalls, of course, Herakles; sometimes Apollo's protégé, sometimes his rival, sometimes perhaps his *alter ego*.

1237 / 1262 *Dreams* These were used in divination. But Iphigeneia's dream, misinterpreted to be sure, was false. Apollo's prophecies, doubted, proved true. Despite his predatory ways, Apollo may here be thought of as advancing culture and civilization over the inarticulate early religion.

1257–473 / 1284–499 *Exodos* with theophany or *deus ex machina*.

1257 / 1284 messenger There may be more than one messenger in a tragedy, but the messenger *par excellence* is the one who arrives late in the play to narrate the catastrophe or decisive event (though in this play the action is not decided until the god appears).

1275 / 1302 *the spokesman* The word means "interpreter." In civilized Egypt, for example, there would probably be bilingual guides who showed Greek and other tourists around the wonderful sights, particularly the sanctuaries. It is rather quaint to think of such an official at the untouristy, not to say anti tourist, sanctuary of the Taurians; yet that may be indicated. Uncertain, I have hedged. Murray thinks the "spokesman" is a stick or club with which the messenger will hammer on the door and force an answer.

1275–79 / 1302–7 See Introduction II. We must have this story. But it does, though full of naturalistic detail, strain credulity. For it will appear within the speech that the two Greek men, hampered by a young woman and an image, whom they have to protect and to carry some of the time, have already given the king's men enough trouble to justify calling out the whole army at once. There will not be just two Greeks but a whole shipload to deal with. See also notes on **1340 / 1367–68, 1395 / 1422, 1408 / 1435.**

1322–26 / 1349–53 After attempting in vain to extract a reasonable reading from the manuscript tradition, I have adopted Platnauer's combination of previous suggestions, although it involves transposing one line and making five other changes. Platnauer also would follow Weil and postulate a lacuna in the middle of 1349 in the Greek, or between **1322** and **1323** in the English. This would make the construction smoother, but I would rather refrain from more surgery than is absolutely necessary. Greeks moored their ships on a beach with the prow facing outward. There were three ways of holding the ship in place: anchors or anchor-stones at both bow and stern and, when these were pulled in, poles.

1340 / 1367–68 *neither they nor we had steel weapons* It is once more a strain on our credulity when we are asked to believe that Thoas' men were not armed. This may at least, however, be why Iphigeneia explicitly asked Thoas to have Orestes and Pylades bound; had they not been, their guards must have been armed.

1387–90 / 1414–18 *Holy Poseidon* In the *Iliad*, Apollo is the chief defender of Troy; in Euripides, Poseidon.

1396 / 1423 *haste* Here at last is that urgency one might have expected at **1298 / 1325** or thereabouts.

1408 / 1435 Athena. Euripides usually closes with the appearance of a god. The god ties up loose ends, explains the action, corrects misunderstanding, and predicts the future—including, usually, the establishment of a cult. The god does not always solve a dramatic problem, though he may do so.

Why did not Euripides simply let the ship escape (as in *Helen*) and have Athena perform her other functions, enlighten and pacify Thoas, and save the women of the Chorus? He seems deliberately to have painted himself into a corner so that divine aid is necessary; possibly because the ultimate benevolence of heaven has been doubted throughout the play. In a happy-ending tragedy the gods must be, in the end, benign.

And why Athena rather than Artemis? Because Artemis is being rescued, in person, in the form of her image?

1418 / 1444 *Poseidon, to please me* Thus in the *Trojan Women* Poseidon and Athena drop their differences and work together (not, this time, for benevolent purposes).

1424–41 / 1450–67 The establishment of the cult, or cults. Two places are involved: Halai and Brauron, on the southeast coast of Attica, a few miles apart. Artemis Tauropolos was worshiped at Halai; Artemis, sometimes called Iphigeneia, at Brauron. We are told sometimes that the Taurian image of Artemis was at one, sometimes at the other. Euripides seems to be trying to do justice to two rival claims. The imitation of human sacrifice goes, here, with the image (1433–35 / 1459–61); Iphigeneia shall serve Artemis the goddess of childbirth (1436–41 / 1462–67). Throughout here, one may discern the original identity of goddess and heroine.

1471–73 / 1497–99 These last three lines also conclude Euripides' *Phoenician Women* and *Orestes*. They sound like an appeal to the judges to vote favorably for the poet who wrote these lines.

ORESTES

Translated by

JOHN PECK

and

FRANK NISETICH

INTRODUCTION

I

Orestes was the young man who killed his mother and got away with it. The matricide is first, the escape second, but the two belong together, particularly in Athens.

Even an Athenian who had never heard of the theater would still be likely to know that Orestes, on his way to salvation, made a stop at Athens. His arrival there had not only been dramatized on the Athenian stage, it had also been enshrined from time immemorial in Athenian religious ritual. During the second day of the festival of the Anthesteria, the Athenians drank their wine in silence, commemorating the time when Orestes, polluted by the blood of his mother, Clytemnestra, was received into their midst but given a separate table and not spoken to—all out of fear of the contagion he bore. On that second day of the festival, everyone in Athens acted as if they, too, were contagious, as if they were, in a word, Orestes themselves.

The young man who killed his mother and got away with it was also the son of Agamemnon, king of Argos, leader of the Greek host that conquered Troy. Agamemnon died the very day he returned in triumph from the Trojan War, stabbed to death in his homecoming bath by his own wife, who had taken up with her husband's cousin during his absence. Wife and lover then usurped the Argive throne, reducing the dead king's alienated daughter, Electra, to servitude and sending his son, the potential avenger, into exile.

Orestes, then, had reasons for killing his mother. She betrayed and murdered his father, married his father's cousin, deprived him of his home and his inheritance. Reasons enough in a situation less charged. Primordial custom made the next of kin responsible for avenging bloodshed, but when the blood had been spilled by the survivor's own mother, what was to be done? The god Apollo, speaking from his oracle at Delphi, gave the answer: let the son kill the mother, come what may. The god would help him deal with the terrifying consequences.

But it was just those consequences that brought Orestes to Athens: he was a fugitive from the Erinyes (Furies), avenging spirits of his mother's blood. Apollo, who had commanded him to kill her, could drive the Furies from his shrine at Delphi, but he could not keep them off the track of their quarry. And so it was that the final settlement between Orestes and the Furies did not come about at Delphi under Apollo's auspices but at Athens under Athena's.

Deliverance at Athens, however, lay in the future. It is, for Orestes in this play (but not the audience in the theater), the hidden part of his own legend. Equally important is the part of the legend that is not hidden from him and the other characters: the history of this tormented family up to the moment the play begins.

II

The founder of the line, Tantalos, appears dimly to Electra in the prologue, more spectacularly in the great monody she delivers later, her own death song. The crime he committed remains undefined, but what it means to Electra is clear enough. It engendered further crime. The family curse begins with Tantalos.

His son Pelops resorts to treachery to secure his bride, then murders the man who had helped him win her. The victim, Myrtilos, who had wanted the bride himself, curses Pelops and his descendants.

As if on cue, the sons of Pelops, Atreus and Thyestes, fall into violence fueled by sexual rivalry. Thyestes seduces his brother's wife, Aerope, and with her complicity gets possession of the throne of Argos. Betrayed by his wife and cheated of his throne, Atreus returns to power with Zeus' help and then expresses the desire to make up with the brother who had wronged him. In the most notorious episode of the entire saga, he takes the two sons of Thyestes, butchers them, and feeds them to their unsuspecting father at a feast of pretended reconciliation. Thyestes, enlightened as to the nature of the food he has eaten, curses his brother.

The curse of Thyestes on Atreus takes hold in the next generation. Atreus' two sons, Agamemnon and Menelaos, both suffer as their father and uncle suffered before them: from infidelity, lust for power, and violence against their own flesh and blood. The stage is set when the two brothers marry the daughters of Tyndareos of Sparta, Clytemnestra going to Agamemnon, and Helen, famed for her beauty, to Menelaos.

Helen runs away with the Trojan prince Paris, precipitating the famous war. Agamemnon assembles the Greek fleet at Aulis and takes command of the expedition, his eyes on military glory and the fabulous wealth of Troy. But one thing stands in his way: the goddess Artemis demands the sacrifice of his daughter Iphigeneia or the ships cannot sail. The ambition of the king stifles the affection of the father. Agamemnon cuts his daughter's throat over the altar so the winds will blow. Of all the reasons Clytemnestra has for hatred, this one alone comes close to justifying her murder of her husband. But the man who joins her in adultery and bloodshed has his reasons, too. He is Agamemnon's cousin Aigisthos, son and avenger of Thyestes.

Stroke and counterstroke, crime leading to further crime, it all transpires in the context of political strife. These are the throes of a dynastic family caught in the struggles of greed, lust, and power, turning on itself and casting its subjects, the people of Argos and of Greece, into the toils of war.

Orestes, born into such a family, lives out its worst propensities. Violence against kin takes its most daring and pitiful expression when he kills his mother. But he does so at a god's behest and, according to tradition, the gods stand by him in the end. He is to be the last of the avengers. Or so the original audience, familiar with the traditional story, had a right to expect. As the play goes on, Orestes acts more and more, not less and less, like his predecessors. He turns, again, on his own flesh and blood. Greed, too, and the lust for power have not yet let go their hold on him. By play's end, he stands on the brink of destruction. Yet, from beginning to end, he has shown redeeming qualities, characteristics that might account for the interference of the gods in his behalf.

III

The usurpers of Agamemnon's throne had reigned for seven years when Orestes returned from exile and killed them. On that very day his uncle Menelaos came home at last from the Trojan War.

Such is the account we find in Homer. Euripides makes one alteration, crucial to his dramatic purposes: he has Menelaos appear on the scene not immediately but six days after Clytemnestra and Aigisthos have fallen in blood. A lot has happened in the meantime.

The Furies of Clytemnestra have launched their attack on Orestes, reducing him, by the time the play opens, to exhaustion. In addition, old enemies of his father have been at work inciting the people against him and Electra. A meeting of the assembly this very day will determine their fate. The most likely outcome is death by stoning. Menelaos has arrived in the nick of time.

"The treatment of the legend is without parallel," remarked an ancient critic.[1] The first new element we notice is the political danger threatening Orestes. Much more than a novel touch, it enables Euripides to introduce two major developments, both of which take the play further and further from the story familiar to the audience.

First is the possibility, almost a certainty by the end of the play, that Orestes will not get out of Argos alive. When he returns from pleading his cause in the assembly, abandoned by Menelaos and sentenced to take his own life or have it taken from him, the play has come within an inch of the impossible. How will Orestes go to Athens, as everyone knew he did eventually, if, instead, he dies in Argos?

The second development is no less in conflict with tradition. Orestes' friend Pylades proposes getting even with Menelaos for his failure to help by killing his restored wife, Helen, the only person who means anything to him. Having arrived in Argos the night before, she is still within the palace, an easy target. There is only one problem, for the audience if not the characters: everyone knew that Helen lived happily ever after with Menelaos in Sparta. According to some accounts, she even became a goddess.

The suggestion to kill her is prompted by despair. Orestes would at least not die unavenged. But now Electra thinks of a plan that may enable them both to get even and to escape. In the prologue, Helen, afraid to venture out of doors, has sent her daughter, Hermione, to pay respects at the tomb of Clytemnestra. The girl is due back at any moment. Electra suggests taking her hostage, threatening to kill her if her father, Menelaos, does not move to save them. Helen's dead body, on display, would show they are in earnest.

By the final moments, Helen, contrary to everything known about her fate, will seem to have died and Orestes, contrary to everything known about his, will seem on the point of dying, taking Hermione, Electra, Pylades, and the palace itself down with him in flames.

IV

So much for the plot, a stunning combination of old and new. The characters, with the sole exception of Pylades, struck one ancient critic as "worthless."[2] Modern critics have expanded the negative judgment to

---

1. Aristophanes of Byzantium *Hypothesis* (preface) 5.
2. *Hypothesis* 21–22. Although the comment is included in the *Hypothesis* attributed to Aristophanes of Byzantium (c. 257–180 B.C.), it may belong to Didymus (c. 80–10 B.C.): M. L. West, *Euripides Orestes* (Warminster, Wiltshire, Eng.: 1987), p. 178. (Hereafter cited as West.)

include Pylades and have made it the basis of a nihilistic reading of the play. Produced in 408 B.C., two years before the poet's death, *Orestes* appears to be an indictment by Euripides of the age in which he lived. Although none of the characters makes what we would call a heroic impression, the tendency to view them as signs of Euripides' final despair of Athens goes too far.[3]

We hear from Electra first. Although it is Orestes who has borne the brunt of the Furies' attacks, Electra has been at his side all along. Her devotion to her brother is complete, perhaps the most appealing thing about her.

She also exhibits formidable presence of mind, an ability to meet the demands of the moment, however unpredictable. Although she keeps things moving in the present, she provides, along with the Chorus, our only source of comment on the legendary past. Her comments have a distinctive flavor, however. She imagines Tantalos' punishment and the prodigies that occurred when Atreus and Thyestes struggled for power in terms suggestive of astronomical speculations and discoveries. We catch, in such moments, a hint of the new learning associated in Athenian public opinion with the sophists.[4]

Helen, the second character to appear on stage, emerges from the palace during the prologue, engages Electra in conversation, and goes back into the palace, not to be seen again until the climax. Although she never fades entirely from our minds, our interest in her intensifies once the conspiracy against her gets underway. Seldom has a dramatist accomplished so much with a character so little seen and heard.

Her daughter, Hermione, says nothing at her first entrance, when Helen summons her from the palace, and very little at her next appearance, when Electra coaxes her back in. We shall see her a third time at the climax of the play, standing on the roof with Orestes, who holds a sword to her throat. She provides the conspirators with the hostage they need to put pressure on Menelaos. That is her role in the plot. She fits, also, into the larger pattern of the legend, resembling the sons of Thyestes killed by their uncle and the daughter of Agamemnon sacrificed by her father—innocents who become the tools of vengeance or the pawns of power.

---

3. W. Arrowsmith, *The Complete Greek Tragedies IV* (Chicago: 1959), 191. (Hereafter cited as Arrowsmith.)

4. The Athenians, for example, mistaking Socrates for a sophist, also assumed he was interested in physics and astronomy.

The Chorus enters next. When it first approaches, Electra refers to it as the partner of her lamentations, suggesting that she and it belong if not to the same household at least to the same social class. We learn later that it consists of daughters of the noblest families in the city.

After Electra has delivered her monody, about two-thirds of the way through, it is up to the Chorus alone to continue reminding us of the legendary framework in which the play is set. There would be nothing exceptional about that if the normal harmony between the legend and the unfolding action were maintained; but dramatic momentum now begins to sweep the characters toward a catastrophe radically different from anything the audience familiar with the legend of the House of Atreus would expect. The temptation to take these reminders (1611–13 / 1537–38, 1620–21 / 1545, 1627 / 1552) as ironical asides by the poet, wry hints at the irrelevance of the myth to the dramatic action, ought to be resisted. The Chorus has said nothing until now that even remotely suggests irony.

v

A good deal of what Euripides wanted Orestes to evoke is suggested by his most constant epithet: he is, from beginning to end, *tlêmon Orestes* (Orestes "the enduring," "the suffering"), the one who has dared (*etlê*) to do something terrible and must suffer terribly in turn. The word has active as well as passive connotations, and both are reflected in the overall structure of the play. In the beginning, Orestes is largely passive; in the middle, under the influence of others, he starts to become active; by play's end, he has taken the reins himself. The general movement resembles that of *Oedipus at Colonus* or *Samson Agonistes*.

This is not to suggest that Orestes makes anything like the heroic impression of a Samson or an Oedipus. He is, we need to remember, a young man on the threshold of adulthood. Like Hippolytos and Pentheus, two other Euripidean adolescents, he has unattractive as well as attractive features. Not all the qualities an ancient audience would have recognized in him enjoy the sanction of modern morality. In particular, his sense of honor and desire for revenge may make us uneasy. To help one's friends and hurt one's enemies: so runs the ancient Greek code of ethics. According to this code, Orestes, striking back at those who have wronged him, demonstrates his self-worth. It is a far cry from the Christian injunction to turn the other cheek, but it would have won the approval of the average Athenian. Nor would the original audience have been put off by the decision to take vengeance on Menelaos through his wife. On the contrary, the misogyny that fuels the attack on Helen, although it may not sit well with us, is yet another motivation that would have struck a responsive chord in the ancient Greek heart.

In Electra and the Chorus, in Menelaos and Tyndareos, Orestes evokes anxiety and solicitude, circumspection and curiosity, horror and loathing. All these responses and the attitudes that attend them derive from the deed he has done and the price he must pay. The burden falls with crushing weight on the shoulders of so young a man, and as the play develops we watch him at first sink into despair and then try to save himself. The goodness or badness of his character may in the end be less relevant than the excitement he generates simply by being the person he is, faced with the situation Euripides has invented for him. What has been ignored in criticism seems to have made itself felt on stage. *Orestes* was Euripides' "most popular play, indeed the most popular of all tragedies."[5]

As for the unattractive aspects of his character, the personal traits that would have made the original audience uncomfortable about him, they are not the ones we meet in modern assessments of him. One critic says that he has "murder...in his heart,"[6] another calls him "a juvenile delinquent of a startlingly modern depravity."[7] This, again, goes too far. Orestes is a young man with a young man's failings, suddenly thrust into a world governed by passions he is ill equipped to deal with, passions that gradually infect him, too, in complex ways, direct and indirect.

VI

The main lines of his characterization are brilliantly laid down in the scene in which he confronts his uncle Menelaos and his grandfather Tyndareos.

Menelaos enters first. Horrified, curious, he keeps his distance from his nephew, son of the man who has done so much for him. Before the conversation ends in a desperate appeal by Orestes for help, Menelaos has taken stock of the political situation in Argos. The people will not allow Orestes to inherit the throne of Agamemnon (**441–42** / 437–38).

We do not know how Menelaos intends to respond to the appeal he has just heard, for no sooner has Orestes made it than Tyndareos enters. King of Sparta, father of Clytemnestra, and father-in-law of Menelaos, he has come to pay respects at his daughter's tomb. As next of kin to the murdered woman, he should be interested in securing her killer's punishment. Two factors, however, operate to keep him from active pursuit of vengeance.

In the first place, the murdered woman, like her sister Helen, was a notorious adulteress. Tyndareos is her father, but he has no cause to feel proud of the fact. In the second place, the man who killed her is no stranger to him. The intensity of his feelings (in stark contrast to the coolness so far exhibited by Menelaos) derives from disappointed love, felt on both sides (463–69 / 459–67). The emotional situation on stage could not be more explosive.

Surprisingly, it is Menelaos, not Orestes, who ignites the explosion. Tyndareos is disturbed to find Menelaos talking with his nephew. Only a Greek corrupted by foreign influences would have anything to do with a polluted person, an "outcast" (484 / 481), Tyndareos calls him. In response, Menelaos attacks such inflexible adherence to custom and law, suggesting that Tyndareos, in his abhorrence of Orestes, shows unthinking conservatism and irascibility, two characteristics typical of old men. This stings Tyndareos, as well it might, and moves him to defend his position at length, arguing that his own attitude toward Orestes, contrary to what Menelaos says about it, is eminently sensible. After all, there can hardly be anything more senseless than matricide.

Orestes then comes forward to defend killing his mother, point by point, as an act that made sense. The emphasis, which may strike a modern audience as peculiar, derives directly from the posture adopted by Tyndareos, the prosecutor in the case before us. The drama of the moment is heightened also by the rhetorical challenge: it will not be easy to prove that killing his mother was, under the circumstances, a reasonable thing to do.

But in addition to appreciating the difficulty facing the youthful orator at this point, the original audience might well have felt a little uneasy about him. He has already, in his conversation with Menelaos earlier, shown a bent for sophisticated paradox and clever repartee. In coming forward now to defend the matricide itself, he resembles a figure all too familiar in Athens at the time, that of the young man corrupted by an education designed to give its pupils the power of making the weaker argument appear the stronger—just the sort of education Socrates would be accused of providing the aristocratic youth of Athens at his trial only nine years later.

The defense of matricide as a sensible act also holds particular dangers for Orestes. His troubled feelings about women have already surfaced well before Tyndareos arrives on stage: in the scene where he first wakes up and engages Electra in conversation. In that earlier episode, Electra tells Orestes that Menelaos has arrived and that Helen is in the palace. The mere thought of Helen touches a sarcastic chord in the brother, as it had earlier in the sister and does again now: the two of them wax eloquent on the theme of Tyndareos' daughters, "notorious throughout Greece" (249 / 250). Electra, however, soon has reason to regret encouraging Orestes in this vein: he looks at *her* now, a woman too, capable, perhaps, of the same monstrous behavior. She notices the change coming over him, but it is too late: the Furies are attacking.

A similar pattern emerges in the clash between grandfather and grandson. First, the misogynistic theme: again and again Orestes brings up Clytemnestra's adultery with Aigisthos. It was that, more than anything else, that seems to have incited him to take action against her. Even the murder of Agamemnon gets less emphasis in his defense, tending to appear more as a natural consequence of female depravity (579–85 / 566–70) than as something with a possible motivation of its own.

So much for the theme. The effect it produces comes close to the one it had in the earlier scene, only now it is Tyndareos who attacks, not the Furies. By the time he quits the stage, he has become the avenger he might not have been but for the provocation we have just witnessed, his grandson's insistence on rubbing in the one thing that bothers him most.

VII

Tyndareos leaves, determined to incite the Argive assembly to pass sentence of death on Orestes and Electra, too. He adds a warning for Menelaos: should he intervene, he will pay a high price—he will no longer be welcome in Sparta. Wealth and power are now at stake.

The characterization of Menelaos was censured by Aristotle as more base than it needed to be for the purposes of the drama.[8] The fundamental dramatic desideratum here is the betrayal of the nephew by the uncle. That alone is required by the plot. Euripides could have motivated it simply out of Menelaos' fear to lose what he already has, his position at Sparta; instead, he goes a step further, adding what Menelaos stands to gain from letting his nephew down: the death of Orestes would secure the vacancy of the throne in Argos. Who but the late king's brother and now only surviving heir would sit upon it next?

---

8. *Poetics* 1454a 28–29, repeated at 1461b 21.

But Menelaos' baseness gets another touch. He is, in addition to being a traitor and a coward under a woman's spell, a Spartan. The brief argument between him and his father-in-law pits one Spartan, old and conservative, against another, younger and full of innovative ideas. The contrast suggests that Spartans are not what they used to be. The old man in fact levels a charge at his son-in-law that would have suggested precisely that to the original audience.

Menelaos' contempt for ancestral ways results, Tyndareos says, from his travels abroad. He has picked up barbarian attitudes and been corrupted by them. The charge has a good deal of resonance. It chimes with the note sounded earlier, when Menelaos first appears on stage, arriving as conqueror of Asia (353–55 / 348–53). From that point onward, the Trojans of Homeric poetry continue to be confused with the barbarians of contemporary Persia, and Troy is the "Asia" conquered by Agamemnon and Menelaos. Before the play has ended, we shall see that Menelaos' household, Helen and her retinue now inside the palace, is infested with such Trojans turned barbarians.

At the time of production, and for some years before and after, one of the burning foreign policy issues under discussion at Athens was the role played by the gold of the Persian king in Greek affairs. It was Sparta that had been enjoying Persian support till then. Athens tried to replace her in the favor of various satraps, without success. Sparta continued to replenish her war coffers with barbarian gold. The satirization of Menelaos as an orientalizing fop must have gone over well with the Athenians. What were their Spartan enemies now but craven dependents of the Great King?

VIII

Orestes, knowing he has been betrayed, sinks into despair when Menelaos leaves. His spirits lift with the arrival of Pylades.

First and foremost a catalyst, Pylades has an immediate energizing effect on Orestes. He provides, also, a foil for Menelaos. The treachery of the uncle stands out in stark relief against the almost fanatical loyalty of the friend.

The contrast is a variation on a major theme of the play, with topical as well as purely dramatic interest. The original audience would surely have applauded Pylades' faithfulness, but not with the whole-hearted fervor of the ancient critic who dismissed everyone else in the play as worthless. They would just as surely have noted a troubling similarity between this young man, so dedicated to proving, through bloodshed, his devotion to his comrade, and the young men, educated by sophists[9]—and bound together in loyalty by their membership in aristocratic clubs—who had played the role of assassins in the oligarchic seizure of the government in 411 B.C., only three years before the play was produced.

The Four Hundred had seized power by entering the Athenian council chamber with daggers hidden in their cloaks, accompanied by 120 young men similarly armed. Euripides may have had that scene from recent history at the back of his mind when he depicted Orestes and Pylades entering the palace, determined to obtain swords inside, hide them in their cloaks, and then terrorize Helen's retinue, killing any who opposed them (1175–78 / 1125–28).

Earlier, on their way to the Argive assembly, Pylades tells Orestes he is not ashamed to appear in public not only walking side by side with the polluted outcast but holding him up, guiding his steps. He disdains what the mob may think of it (840 / 801), just as Menelaos, earlier, had looked down on Tyndareos' reservations about talking with Orestes. The reasons differ: Pylades acts out of loyalty, Menelaos out of what he would call intelligence, an enlightened attitude. But both express disregard of the common outlook. The antidemocratic sentiment occurs again later, when Pylades suggests killing Helen and Orestes bursts into praise. One comrade like Pylades, he says, is worth more than the favor of the mob (1203–4 / 1156–57).

IX

Comrades in aristocratic pride and disdain for the mob, Orestes and Pylades go off together, hoping to sway the popular assembly to their side. They are, like the assembly itself, a volatile mixture of the contemporary and the mythical. The combination of the two is one of the most fascinating features of Euripides' dramatic achievement in this play. But which comes first? Does the myth remind him of the climate of Athens at the time, or is it the other way around, the contemporary scene inviting a new presentation of the myth? Whatever the answer, contemporary history does not seem far removed from the ancient story as Euripides presents it.

Tyndareos' insistence on the primacy of law, for example, has a good deal of contemporary resonance. In 409 B.C. the Athenians began a revision of their laws. The year *Orestes* was produced, the law of Draco

9. Pylades has not as much time as Orestes and Menelaos to display his sophistry. It does not matter: one near quotation of Gorgias on the primacy of seeming over being suffices, in combination with the other touches, to make the impression intended. See note to 820 / 782.

on homicide was being copied and put on public display. Political killings had paved the way for the revolution of 411 B.C. When the democracy returned to power, the body of one of the traitors, Phryni- chos, was disinterred and cast out of Attica, and those who fled to the Spartans were declared outlaws. An imprecise but suggestive parallel between the citizens who struck at Athenian democracy and the young man who shed his mother's blood may well have figured in Euripides' thoughts as he composed the play. Tyndareos, at any rate, views Orestes as an abomination, an outcast.

The question as to what to do with those who have such crimes on their heads—when, if ever, to let them return to normal life—was anything but academic at the time. In July 410 B.C., just under two years before the first performance of *Orestes*, the Athenians passed a law making it legal to kill anyone who had been an enemy of the democracy, stipulating that to do so would not incur blood guilt.[10] The harassment of those who had participated in the coup of 411 B.C. con- tinued for several years; it was still being lamented by Aristophanes as late as 405 B.C., in the parabasis of his *Frogs*. Three years before, in our play, Orestes and Pylades, "young aristocrats beleaguered and hounded to death by an enraged demos,"[11] would have roused uneasy memories by their fanatical loyalty to each other; at the same time, their rescue by Apollo would have done more than merely fulfill the expectation that their persecution *had* to end short of their deaths. It would also have satisfied a feeling that it *should* end for the good of all.

X

Apollo's appearance at the end of the play, however, seems to have satisfied no one. It has been called "an apparent resolution which in fact resolves nothing"[12] even though, in fact, it resolves everything.

The gulf between what Euripides has done and what modern critics make of it results directly from the exaggeration of the baseness of Orestes' character. Once he has been cast in the role of a criminal psychopath, the god who rescues him loses all claim to respect. Apollo cannot be real. His appearance at the end must have left everyone in the theater depressed by the thought that reality is the chaos in Argos, and Argos equals Athens. It is mere myth or dream or illusion that descends from heaven in the guise of Apollo, bringing about a blatantly mechan-

10. The law of Demophantos, quoted in Andokides 1.96–97. Blood guilt is a major theme of the play.
11. West, p. 36.
12. Arrowsmith, p. 190. Often repeated.

ical resolution of the all-too-human problems unleashed by the drama. And it is with those problems, not their solution, that the audience leaves the theater.

The play, on this view, has a modern, even absurdist, feeling about it. Euripides brings in a god to remind us that gods, if they exist, are *not* in the habit of rescuing people from the consequences of their own evil actions. The Athenians, of course, were perfectly aware of this. What reason could Euripides have for reminding them of it, if not to deprive the myth of its meaning and the god of his dignity?

It is easy enough to leave the play with such feelings of disillusionment. They accord nicely with our sense of Euripides' sophistication. Indeed, his popularity in modern times owes not a little to the invitation he seems to hold out to us: to read him as if he were a modern dramatist. To do so, however, requires forgetting a number of factors that would have conditioned the impact of the original performance.

In the first place, Apollo's intervention does not involve anything impossible or unprecedented. In the second place, it is absolutely necessary, both in itself and in its manner and timing.

Greek gods act in their own interest and at their own prompting. Orestes is unhappy that "Apollo takes his time" (422 / 420), but he does not deny that it is his privilege to do so. More important, if Apollo did not take his time, we would have no play. His failure to fortify Orestes against his enemies in the beginning is the dramatic premise for everything that follows. By the same token, Euripides could not have composed the play if Apollo were not available to resolve everything in the finale. A play about to end with Helen apparently dead and Orestes going down in flames is inconceivable without a god to put a stop to it. Apollo (absent in the beginning and arriving at the end) is the cornerstone. Take him away and all collapses.

XI

Orestes, however, makes one comment—his last utterance but one in the play—that might seem, at first, to confirm an absurdist interpretation. He admits to wondering at times whether the god prompting him to act was a god at all (1741–43 / 1668–69). When, in the next breath, he says that all that is over now, and "everything has turned out well" (1744 / 1670), we may be tempted to take his new confidence for delusion. His old misgivings seem more like the sort of thing Euripides the ironist would want to leave us with.

But there are good reasons, remote and immediate, for hesitating to take Orestes' words ironically. To deal with the remote reasons first, even the feelings Orestes has expressed before in regard to Apollo are not as vehement as one would expect from the hero of a play in which the god comes in for a critical drubbing.

Orestes first mentions Apollo during the onset of the Furies' attack. It is an implicit cry for help (**259** / 260). Before the attack has ended, he orders the Furies to accuse Apollo's oracles (**277** / 276). He returns to the idea later, when the Furies have left. Apollo (through his oracles) told him to kill his mother and ought to bear responsibility for it (**287–89** / 285–87).

The striking reflection that follows, that the dead Agamemnon would have pleaded with him not to kill his mother (**290–95** / 288–93), is less an indictment of Apollo than a sign of Orestes' despondency. Apparently abandoned by the god who moved him to do what he has done, he wishes that he had not done it. The emphasis falls not on the act itself but on its futility (**294** / 292: it has not restored Agamemnon to life) and on its consequences (**295** / 293: his own desperate plight). We are dealing with two negative moments, but only one criticism.

There are no others from Orestes in the rest of the play, a fact that has not been appreciated. The example just described occurs, also, in private; Orestes confides his doubts to Electra, the person closest to him. Later, in conversation with the skeptical Menelaos, he defends taking the god at his word. He wants not to appear entirely naive for having done so, but the defense itself rests on traditional attitudes of mortal deference to the power of the gods who act, after all, if and when it pleases them (**418–22** / 416–20). Finally, Orestes asserts the god's patronage as his most powerful defense in the debate with Tyndareos on stage (**612–21** / 591–99) and, presumably, off stage as well in the assembly (**992–93** / 955–56).[13]

The last mention of Apollo before the finale is made by the messenger from the assembly. It is he, not Orestes, who concludes that the god has abandoned him. When Apollo finally makes good on his promise to stand by Orestes, he has not come to the rescue of a youthful blasphemer.

So much for Orestes' feelings about Apollo up to the moment Apollo intervenes to save him. The immediate reason we should hesitate before attributing his misgivings and final confidence to irony or delusion is the way he expresses them. He says that at times he feared it might not be a god but a fiend, an *alastor*, prompting him to act (**1741–43** / 1668–69). The feeling is natural enough, given all the suffering and confusion that

13. See note to **992–93** / 955–56.

have come upon him since he obeyed Apollo's command to kill his mother. He might well have feared being overtaken by Clytemnestra's fate, both in the sense in which Tyndareos says he deserves it (505–8 / 504–6) and in the Aeschylean sense that he, too, may prove to have been only one more member of this family destined to embody an *alastor* or avenging spirit.[14]

The Chorus at one point sees the whole line of Atreus under the influence of such a spirit (339–43 / 335–39); at another point, it sees Orestes and Pylades as *alastores* about to destroy themselves and the palace of the Atreids (1622 / 1546). Orestes' recollection that he feared at times mistaking what was really an *alastor* for the god Apollo, far from implying an ironical presentation of the myth affirms its meaning one more time before the end. Orestes *would* have perished as his forebears did were it not for the favor of the gods. To the others they sent only *alastores*; to him they also sent Apollo, one of themselves.

XII

Whatever else we may think of it, Apollo's appearance at the end brings the play to the most spectacular climax in all Greek tragedy. Standing on a platform, the god addresses Orestes on the roof and Menelaos on stage. At ground level, in the orchestra, the Chorus watches, silent till it speaks the closing formula. All four available regions of space are occupied: the ground, the stage, the roof, the sky.

The stage, moreover, is thronged with silent extras. Menelaos summons armed men to help him as he rushes the palace doors, sword in hand. The roof, too, is crowded: Electra stands to one side of Orestes, Pylades to the other, both holding torches. Orestes himself holds a sword to the throat of Hermione, who makes a fourth figure on the roof. A few moments after Apollo has stepped into view, bringing everything to a sudden halt, the radiant figure of Helen joins him on the platform.

"The play is one of those that enjoy popularity on stage," remarked the ancient critic,[15] and we can see why. Yet it was not only the extraordinary tableau at the end that made it a hit with ancient audiences. Euripides' stagecraft and masterful employment of the conventions of the theater work to powerful effect from beginning to end. The play would have had a brilliance in performance that can only be suggested here.

It opens with the weary Electra keeping watch beside the bed on which her brother lies unconscious. The Chorus enters, alarming her.

14. Aeschylus *Agamemnon* 1497–1504.
15. *Hypothesis* 21.

Perhaps it will disturb Orestes and precipitate another fit of madness. The usual uneventful entry of the Chorus thus becomes a miniature drama, intriguing in itself but also serving to prepare us for the attack by the Furies, which then ensues.

The attack itself involves more activity than an ancient audience was used to seeing occur on stage. Not only the symptoms of the madness (Orestes leaping about, hallucinating, aiming imaginary arrows at invisible assailants) but also the effect of its outbreak on Electra (who tries to restrain him, to get him to lie down on his bed again, only to be thrust aside, helpless before the onset of the attack) must have been spellbinding.

Perhaps the most striking combination of the familiar and the unexpected occurs later, when the conspirators have all entered the palace and the Chorus is left in the orchestra, wondering what to think. There have been noises from within. Helen has cried out, apparently on the point of death. The audience knows that Helen cannot die, but the Chorus does not share in this certainty. It waits for the doors to open, for Helen's body to be wheeled out or for someone to emerge from the palace and describe how she died. The Athenians would have witnessed such scenes in other plays many times before.

But instead the doors open and a Phrygian slave stumbles out, frantic, in fear for his life. It is from him that the Chorus leader tries to elicit a description of what went on inside. The scene has its own dynamics, intriguing in themselves, but they are enhanced when we take the conventions of the tragic theater into account.

Here is a messenger, the second to appear in the play. The first comported himself in the conventional manner. He came with news and gave it without hesitation, in iambic trimeter, the normal meter of spoken verse. When he was done, Electra had a clear idea of what transpired in the Argive assembly to which Orestes and Pylades were going when we last saw them. In contrast, the Phrygian, running away, scared to death, has to be stopped in midcareer and made to tell his story, and when he is done it is still unclear what has happened to Helen. Most surprising of all is his delivery. He does not speak, he sings. He is the only singing messenger in Greek tragedy.

We can hardly imagine the impact of such a novelty on the original audience. Yet it is not there for mere effect; it serves Euripides' dramatic purposes. Lyric, the language of emotion, may be more vague and allusive than spoken verse. The Phrygian sings because he is a bundle of emotions *and* because Euripides wishes to keep us in the dark as to the fate of Helen. What better witness of events whose outcome must be blurry than a hysterical foreigner? In addition, the Phrygian, threatened by Orestes' sword, manages to survive. So will Hermione on the roof in a few moments; so will Orestes himself. The Phrygian scene prepares us for the ending, which cannot be disastrous for any of the characters the dramatist has brought to the brink of disaster.

The poet's handling of stage properties is equally impressive. On a monumental scale, the palace stands in the center of the stage, a reminder, always, that we are watching a play about the notorious House of Atreus. Orestes and Menelaos engage in an unnerving duel to see who will inherit it. In the final moments, it is even in danger of destruction. And all the while Helen is inside, target of conspiracy, focus of uncertainty: Will she emerge again, alive or dead?

On a much smaller scale, once Orestes has gone to the assembly, we hear and presumably see no more of his bed. His passive phase is over, his active phase is in full swing. The bed on which he has been lying since the play began disappears with his passivity.

The early scenes of the play, all performed with the bed in view, enact a kind of overture. The quiet enjoined by Electra on the entering Chorus gives way to the outburst of activity as the Furies attack Orestes. When the attack has ended, Electra goes into the palace to rest. A long stretch of dramatic time now elapses, during which very little action occurs on stage. We see Orestes make his first appeal to Menelaos, fall silent when Tyndareos enters, deliver a speech in response to his grandfather's attack, appeal to Menelaos again and then collapse on his bed only to be roused by Pylades to take his fate into his own hands. What happens afterward leads to an explosion of stage activity that makes the Furies' attack earlier seem mild.

No wonder *Orestes* was performed more often than any tragedy in the ancient world. Given the chance, it should do well in modern theaters, too.

FRANK NISETICH

TRANSLATOR'S NOTE

Because the tonalities of this play span a nearly operatic range, my guide and chastener, himself a seasoned translator and poet, has often shared my role. Our rendering is a full collaboration.

JOHN PECK

ORESTES

Translated by

JOHN PECK

and

FRANK NISETICH

CHARACTERS

ELECTRA   sister of Orestes

HELEN   wife of Menelaos

HERMIONE   daughter of Helen and Menelaos

CHORUS   noble Argive women, sympathetic to Electra and Orestes

ORESTES   son of Agamemnon

MENELAOS   brother of Agamemnon, husband of Helen, uncle of Orestes and Electra

TYNDAREOS   maternal grandfather of Orestes and Electra

PYLADES   companion of Orestes, betrothed to Electra

MESSENGER   old retainer of Agamemnon's

PHRYGIAN   one of Helen's slaves

APOLLO   god of prophecy and purification

Line numbers in the right-hand margin of the text refer to the English translation only, and the Notes beginning at page 259 are keyed to these lines. The bracketed line numbers in the running heads refer to the Greek text.

Before the palace of Agamemnon in Argos. Orestes lies unconscious on a small bed, his sister Electra seated at his feet, keeping anxious and wearied watch. Time: six days after the killing of Clytemnestra.

ELECTRA No terror one can name—
    no suffering of any kind, no not even
    affliction sent by a god, is so terrible
    that human nature couldn't take it on.
    Tantalos, whom everyone called
    the happiest of men, the son, they say,
    of Zeus himself (and I don't mean
    to ridicule his fate), now
    shoots through the sky, terrified
    by the huge rock looming over his head.   10
    This is the price he pays, and why?
    According to the story, when he sat
    with the gods at the same table, a mere man
    banqueting with them as an equal,
    sick with insolence, shamefully
    he let his tongue run away with him.
    He had a son, Pelops, who in turn had a son
    born for strife with his own brother.
    But why do I have to go through
    the unspeakable again? Atreus   20
    butchered Thyestes' children and served them to him.
    I'll leave aside what happened after that
    and come to the sons of Atreus
    by Kretan Aerope: Agamemnon
    the glorious (if glorious is what he was)
    and Menelaos. Now Menelaos married
    Helen, whom the gods hate,
    while Agamemnon, lord of men, won
    Clytemnestra for his bride, the talk of Greece.
    Three girls were born to him—   30
    Chrysothemis, Iphigeneia, and myself, Electra—
    and a son, Orestes,
    all from one abominable mother

who wound her husband in an endless robe
and killed him, for reasons that a young woman
shouldn't mention. I'll leave them vague, then—
people know and may judge for themselves.
As for Apollo's injustice, what point is there
in my bringing charges against it? Still,
he persuaded my brother   40
to kill the woman who bore him.
Not everyone approves, but all the same
he obeyed the god: he murdered her, and I
did what a woman could, I helped him kill her.
    Since then he has been sick.
Orestes lies here savagely ill,
collapsed in his bed, and Mother's blood
whips him from it into fits of madness—
I say "Mother's blood" because
I dare not name the dread goddesses   50
who frenzy him. It's been six days, now,
since Mother's bloodstained body was cleansed by fire,
six days since he has eaten or washed himself.
Whenever the pain eases a little
and lets him come to his senses, he sobs there
buried under his robes, or sometimes
races from bed like a colt
bucking free of its yoke.
    Here in Argos they have decreed
that no one can shelter us,   60
or warm us at their fires, or even
speak to us, the matricides.
And this is the day set aside by the assembly
to determine if they'll stone the two of us to death.
But we still have some chance of escape.
Menelaos has landed from Troy,
rowing into harbor at Nauplia,
home at last from the war and long wanderings.
And the cause of all the bloodshed, Helen,
he sent ahead to our palace, waiting till darkness   70
for fear those who lost their sons at Troy,
seeing her in broad daylight, would stone her.

She's in there now, bewailing
her sister's death and the ruin of the house.
Yet she has some consolation:
her daughter, Hermione, whom Menelaos
brought from Sparta and left in my mother's care,
gives her delight, helping her to forget.
      But I am keeping watch,
I look everywhere, hoping to catch sight   80
of Menelaos, for our shaken strength
won't carry us through unless somehow
he saves us. A house brought down lies helpless.

                              Enter HELEN *from the palace.*

HELEN Ah, Electra, daughter of Clytemnestra and Agamemnon!
      Still unmarried, after all these years,
      how are you, and how is your brother?
      Speaking with you won't contaminate me,
      for I ascribe the crime
      to Apollo. Yet I mourn for Clytemnestra, my sister—
      I never saw her again, once I had sailed off to Troy.   90
      Fate and madness, sent by the gods, drove me there.
      But now I feel her loss, and the sting of sorrow.

ELECTRA Do I have to spell out, Helen,
      what you can see for yourself?
      Here I am, sleepless, watching over a miserable corpse—
      he might as well be dead, he's hardly breathing:
      I wouldn't ridicule his sufferings.
      But now you've come, you
      in all your happiness and your husband in his
      as if to gloat on our misery.   100

HELEN How long has he been lying here?

ELECTRA Ever since he shed his mother's blood.

HELEN Poor man! And his poor mother, the way she died!

ELECTRA That's the way it is—evil overwhelmed him.

HELEN Would you do me a favor, though, Electra?

ELECTRA I would, but it depends: I must tend to my brother.

HELEN Won't you, just for me, go to my sister's grave ...

ELECTRA My mother's grave, you mean—what for?

HELEN ... to carry my libations and this offering of my hair?

ELECTRA Shouldn't you pay respects, yourself, at the tomb of a
loved one? 110

HELEN Well, I'm ashamed to show my face in this city.

ELECTRA It's about time. You ran off in disgrace before.

HELEN There's truth in what you say, but no consideration.

ELECTRA So you feel shame among the Mycenaeans. I wonder why?

HELEN I fear the fathers of the dead left at Troy.

ELECTRA As well you may: they curse your name here in Argos.

HELEN Free me from fear, then: please, go in my place.

ELECTRA I couldn't bear to look on my mother's grave.

HELEN Yes, but how disgraceful, for a servant to take these things!

ELECTRA Then why not send your daughter, Hermione? 120

HELEN An unmarried girl shouldn't venture into the streets.

ELECTRA But she should visit the grave of the woman who raised her.

HELEN That's true, my dear. What you say is convincing.
　　　　Hermione, Hermione—

　　　　　　　　　　Enter HERMIONE *from the palace.*

My darling child, take these libations and my hair,
go to Clytemnestra's grave, pour out
the honeyed milk and the wine, and standing over the mound
speak these words: "Your sister bestows these,
who dares not come herself, living in fear of the Argives."
And bid her not to look unkindly   130
on me, you, my husband,
and this sorry pair, destroyed by the god.
Assure my sisterly observance
in all things due to the dead.
There, off with you now, perform the rites, then hurry back.

　　　　Exit HERMIONE *offstage; exit* HELEN *into the palace.*

ELECTRA (*to herself*)
　　　　Nature! How your evil shows
　　　　　　　　in human beings!

　　　　　　　　　　　　　　　　(*to the audience*)

Did you see her,
barely trimming her locks to save her looks!

　　　　　　　　　　　　　　　　(*to herself again*)

She's the woman she always was.   140

　　　　　　　　　　　　(*looking back at the palace*)

　　May the gods pour their hatred on you
for destroying me, and him here, and all Hellas!

The CHORUS *approaches.* ELECTRA *rises in alarm.*

193

Oh no, here come my friends,
the women who echo my laments—
they'll wake him, start him raving, and me weeping.
    Women, step lightly, keep silence,
I know you mean well, but waking him
will destroy me.

Full entry of CHORUS.

CHORUS AND
    ELECTRA (*together*)

strophe a

CHORUS Softly, step softly, make no sound.

ELECTRA Away, away from the bed!   150

CHORUS See, we obey!

ELECTRA And please, speak as gently
                as the slender pipe.

CHORUS There ... we'll whisper, like wind
                among the reeds.

ELECTRA Good. But lower still.
            And now, come closer, quietly,
                and very quietly say
                what you have to say,
            for at last he's at peace, he sleeps.   160

antistrophe a

CHORUS How is he, Electra? What happened? What's wrong?

ELECTRA He still breathes, but in gasps.

CHORUS What's that? I'm afraid.

194

ELECTRA Hush! If you drive sleep from his eyes,
                the one sweet grace he needs, you'll kill him.

CHORUS He took on horrors from the gods
                and suffers horribly.

ELECTRA   Ah, the pain of it!
                And the crime—yes, it was crime
                    Apollo himself screamed for
                    from the tripod of Righteousness,   170
                    passing sentence of murder on our mother
                    in return for murder!

                                                            strophe b

CHORUS Look at the covers—he's moving!

ELECTRA Yes, your cries disturbed him—hush!

CHORUS We thought he was asleep.

ELECTRA Circle back there, get back,
                away from the palace,
                and be quiet!

CHORUS But now he's resting. He'll sleep.

ELECTRA   So I pray!

                        (*in the shrill intonation of a dirge, but softly*)

            Oh majesty, Queen Night,   180
            bearer of sleep to toiling men,
            come, come from your darkness,
            lift yourself from your deeps, great power,
            and stretch wing to Agamemnon's palace,
                for pain and ruin are here,
                breaking, crushing us . . .

195

ELECTRA *turns to the* CHORUS *now approaching again.*

Too loud! Won't you quietly
    back away from his bed, my friends, won't you let
    sleep do its gentle work?

antistrophe b

CHORUS But tell us, what is in store—where will these evils end?   190

ELECTRA In death. What else? He won't even eat.

CHORUS Clearly, then, he will die.

ELECTRA Die at Apollo's hands—he sacrificed us
        with that black oracle of bloodshed
        overtaking bloodshed, to kill
    our father's killer, our mother.

CHORUS Justly!

ELECTRA   And hideously!

        You killed and died for it, Mother
        who gave me life, you destroyed
        Father and these children   200
        of your blood, leaving us lost,
        among the dead—Orestes
        a corpse already, and me
    with nothing to live for, weeping
        through the long nights,
        sorrowing through time.

CHORUS LEADER Electra, you're next to him, look at your brother.
        His stillness frightens me.
        He may have died without your knowing it.

                ORESTES *wakes suddenly, uncovering himself.*

ORESTES   Oh precious charm of sleep, the nurse of sickness,   210
          how sweetly you came to me when I needed you!
             Great queen of forgetting, wise power
          the afflicted wisely pray to . . .

                                              He looks about him.

          But where have I been? How did I get here? Nothing
          of that comes back to me, it's been swept away.

ELECTRA   Orestes, how glad I was to see you resting!
          Do you want to get up now, shall I help you?

ORESTES   Yes, give me your hand, help me up, and wipe
          the scum from my eyes and mouth.

ELECTRA   Let me, then: it's not beneath me   220
          to tend my brother this way, with my own hands.

ORESTES   Come, hold me up, and brush away
          this matted hair. I can hardly see!

ELECTRA   What a tangle of curls: how filthy! You've become
          a wild animal, going so long without washing!

ORESTES   Let me lie down again. When these seizures pass,
          my arms and legs go limp, I have no strength.

ELECTRA   There, now, when you're sick a bed is like a friend:
          a good thing to have, but painful to need.

ORESTES   Wait, prop me up again. And turn me around.   230
          Helpless! The sick are so hard to please.

ELECTRA   Do you want to swing your feet over and try
          walking at last? A change can always help.

ORESTES   Sure, if only to make a show of health—
          it's better to seem so, even if you're not.

197

ELECTRA Orestes, I have something to tell you. Listen to me,
while the Furies leave you some peace of mind.

ORESTES I hope your news is good news.
I've had my fill of the other kind.

ELECTRA Our uncle, Menelaos, is here.   240
His ship is anchored at Nauplia.

ORESTES Do you mean our troubles are over? Light at last?
Our uncle here, who owes our father so much?

ELECTRA He's here, and—take this as proof of what I say—
he's brought Helen with him, from the walls of Troy.

ORESTES He'd be a man to envy if he'd survived alone!
He brings disaster with him, bringing that wife.

ELECTRA A fine pair of daughters Tyndareos sired,
reviled at home, notorious throughout Greece!

ORESTES You, now! See that you don't take after them!   250
You say you won't, but in your mind...

                                         ORESTES *rises, staring.*

ELECTRA Orestes! Now your eyes are wild...here it is
again, the madness, and a moment ago you were fine!

ORESTES Please, Mother, no! Don't sic them on me,
those girls with eyes of blood, with snakes...

ELECTRA Easy, easy now. Back into bed. You can't really
be seeing them, however real they seem to you.

ORESTES I *do* see them. There they are, there, leaping at me!
They'll kill me, Apollo—those bitch-hound faces
and gorgon eyes, those priestesses of the dead! The
                                         goddesses!   260

ELECTRA *tries to force him onto the bed.*

Let go! You're one of them, you're one of my Furies
grabbing me, wrestling me down to hell!

ELECTRA I won't let go of you! I'll lock
my arms around you until it's all over . . .

ORESTES *breaks free.*

Ah, what help can I call on now?
The gods themselves are against us.

ELECTRA *veils her face.*

ORESTES Bring me the horn-tipped bow, Apollo's gift,
the weapon he told me would drive the goddesses away
if they tried to terrorize me with their ravings.

ORESTES *draws the invisible bow.*

You may be goddesses,   270
but if you don't get back, out of my sight,
one of you is going to bleed
at a man's hands. Hear me?

He shoots.

There! Don't you see the feathers
flash from his distance-devouring bow?
Go on, graze heaven with those wings!
Blame Apollo's oracles!

He stops himself.

What came over me? Why am I
gasping? What drove me from bed? For now
the storm has passed, the great waves gone, it's calm again. 280

He sees ELECTRA *sobbing under her robe.*

    Electra, why are you crying? Don't shroud your face.
The shame is mine, that you must feel my pain, you,
a young woman, having to put up with my sickness.
Don't weep that way because of me
and what I did! Yes, you agreed to it
but the blood, Mother's blood, was spilled by me.
It's Apollo I blame—
he put me up to the abomination, with everything he said
he cheered me on, but he's done nothing!
I now believe that if I'd gone to Father   290
and asked him face to face whether
to kill her, he would have begged me,
pleaded with me not to put a mother
to the sword. Could it bring him back to life?
Or not plague me as it does now?
But come, Electra, uncover your face,
don't cry anymore, no matter how bad it is.
When you see me losing heart, nurse me
out of my terror, my madness, and comfort me;
and when I hear you crying, I'll be there.   300
So should those who love each other help each other.
Go on into the palace, now, and get some rest,
bathe, eat, give your tired eyes some sleep.
If you abandon me, or fall sick caring for me,
I'm lost, I have no help but you—everyone else,
as you see, has deserted me.

ELECTRA No, I can't leave—my place is here with you,
whether I die or live: it comes to the same thing.
For if you were to die, what would I do? A woman
without brother or father or friend,   310
how could I survive alone?
But if you think it best, of course I shall go in.
Meanwhile, you must lie down again yourself.
And if the terror and confusion come back,
hold them off, don't leave your bed.
Even an imaginary illness, a sickness

living only in the mind, feeds on the mind's belief
and so winds a man deeper in its toils.

ELECTRA *exits into the palace.* ORESTES *lies down.*

CHORUS

strophe

Wind-running and
down-swooping   320

goddesses of the abyss, banded together
in dark orgies of weeping and keening,
Eumenides robed in blackness
who drum across the stretched air
calling down blood punishment
and punishment for blood shed,

we pray, we pray you, free
the son of Agamemnon
from his seizing
onspinning madness!   330
                    Ah, the pain
you wrestled and were crushed,
obeying the word Apollo

screamed from the tripod, in hushed
precincts where they say the earth

chambers her center.

antistrophe

Great God! What torment, what
suffering will it end in,

this gruesome agony driving you on?
Some avenger
hounding the whole line   340
pours stream on stream of misery

into your sobbings, maddening you
for your mother's blood!

We grieve for you, we mourn!
Great human happiness cannot last—
some god topples it,
shakes the little sail
and punches the boat over
into the pounding waves, the swells of pain.

Or could we honor some other house   350
more than this one, sprung from Tantalos

and grown in the beds of the gods?

CHORUS LEADER And now, here comes the king, Lord Menelaos.

Enter MENELAOS *with retinue.*

Welcome, O King, who launched
the fleet of a thousand ships against Asia!
No need to pray for good luck
in your coming: it stands beside you.
You have achieved what you asked from the gods.

MENELAOS House of my fathers! Looking on you at last
and back from Troy, I am a happy man. Yet   360
I must greet you sadly, for never have I seen
more evils besiege, close in on a house!
Coming toward Cape Malea, I learned of Agamemnon's fate.
Out of the waves rose Glaukos
son of Nereus, sailor's prophet, unlying god,
who proclaimed it, right before my eyes:
"Menelaos. your brother lies dead
in the last bath his wife will draw for him."
I broke down at this, my men, too,
and wept. But when I came ashore at Nauplia   370
and sent my wife on ahead, expecting
before long to put my arms

around Orestes and his mother,
finding them both well,
I heard the news—an old salt told me—
of the abominable murder of Tyndareos' daughter.
All the same, young women, tell me where he is,
Agamemnon's son, the man
who nerved himself to this horror.
When I left these halls on my way to Troy,   380
he was still a babe in Clytemnestra's arms
and so I wouldn't know him if I saw him.

> ORESTES *rises from his bed and steps forward.*

ORESTES Here I am, Menelaos, the man you're asking for.
I'll gladly testify to my horrors, but first
I appeal to you—

> *He kneels and touches* MENELAOS' *knees.*

I lack the suppliant's branches, so let me
hang my prayers here, let me implore you,
save me from disaster! You've come just in time.

MENELAOS O gods, what am I looking at? Someone back from the dead?

ORESTES That's right: I've been in hell. I'm there still.   390

MENELAOS The filth in your hair! Like a wild animal's.

ORESTES I'm finished. Nothing's left but my name.

MENELAOS Your eyes are frightening, burnt out.

ORESTES It's not my looks that disfigure me, it's what I've done.

MENELAOS What a ghastly sight! Nothing prepared me for this.

ORESTES Still, it's me, killer of my mother, such as she was.

MENELAOS I've heard about it. The less said, the better.

ORESTES However I hold back, the god has more.

MENELAOS What is it? What sickness is destroying you?

ORESTES My own mind. It sees what I did.   400

MENELAOS What does that mean? Be sensible, don't speak in riddles.

ORESTES Pain is one way of putting it, yes, pain . . .

MENELAOS A grim goddess, that one. But cures can be found.

ORESTES . . . and madness, the workings of my mother's blood.

MENELAOS When did it start? What day was it?

ORESTES The day I raised her burial mound.

MENELAOS Did it come over you at home, or at the pyre?

ORESTES The pyre, at night. I was waiting to gather her bones.

MENELAOS Was anyone else there, watching beside you?

ORESTES Pylades, who helped me kill my mother.   410

MENELAOS What kind of visions bring on the madness?

ORESTES I seemed to see three women. Women like the night.

MENELAOS I know who they are, but I'd rather not name them.

ORESTES They do inspire silence, those three. Best refrain.

MENELAOS It's they who drive you mad, for murdering your mother.

ORESTES But I can escape them. I've got a way out . . .

MENELAOS I hope you don't mean death. There's no sense in that.

ORESTES ...through Apollo. He ordered me to kill her.

MENELAOS Yes, with scant regard for seemliness and justice.

ORESTES We're only slaves to the gods—whatever the gods are.   420

MENELAOS And what of Apollo? No help from him yet?

ORESTES Apollo takes his time. That's the way a god works.

MENELAOS How many days since your poor mother died?

ORESTES Six. The embers are still warm.

MENELAOS How quickly the goddesses visit her blood on you!

ORESTES Yes, they hound me, snapping at me, bringing me down!

MENELAOS Terrible acts have terrible consequences.

ORESTES I might have known better. Instead, I was true to my own.

MENELAOS You avenged your father, but what have you got to show for it?

ORESTES Nothing, yet. Help to come I call no help at all.   430

MENELAOS How are things with the city after what you've done?

ORESTES They shun us. They won't speak to us.

MENELAOS You haven't cleansed your hands of bloodshed, according to
                                                        custom?

ORESTES No. Wherever I'd go, they'd shut the door in my face.

MENELAOS Who's behind this? Who's hounding you out?

ORESTES Oiax, shifting the hatred of Troy onto my father.

MENELAOS I see: he's avenging the death of his brother Palamedes.

ORESTES Which wasn't *my* doing. But there's still a third blow.

MENELAOS From what quarter? The party of Aigisthos?

ORESTES Yes, them, too. And they've got the city's ear.   440

MENELAOS Will Argos let you keep Agamemnon's scepter?

ORESTES How, when they won't let us keep our lives?

MENELAOS What action are they taking? Be specific.

ORESTES A vote, today—against us.

MENELAOS And you haven't gotten out of the country yet?

ORESTES We're penned in on every side by swords.

MENELAOS Whose? Personal enemies, or Argive troops?

ORESTES The whole populace, out for my blood. There you have it.

MENELAOS Poor man, you're at the end of your rope.

ORESTES But you can get me out, you alone.   450
       Come, now: here you are, flushed with success—
share some of it with us, your own kin
struggling to survive: don't hug it
to yourself, don't refuse
your own part in these troubles, but pay
your debt to our father, as you should.
Friends who aren't there when it counts
aren't worth the name.

CHORUS LEADER Here comes Tyndareos of Sparta,
       striving on at the stiff pace of age,   460

all in black and his hair shorn
in mourning for his daughter.

ORESTES Menelaos, I'm lost! It's Tyndareos. He's here!
Shame at what I did drives me from his sight, his
above all others! He raised me when I was little,
showered me, "Agamemnon's boy," with affection,
cradled me in his arms, he and Leda both,
making as much of me as of their own sons.
Heart and soul! I've not returned their love.

Moving aside, ORESTES *covers his head.*

Where is the darkness, where is cloud thick enough   470
to hide me from that old man's eyes?

Enter TYNDAREOS *with attendants.*

TYNDAREOS Where is my daughter's husband,
where may I lay eyes on Menelaos?
While I was pouring libations over Clytemnestra's grave,
I heard that he had come home,
landing at Nauplia safely with his wife
after all these years. Show the way,
I want to take his hand in welcome,
face to face at last.

MENELAOS Greetings, Sire, who shared your wife with Zeus.   480

TYNDAREOS There you are, then! Greetings also to you, my son.

He catches sight of ORESTES.

What's this! That snake who killed his mother, right here,
his sick eyes gleaming—I can't stand the sight of him.
Menelaos, you aren't talking with this outcast, are you?

MENELAOS What if I am? He's the son of a man who was close to me.

TYNDAREOS Agamemnon's son, you say, when he's turned out like this?

MENELAOS Yes, his son, and if his luck is down he's still to be honored.

TYNDAREOS All those years among barbarians have made you one yourself.

MENELAOS It's always been Greek to honor your own kin.

TYNDAREOS Yes, and not go in for lawlessness.   490

MENELAOS Only slaves do nothing but obey—that's the enlightened view.

TYNDAREOS You can keep such notions to yourself, I'll have none of them.

MENELAOS No, because your temper and your age don't make for good
                                                              sense.

TYNDAREOS Sense! There's some dispute about that in *his* case.
        Look: If everyone knows right from wrong
        then who on earth has shown less sense than he?
        To begin with, justice meant nothing to him:
        he spurned the practice followed by Greeks everywhere.
        When Agamemnon was struck down by my daughter—
        and I shall never excuse that atrocity—   500
        Orestes should have punished her, yes, but
        in a way respect for the gods demands:
        by casting her out. Then he would have kept
        a name for sanity, holding to law
        and righteousness. But as it is,
        his mother's own fate has claimed him.
        Yes, he was right to believe her damnable, but when
        he killed her, he damned himself twice over.
        Menelaos, let me put it this way.
        Suppose this man should be murdered by his wife.   510
        Their son in turn would then kill his own mother,
        and then his son in the next generation
        once again pays murder off
        with murder. I ask you, where would it end?
        Our ancestors found the way that works.

They commanded everyone to avoid contact
with a murderer, not even to look at him,
but to secure the favor of heaven again
by banishing, not killing him in turn.
The other way, someone would always   520
be taking the pollution onto his own hands.
    As for me, I loathe sinful women,
first among them my daughter, who slew her husband.
And Helen, too, your wife, I shall never approve,
I would not even speak to her.
Nor can I say you did well
going to the plain of Troy to get her back.
But with everything I can, I am committed
to defending the law and stopping this blood lust
that always turns men into beasts,   530
destroying cities and polluting the earth.

He turns suddenly on ORESTES.

And *you*, what kind of heart was beating inside you,
if you had any, when your mother begged you
to let her live, baring her breast to you?
These old eyes of mine saw nothing of that horror,
but even as I think of it now the tears well up...
    One thing bears out what I say.
You are hated by the gods themselves, you are paying
the penalty for what you did to her,
straying among terrors and driven mad. Do I need   540
witnesses to tell me what I can see for myself?

(turning to MENELAOS *again)*

So I hope it's clear, Menelaos:
don't go against the gods
by acting on your impulse to protect this man.
My daughter is dead. And she deserved to die.
But it was beyond all bounds for her to die at *his* hands.
    I've been a happy man in everything
except my daughters: in them I was unlucky.

CHORUS LEADER A man whose children are a blessing is fortunate.
Not so the one on whom they bring ruin and shame.   550

ORESTES *comes forward.*

ORESTES Sir, I am afraid to answer you
in a situation that guarantees offense.
If your great age were not before me,
I might not choke back my words. As it is,
your gray hair makes me tremble.
    As I see it, the law brands me an outcast
for killing my mother, but also embraces me
with another designation: my father's avenger.
What was I to do? Let's weigh
the factors involved, two sets of them.   560
Father sired me, while your daughter bore me;
his was the seed and hers the empty field.
In coming to his defense, then, I decided
to give priority not to the one who simply
nurtured me, but rather the one who gave me life.
And now the second point: your daughter—
shame prevents me from calling her "mother"—
took herself a man. It was a private wedding,
but not a decent one.
In saying this about her   570
I blacken my own name, but say it I will.
Aigisthos was her closet husband. I killed him
and added my mother's death to crown that sacrifice,
bringing pollution and treatment as an outcast
upon myself, but avenging my father.
    As for the grounds on which you and others
threaten me with stoning, listen to this:
they make me Greece's benefactor.
If women can muster the audacity
to kill their own lords, fleeing   580
to their children, baring their breasts
to excite "pity," as you call it,
then husband murder will count

for nothing, they'll resort to it
on the slightest pretext.
By my "dreadful crimes," as you loudly proclaim them,
I've put a stop to that sort of precedent.

    In hating my mother, and killing her, I did justice.
She betrayed her husband while he was away from home
leading the combined Greek armies as commander-in-
                        chief—   590
betrayed him, defiled their bed! And then, seeing
where all this was leading her,
she didn't punish herself; instead,
to avoid paying for her crimes,
she punished *him*, she killed my father!

    It was *you*, Sir, who destroyed me—yes, *you*,
by fathering that evil daughter. Only because of her
outrageousness did I lose my own father and become
what I am: a matricide.
You see? Telemachos hasn't killed *his* mother, but then   600
neither has Penelope run around adding
husband to husband. Odysseus' wife
behaves. Her marriage bed stays undefiled.

    By the gods!—or maybe I shouldn't mention gods:
it's they who execute blood justice.
But if I had condoned my mother's actions
by holding my tongue, what would my father's ghost
have done to me? Hated and driven me mad
with his own Furies, no?
Or do you suppose that my mother   610
has gods of her own when he, wronged far more, has none?

    And what of Apollo, isn't *he* there,
enthroned at Delphi, center of the world, giving
sure oracles to us all? When I killed
my mother, I was obeying him.
Treat *him* as an outcast, all of you, kill *him!*
I'm not at fault, he is. What was I to do?
Will the god not stand by his word
and cleanse me of pollution? How on earth
could anyone escape if the same god   620

who commanded me to kill won't save me from being killed?
    Don't say, then, that what I did was terrible,
but that for me it has turned out terribly unlucky.

CHORUS LEADER Women are always getting themselves involved
in the lives of men, and seldom for the better.

TYNDAREOS Outrageous, are you? Refuse to curb your tongue,
do you? Answer in just the way
to gall me, will you? Well, then: you'll fire me
all the more to bring about your death!
I'll consider it an extra piety, a nice   630
companion to the act of homage
at my daughter's grave for which I came here.
The Argives are meeting in emergency session.
I'll go before them—they're eager enough—
and sic them on you, the whole city,
till I hear you both condemned to death
by stoning—you, and your sister.
Yes, her, too! If anything, she deserves it more.
It was she who unleashed you against your mother,
baited you with tales to swell your hatred,   640
harping on the scandal of Agamemnon's death
and that affair with Aigisthos—I hope
it reeks in Hades, it was a stench in our faces here—
all fuel to the fire she kindled, your sister,
until the whole house went up in flames.
    As for you, Menelaos,
I have this to say, and I mean it:
if you care at all about being in my good graces,
don't go against the gods for the likes of him.
Let the people stone him to death! Try to prevent it   650
and you will never set foot in Sparta again.
Mark my words, and don't embrace
a blasphemer, or you'll put a lot of distance
between yourself and your more decent friends.
Men, lead me away from here.

Exit TYNDAREOS, *left*.

212

ORESTES   Yes, go! What I have to say to Menelaos
          I can say as I please, with your old age out of the way.

                              He turns to MENELAOS, *who is*
                              now walking back and forth.

          Menelaos, why are you pacing up and down,
          lost in thought? Is something troubling you?

MENELAOS Quiet. Something *is* on my mind. I don't know   660
          which way to turn in this situation.

ORESTES   Don't decide too hastily. Hear me out
          first, and then make up your mind.

MENELAOS All right, go ahead. Sometimes it's better
          to listen, at other times to talk.

ORESTES   With your permission, then, I'll speak at length:
          a longer speech makes for greater clarity.
              Menelaos, I'm not asking you
          for anything of yours. Return, instead,
          the favor you owe my father. Save   670
          what I value most, of all that's mine: my life.
              I have transgressed.
          What my guilt requires is a corresponding
          transgression from you.
          When my father Agamemnon assembled the invasion fleet
          and went to Troy, he, too, was in the wrong
          but not on his own account.
          It was the sin of Helen, your wife's crime,
          that he was mending. Like the true brother he was,
          Agamemnon stood by your side, shield to shield,   680
          and fought to retrieve your wife. Pay back to me, then,
          what you got there: stand and fight, our savior
          not for ten long years but one short day!
              As for what Aulis took, also through my father—
          the sacrifice of my sister—I ask no return for that, you
          need not lift a hand, yourself, against Hermione.

213

My situation being what it is,
the advantage must remain yours
and I must make allowance.
Offer, instead, my life to my poor father.   690
Do it to repay him, for if I die
his house, the house of Agamemnon, will be orphaned.
    Hopeless, you may say.
Exactly. But it's during crises
that we help each other, not in good times.
Who needs family when the gods make things smooth?
When those powers prove willing, it is enough.
    Everyone knows you love your wife.
I don't mean to disarm you
with flattery, Menelaos,   700
by begging you in her name.
Yes, beg: it has come to that.
What choice have I left?
I'm pleading for the house itself, root and branch.

                    ORESTES *adopts a suppliant's posture.*

Oh you who have my father's blood in your veins,
Uncle, imagine that in the dead underearth
Agamemnon hears this now, a ghost
fluttering over you, and that he finds
his voice in mine!

                              (*rising to his feet again*)

    These are my claims. You've heard my case.   710
I'm pleading for my life, as any man would.

CHORUS LEADER I, too, though I am only a woman, beg you
               to help them in their need, for you have the power.

    MENELAOS   Orestes, I, as you know, hold you
               in high regard and I very much want
               to share in your ordeals. Honor requires one

to take up a kinsman's troubles and carry them
to the end, if the gods grant the power, and even
to die, provided one's enemies die also.
But I'd have to get that power from the gods,   720
for I've come with barely a few fighting men,
worn out, myself, by the endless stress of wandering
and not able to count on the friends I left behind.
Force of arms, then, is not the way to win
ancient Argos. But if we try, by means
of gentle persuasion—*there* we have a fighting chance.
How can one hope to attain mighty ends
with meager resources?
Even wanting to do so is silly.
When anger sweeps the people and is still   730
rising in them, resistance
is like fighting a raging fire.
Yet if, biding his time, a man will calmly
ride out their fury, watching for the right moment,
the tantrum may blow over; and then you can easily
get what you want from them, as much as you want.
There is pity in the people, and powerful emotion—
picked prizes for the man with a sense of timing.
That being the case, I'll go and try to persuade
Tyndareos and the assembly not to carry things   740
too far. It's the same way with a ship:
when you rein her in, straining the ropes,
she heels over; let go, and she lifts again.
The gods hate overdoing it, so do the people.
I must save you, not by
resisting those who are stronger, but by being
clever. Using force, as you would perhaps
have me do, isn't the way—my spear alone
won't put your troubles to flight.
Nor would I ever choose the delicate approach   750
without good reason. As things are, if we're sensible,
we'll admit that we're the slaves of chance.

Exit MENELAOS, *left.*

ORESTES O mighty campaigner, when the cause is a woman,
but useless when it's your own kin, there you go
turning and running—can't wait to be off? And do
Agamemnon's claims count for nothing?
You lost your friends, Father, when you lost your luck!
    I am betrayed, I have no hope
of finding safety from death in Argos:
that uncle there was my last refuge.   760

> ORESTES *sinks back down on his couch, exhausted,*
> *then looks up, sensing the approach of someone.*

But wait! Here comes Pylades, my best friend
back from Phokis, running at full stride.
How good to see him! A person you can count on
in times of trouble is better than the sight of calm
to desperate sailors.

> *Enter* PYLADES *from the right, running.*

PYLADES I came as fast as I could, rushing through town
when I heard the news—all too true,
as I saw for myself—that the citizens were meeting
to kill you and your sister, this very day.
What is all this? How are things with you?   770
How are you doing, comrade, friend, cousin—
for you're all these to me.

ORESTES We're lost. That—in a word—sums up my ruin.

PYLADES Then take me down with you. Friends are friends through
thick and thin.

ORESTES Menelaos is a traitor to me and my sister . . .

PYLADES I wouldn't expect a whore's husband to be much of a man.

ORESTES . . . and might as well not have come back at all.

ORESTES					[739–57]

PYLADES It's true, then—he has returned? To this very place?

ORESTES At long last. But he wasn't long in dropping his own.

PYLADES And what of Helen? Did he come back with her on board? 780

ORESTES The other way around—she brought him.

PYLADES Where is she now, that woman who nearly wiped out Greece?

ORESTES Inside my palace—if I can still call it mine.

PYLADES And what did you ask from your father's own brother?

ORESTES Not to stand by watching the people kill me and my sister.

PYLADES Well, by god, what did he say to that, I'd like to know?

ORESTES He advised "caution," like the typical bad friend.

PYLADES What excuse did he reach for? That tells it all.

ORESTES Onto the scene walked that old sire of such fine daughters.

PYLADES You mean Tyndareos, furious, no doubt, because of
					Clytemnestra.		790

ORESTES Right. Menelaos preferred his "good graces" to my dead father.

PYLADES And he refused, point blank, to share in your struggle?

ORESTES He's not much with a spear, except among the ladies.

PYLADES You *are* in trouble, then. But does death have to be the out-
					come?

ORESTES That's for the people to decide. We're charged with murder.

PYLADES What will their vote determine? Tell me. I'm full of dread.

217

ORESTES Life or death. A few words, but they mean a lot.

PYLADES Then take your sister and escape! Leave these halls behind!

ORESTES But haven't you seen them? Armed men on guard, every-
                                                            where.

PYLADES I did find street after street fenced with spears.   800

ORESTES We're like a towered city holding besiegers at bay.

PYLADES Put some questions to me, now. I, too, am ruined.

ORESTES And who has added this to all my troubles?

PYLADES Strophios in his fury has banished me, my own father.

ORESTES In a private matter, or a public one? What was the charge?

PYLADES That I took your mother's blood upon myself. He calls me
                                                            "outcast."

ORESTES Just like me! All my sufferings, it seems, are to be yours.

PYLADES I'm not nimble, Menelaos. I'll face what I must.

ORESTES What if the Argives want to kill you as well?

PYLADES It's not their affair; only Phokis has jurisdiction.   810

ORESTES Well, then: it's time we considered . . .

PYLADES   . . . what needs to be done?

ORESTES Suppose I went to the assembly and said . . .

PYLADES   . . . that you were justified . . .

ORESTES . . . as my father's avenger?

218

PYLADES   They may not welcome you with open arms.

ORESTES Should I grovel here instead, and die without speaking up?

PYLADES   A coward's way.

ORESTES Well, then, what should I do?

PYLADES   If you don't go, can you escape death?

ORESTES No.

PYLADES   And if you do, have you any chance of being saved?

ORESTES Perhaps, with luck.

PYLADES   Then that seems the better choice.

ORESTES Shall I go, then?

PYLADES   Yes. Even if you die you'll die nobly.

ORESTES You're right. That way I avoid cowardice.

PYLADES   More so than otherwise.

ORESTES My cause is just, too.   820

PYLADES   Pray only that it seem so.

ORESTES And some may take pity on me...

PYLADES   ...considering your high birth...

ORESTES ...and feeling outrage at my father's death.

PYLADES   I see it all coming.

ORESTES I must go, if only to die like a man!

PYLADES   Yes! I'll second that.

ORESTES But then there's my sister. Shall we tell her?

PYLADES   *I* wouldn't.

ORESTES You're right. There'd be a scene.

PYLADES   A bad omen, for sure.

ORESTES It's better, obviously, to say nothing.

PYLADES   And the time saved will help.

ORESTES Only *them, them* in my way—

PYLADES   What is it, what do you mean?

ORESTES The goddesses. They might drive me mad.

PYLADES   But I'll be right beside you.

ORESTES It's difficult, touching a sick man.

PYLADES   Not for me, with you.

ORESTES But take care: my madness might infect you, too!   830

PYLADES   Never mind that.

ORESTES Then you won't hold back?

PYLADES   Hesitation and friendship don't mix.

ORESTES Very well, then. Steer me on my way.

PYLADES   Gladly, with a friend's care.

220

ORESTES *rises from the couch, assisted by* PYLADES.

ORESTES And take me to my father's grave.

PYLADES   But what for?

ORESTES To pray to him for deliverance.

PYLADES   Yes. That he'll listen to.

ORESTES As for Mother's grave, I wouldn't look on it.

PYLADES   No—she was your enemy.
But quickly—or the Argives
may condemn you first: here, take my arm,
let my strength support your weakness,
and come with me right through town—
I don't care about the mob,   840
I'm not ashamed to suffer with you.
How will I ever prove my friendship if I don't
prove it now, when you're facing the worst?

ORESTES That's what I meant—friends are better than family!
A man whose mind mirrors your own, though there's
no blood tie, is better than an army of relatives.

                    Exit ORESTES *and* PYLADES *to the right*.

CHORUS

                                                        strophe

                    The vast prosperity, the prowess
                    vaunting itself through Greece
            and on to Troy by the banks of Simois
                    has ebbed again for Atreus' house,   850
                            drawn down
                    by the old violence

221

bursting out among the Tantalids
      over the golden lamb,
      gruesome banquetings
      and dismemberings of princes,
         grief after grief
      traded in blood until
      now it envelops the divided
      heirs of Atreus!   860

antistrophe

      To call the hideous slashing
      of a mother's flesh "good,"
and the lifting of the sword black with her blood
        into the sunlight "noble"—
          is this not
        perverted piety
in those who do evil and madness in those who conceive it?
        For in her terror of death,
        Tyndareos' daughter cried out,
        "My son, the gods have no part   870
          in your daring.
        Don't, for your father's sake,
        steep yourself in infamy
          forever!"

epode

      Can earth show any sickness, misery, grief
      greater than this dipping
        of a son's hands
        into a mother's blood?
      That is what he did, and now
      the Furies hunt him, now   880
      his eyes, red with death, flash
      this way and that, demented,
        the son of Agamemnon.
      The pity of it
          when, seeing

her breasts, seeing her bare them
through gold-brocaded robes,
he slaughtered his mother for
          his father
in fate's grimmest trade!   890

                    ELECTRA *enters from the palace.*

ELECTRA Women! Am I right? Orestes ran away
          in a fit of madness, driven by the goddesses?

CHORUS LEADER No, that isn't it. He's gone before the Argive people.

ELECTRA Oh no! Why on earth? Who persuaded him to do that?

CHORUS LEADER Pylades.

                    Enter a MESSENGER *from the right.*

          It shouldn't be long, though, before
          this messenger tells us what happened to your brother.

MESSENGER Noble Electra! Daughter of Agamemnon,
          hear what I have to say, unlucky though it is.

ELECTRA We're lost, then! Your words are all too clear.

MESSENGER The Pelasgians have decreed that your brother,   900
          and you with him, poor woman, must die today.

ELECTRA It has come, the thing I've dreaded so long,
          wasting away in fears of the future. It has come!
              But enough of that. Tell me about the trial.
          When the Argives condemned us, what speeches
          set them on giving us death?
          Speak, Sir: is it stones or the sword
          that will drive the breath of life from my body
          when I and my brother go down together?

MESSENGER I happened to be coming through the gates from the fields,   910
           wanting to see how things stood with you and Orestes.
           For I always loved your father, and your house always sup-
                                                          ported me.
           Peasant though I am I treat my friends nobly.
             There was a crowd, then, going up the hill and filling the
                                                                  seats
           where they say Danaos called the very first assembly,
           when Aigyptos pressed his claims there. Seeing
           all the citizens gathering, I asked one of them,
           "What's happening in Argos? Has some threat of war
           come from our enemies? Why all this disturbance?"
           And he said, pointing: "Don't you see Orestes there,   920
           coming this way, to run his deadly race?"
           And then I saw a sight I didn't expect and wish
           I'd never seen: Pylades and your brother on their way,
           one limp and dejected, the other suffering with him
           like a brother, helping and watching over him.
             When there was a full crowd, a herald stood up and asked:
           "Who wants to speak to the issue, whether or not
           Orestes must be put to death
           for killing his mother?" And thereupon
           Talthybios rose, your father's henchman at Troy.   930
           Always one to kowtow, he spoke both ways at once,
           extolling your father but disparaging Orestes,
           interweaving noble sentiments with vulgar ones,
           to the effect that customs established by Orestes
           would not bode well for parents. And he kept on
           glancing and smiling at Aigisthos' men.
           That's his type: heralds always go for the main chance.
           Him, too, sidling up to those in power.
             After that Lord Diomedes addressed them.
           He advised the city not to execute you and your brother,   940
           but to do what religion demands, that is to banish you.
           Shouts of approval greeted this, but others dissented.
             And after that there rose the kind of man
           who will say anything at all to get his way,
           patriotic when it suits him, a hireling,
           ready to stir up a row with his loose talk,

224

sure to entangle his audience in some crime.
He exhorted them to kill you and Orestes
by stoning; and it was Tyndareos
who coached your executioner.   950
    Then another—not much to look at
but every inch a man—stood up and spoke against him.
Seldom seen in town or marketplace, he works the land
for himself, the kind of man our country relies on,
shrewd, though, and willing to press his points home.
Corruption couldn't touch him, not the way he's lived.
He said that Orestes, son of Agamemnon, ought
to be decorated for having dared to avenge
his father, to kill a whore and godless woman
who would have kept us from arming ourselves and going 960
off to war, afraid the stay-at-homes
would debauch the women while the men were gone.
He seemed to carry his point, too, at least
with respectable people.
                              And then
not a soul spoke up in support.
Your brother came forward
[and said, "Citizens of Argos,
holders and protectors of the land
given to our fathers by Inachos,
in *your* defense, no less than my own father's,   970
I slew my mother. For if women get away
with killing men, if they are condoned, you are all
as good as dead, or you must become
slaves, women's slaves. You will be doing
the opposite of what you should do.
As of now, the woman who betrayed my father's bed
has died. But if you are bent on killing me,
the law becomes a mockery, and any man
is as good as dead. Mark my words:
they won't hold back from it."]   980
But he didn't sway the crowd, for all his eloquence.
That scoundrel won—he carried the majority,
exhorting them to put your brother and you to death.
All that poor Orestes could do, to persuade them

to mitigate the sentence of public stoning, was to promise
that today both of you would take your own lives.
Pylades helped him to leave, weeping as he did so,
and other friends have joined them, commiserating, crying,
all on their way here now, a bitter spectacle.

    So now you must prepare. Get a sword or a rope,   990
to make your way from the light. Noble birth has not saved
                                       you,
not even Pythian Apollo throned upon his tripod
has been your savior, but rather your destroyer.

                    Exit MESSENGER. ELECTRA *and the* CHORUS *join in*
                                              lamentation.

                                                strophe

ELECTRA   Pelasgia! I take up
                          the wail, raking
                my face bloody and beating,
                          beating my head
                to render my due
                          to Persephone of earth's dark,
                          Queen of the dead!   1000

CHORUS   Let this land walled in
                          by giants, taking
                the knife to its hair
                        in lamentation for
                        the losses of this house—
                for such, such is the pity of it—mourn
                      those who are going to die,
                          once captains of Hellas!

                                            antistrophe

ELECTRA   For it's gone, gone,
                        the line of Pelops erased,   1010
                a house once envied for its happiness:
                      the jealousy
                of the gods destroyed it,

and the votes cast
murderously by the many.

CHORUS   Little race living for a day
clamorous with pain,
see how fate presses
steadily against your hopes!
With length of years   1020
a man runs through his share of sorrows—
to live is to have
no certainty.

ELECTRA *moves to the center and sings the epode alone.*

epode

ELECTRA   Let me fly to the rock
hanging in the sky
on chains of gold,
spinning there
in whirlwinds, crag
blasted from Olympos,

to howl my black dirge   1030
to the great forefather
Tantalos, founder of the house, what
horrors it has seen!
—the four whipped
horses shearing the air

as Pelops drove
over the sea, flinging
the corpse of Myrtilos
into the waves at Geraistos.
hurtling above the slam of the surf,
the foam of the beaches.   1040

From that the curse came
into our house!

227

Spawned in the flocks of Hermes,
that fleece-gold lamb's back flared
its ruinous wonder through
the fields of Atreus, breeder of horses.

From that moment Strife
set the soaring
                    chariot of the sun
on its lonely road to dawn
and evening both at once,   1050
            and sent the seven

Pleiades plunging
onto a different track, and then,
        dealing death for death,
            comes the flesh feast
named for Thyestes, and the bed
faithless Kretan Aerope
fouled with her couplings!
                                    until
        it all bears down
on me and my brother, driven   1060
        upon us by the fate
            in our blood.

CHORUS LEADER And now here comes your brother,
            under sentence of death,
            and Pylades, still faithful
            when others fall away,
            all that a brother could be,
            trace horse leading the sick man.

Enter ORESTES *and* PYLADES.

ELECTRA Brother! To see you on the verge of the grave,
        before the gates of the world below!   1070
            Looking on you for the very
            last time, I can't bear it!

ORESTES Quiet, Electra! Won't you accept necessity
without womanish wailing? It's painful, but all the same...

ELECTRA And how can I *not* cry? We'll never see
the sun again, not you and I, ever.

ORESTES Haven't the Argives done enough? Must you
be killing me, too? No more talk about it!

ELECTRA Your youth, Orestes—your sorry fate, your
untimely death! You should *live*, and you can't.   1080

ORESTES For god's sake, don't make a coward of me!
I'll cry, too, if I think of it too much.

ELECTRA We're going to die! It's impossible not to weep,
everyone counts his own death a sorrow.

ORESTES Today is the day. We must choose between
noosing a rope and sharpening a sword.

ELECTRA I want *you*, Brother, to kill me, don't let some
Argive do it, heaping insult on Agamemnon's house.

ORESTES It's enough having Mother's blood on my hands: I won't
have yours, too. Choose your own way, and do it yourself. 1090

ELECTRA I choose the sword, then, and I won't lag behind you
in using it. But now, let me take you in my arms...

ELECTRA *embraces* ORESTES.

ORESTES Enjoy that empty pleasure, if in the face of death
people still enjoy embracing one another.

ELECTRA You are body and soul to me, Orestes,
all that's lovable, all that's sweet!

ORESTES Now see how you've melted me! Come,
let me hold you, why should I go on resisting?

Oh sisterly warmth, these embraces are the only
marriage bed and children we shall ever have!   1100

ELECTRA O that we could die by the same sword
and lie together in the same coffin!

ORESTES Nothing would please me more, but as you see
there's none of our family left, to bury us together.

ELECTRA Didn't he speak up for you, even to save your life,
Menelaos—that coward, who betrayed our father?

ORESTES Never showed his face. Pinning his hopes on the throne,
he took care not to save his brother's children.
    But come, let us die
in a manner worthy of the name   1110
and deeds of Agamemnon! I'll show the Argives
what nobility is, plunging a sword through my heart!
And you must dare the same.

(turning to PYLADES)

Pylades, you be the one to judge
the way we die, and lay out our bodies;
bury us in one tomb, beside our father's.
And now, farewell. I go, now, to accomplish the deed.

ORESTES moves toward the palace.

PYLADES Wait! One thing, to begin with, bothers me
in what you've said: Did you think
I'd care to go on living after you die?   1120

ORESTES I assumed you would: Why must you die with me?

PYLADES You ask me that? What is life without your friendship?

ORESTES You didn't kill your mother, as I did mine.

PYLADES I helped you, though, and ought to suffer as you do.

ORESTES Go back to your father. Forget about dying with me.
Look: you have a city to return to,
I have none. You have a home
to inherit, and the haven of great wealth.
There's marriage ahead for you, though not—
as I had pledged in honor of our friendship— 1130
with this ill-starred girl. Another woman
will be your wife and bear you children.

ORESTES *makes as if to leave again.*

Farewell, then,
best of friends, while you can, and we cannot:
we dead are done with faring well.

PYLADES How far you are from knowing what I have in mind!
May the earth reject my blood, and the sky my soul,
if ever I betray you, and get off free myself!
Not only did I take part in the murder;
I was the one who planned everything
for which you're now paying the price. 1140
It's right for me to die with you
and with her: I said I'd marry her—
as far as I'm concerned, she's my wife already.
And how would I put a good face on things
if I went back to Delphi, the citadel of Phokis?
Tell them I was your friend before, but not
when troubles came? Impossible.
Our fates are intertwined, and since we must die,
let's see to it that Menelaos suffers with us.

ORESTES If only we could! I would die happy 1150

PYLADES Then trust me, and don't use that sword just yet.

ORESTES All right, if somehow I can pay back my enemy!

231

PYLADES Keep your voice down. I put small trust in women.

ORESTES Don't worry: these women are here as our friends.

PYLADES Let's kill Helen—that will get Menelaos where it hurts.

ORESTES How? I'm ready, if we can bring it off.

PYLADES We'll cut her throat. Isn't she hiding here, in your house?

ORESTES She's in there, all right, putting Menelaos' seal on the
                                                                      property.

PYLADES Not anymore, she isn't. Her new husband is Hades.

ORESTES And how are we going to kill her? She has her entourage. 1160

PYLADES What sort of entourage? I'm not afraid of any Phrygians.

ORESTES Ministers of mirrors and creams and perfumes.

PYLADES What? She brought her Trojan luxuries home with her?

ORESTES She always found Greece too small to suit her needs.

PYLADES No matter, slaves are nothing to a free man.

ORESTES Just let me do it. I'd gladly die twice.

PYLADES Same here, if I can see you avenged.

ORESTES Lay out everything in detail.

PYLADES We'll go in as if we're really going to kill ourselves.

ORESTES I follow you so far. But what comes next?   1170

PYLADES We'll weep and wail and tell her all our sorrows.

232

ORESTES So that she'll burst into tears, while gloating inside.

PYLADES Yes—and we'll be feeling the same way at the same time!

ORESTES What's the next phase of the action?

PYLADES We'll get swords and hide them here, inside our robes.

ORESTES But how do we dispose of her servants first?

PYLADES We'll scatter them, and lock them out.

ORESTES Right: and anyone who isn't quiet, we kill.

PYLADES After that, the deed itself shows the way.

ORESTES Killing Helen, you mean: I'm with you there.   1180

PYLADES Yes, you are. But listen, now, to the beauty of my plan.
         If we were putting a lady to the sword, one with a little
         character, her murder would be a disgrace. But
         as it is, she'll finally pay for emptying Greece
         of fathers and sons alike, and turning brides into widows.
         There will be a cry of thanksgiving, bonfires
         piled to the gods, blessings prayed
         on both of us because we shed that bitch's blood.
         No longer will they brand you "Mother Murderer." Instead,
         they'll crown you with the title, "Slayer of Helen who
                                             slew Hellas."   1190
         And Menelaos must not, no, must never thrive while
         your father and you and your sister die, and your mother—
         but enough said—he *mustn't* inherit your palace
         now that he's got his wife back through Agamemnon's spear.
         I'll be damned if I don't run that woman through!
         Even if we don't succeed in killing Helen, we can still
         set fire to the palace and die in the flames!
         One thing's for certain: dying nobly
         or nobly bringing it off, we'll win great fame.

233

CHORUS LEADER The daughter of Tyndareos deserves the hatred   1200
               of every woman alive. She has shamed her sex.

ORESTES Nothing's better than firm friendship, neither great wealth
         nor supreme power. And as for the mob, it's
         worthless in the tally next to one noble friend.
         You, no one else, laid the deadly trap for Aigisthos
         and shared every danger with me, and again it's you
         delivering my enemies to me, standing at my side!
         But I won't go on: praise, too, can be overdone.
         As I'm going to die, I want to do something
         to my enemies first—destroy my betrayers,   1210
         let them suffer pain who caused me pain!
         I am, after all, the son of Agamemnon,
         the man whose worth lifted him over all Greece,
         no tyrant, but all the same he had a godlike power.
         I shall not tarnish his name by dying
         like some slave, but yield up my life
         like a free man, and punish Menelaos.
         That alone would make us fortunate.
         And if we also escape, killing Helen
         and not dying ourselves, salvation   1220
         somehow falling our way—well, I pray for that.
         It's sweet, and costs nothing, to let desire find a voice.

ELECTRA That's it, Orestes! and I can see it coming true:
         safety for you, and him, and me—all three.

ORESTES Inspired words, but what do they mean?
         I've never known you not to have your wits about you.

ELECTRA Then listen to me—and you, too, Pylades.

ORESTES Go on. Why hold back what's good to hear?

ELECTRA Remember Helen's daughter?—as if I needed to ask.

ORESTES Of course, Hermione. Mother took care of her.   1230

234

ELECTRA She's gone to Clytemnestra's tomb.

ORESTES For what purpose? And what's in it for us?

ELECTRA To pour libations over Mother's grave.

ORESTES And what's that got to do with our escape?

ELECTRA Take her hostage when she returns.

ORESTES How does that help the three of us?

ELECTRA Once Helen is dead, if Menelaos threatens you,
or him or me—we're in this together—
then say you'll kill Hermione. Draw your sword
and hold it against the girl's throat.   1240
If, seeing Helen's bloody body lying there,
he wants to save his daughter's life and gives his word
that he'll save *us*, then let the girl go,
let her run to her father's arms. But if his fury should
get the better of him and he tries to kill you, then
respond in kind, make as if to slit the girl's throat.
If he puts up a show of force at first, my guess is
he'll soften soon enough. He's neither brave nor strong.
There's my plan for saving us. I've said what I have to say.

ORESTES A man's intelligence, matched with womanly grace: 1250
how you deserve to live rather than to die!
Pylades, what a loss—or, if you both survive,
what a wife she'll make you!

PYLADES So be it! May she come to Phokis
honored by the singing on our wedding day!

ORESTES But when will Hermione return?
Everything you've said is fine, if only
we can trap that filthy father's cub.

ELECTRA I think she ought to be approaching
at any moment. She's been gone long enough now.   1260

235

ORESTES Good!
> Electra, you stay here in front of the palace,
> waiting for the girl to come. Be prepared,
> if anyone gets inside before the murder,
> to shout, or bang on the doors, or get word to us.
>   Pylades, we'll go in and arm ourselves with swords
> for the final contest.

He makes formal supplication.

> Oh Father below, in the vast halls of night,
> your son Orestes implores you: come, come to our aid!

ELECTRA joins him:

ELECTRA Oh Father come, come if you hear underground
> your children calling you, dying in your cause!   1270

PYLADES also.

PYLADES My father's kinsman, great Agamemnon,
> hear my prayers also: save your own children!

ORESTES I slew Mother!

ELECTRA   And I took the sword in my hands!

PYLADES I set things in motion, I nerved them to act.

ORESTES I did it for you!

ELECTRA   And I did not betray you!

PYLADES Hear them reproaching you? Won't you save them?

ORESTES I've poured out my tears for you!

ELECTRA   And I my lamentations!

PYLADES Enough now! It's time for action.
If prayers carry like thrown spears, piercing down through earth,
he hears.

PYLADES *makes supplication.*

Oh Zeus, ancestral Father, and you, Awesome
Justice, 1280

grant success to Orestes, and his sister, and me!
The three of us face one trial: we must live
or die together in a single judgment!

Exit PYLADES *and* ORESTES *into the palace.*

ELECTRA *and*
CHORUS (*together*)

strophe

ELECTRA   Women of Mycenae, friends,
first rank of Pelasgia's first city . . .

CHORUS   What is your wish, my lady?
In the city of Danaos, we stand by you still.

ELECTRA I want some of you posted on the road here,
and the rest on the road there, to guard the palace.

CHORUS   Good lady, why?   1290
Why ask us to do this?

ELECTRA   I'm worried that someone, seeing
my brother poised for the kill,
will make our troubles greater than they are.

Halves of the Chorus follow their leaders to each side.

LEADER *of*
SEMICHORUS A (*speaking from the left side*)
Take up position, women! We'll watch this road
where day breaks . . .

237

LEADER *of*
SEMICHORUS B (*speaking from the right side*)
        And we'll guard this one, to the west.

ELECTRA   But look around! Keep scanning
           left and right,
      here and there and back again!

BOTH
SEMICHORUSES (*together*)
                        We're doing as you say. 1300

                      antistrophe

ELECTRA   Keep those eyes moving, now,
      and take in everything, everywhere!

SEMICHORUS A   Look: here comes someone! Who can he be,
      stalking about the palace—a hunter?

ELECTRA We're finished, then! He'll tell our enemies
      about our young lions, hidden, waiting to spring!

SEMICHORUS A   There's nothing to fear, good lady,
          the road is empty, after all.

ELECTRA (*to* SEMICHORUS B)
          How are things over there?
          Tell me whether   1310
          your side of the palace is still deserted.

SEMICHOURS B   All clear. (*to* SEMICHORUS A) But keep a sharp lookout
      on *your* side too: ours is secure.

SEMICHORUS A It's the same here: no sign of trouble.

ELECTRA   I'd better go listen at the door.

                ELECTRA *puts her ear to the door.*

BOTH
SEMICHORUSES (*together*)
> You in there! All's quiet!
> What's stopping you
> > from slashing the victim?

epode

ELECTRA They don't hear you! And I can't do a thing!
> Are they standing there
> > staring at her good looks,   1320
> their swords dangling?

BOTH
SEMICHORUSES (*together*)
> Any minute now, some Argive soldier
> will go for the palace to save her!

ELECTRA Keep your eyes peeled! This is no time to relax!

(*to each* SEMICHORUS, *separately*)

> You circle over here, you over there!

BOTH
SEMICHORUSES (*in process of changing positions*)
> We're on our way,
> we're looking all around.

The SEMICHORUSES *merge and stop at the sound of*
HELEN's *voice.*

HELEN (*inside*)
Argos! Argos! Treachery! Murder!

ELECTRA Hear that? Our men have their hands in it now!
> That shriek was Helen's!   1330

CHORUS Zeus, Zeus, shoot your
> everlasting force into their arms!

HELEN Menelaos, I'm dying! Where *are* you?

CHORUS   Cut her down, kill her now—
          slashing with both your
              double-edged swords,
          strike, pay her back for leaving
              husband and father, slaughtering
          Greeks by the thousands, all those who fell
              cut down by the flash of steel   1340
          on the banks of Skamander,
              the river of tears!

CHORUS LEADER Quiet, quiet now! I heard a sound—
          someone on the road, approaching the house.

ELECTRA Just in time! Right at the middle
          of the killing, in she comes: Hermione!
              No more shouting now! Compose yourselves, seem to be
          at ease, and don't let blushing faces
          betray your knowledge of what's gone on in there.
          I'll look downcast myself, as if I didn't know what
                                        happened.   1350

                    Enter HERMIONE *from the left*.

ELECTRA My girl, are you coming back from laying wreaths
          at Clytemnestra's tomb, and pouring out the funeral wine?

HERMIONE Yes, I've secured the blessings of the dead.
          But when I was returning, still some distance away,
          I grew frightened. I heard an outcry from the palace.

ELECTRA What's happening now might well make us cry.

HERMIONE Say it isn't so! What is the news?

ELECTRA Argos has decreed that Orestes and I must die.

HERMIONE No, never! Not my own flesh and blood!

ELECTRA They have spoken. We stand under the yoke of necessity. 1360

HERMIONE Is that why there was crying inside, too?

ELECTRA Yes. He fell at Helen's knees, and cried aloud, begging . . .

HERMIONE Who fell at her knees? I can't follow you.

ELECTRA Poor Orestes, imploring her to save him from death, and me,
                                                                              too.

HERMIONE No wonder, then, the house broke into wailing.

ELECTRA Yes, what greater cause for outcry?
                But come, join in supplication
        with those near and dear to you!
        Go in, and kneel before your mother, Helen,
        fortune's darling, pleading with her that Menelaos   1370
        not let us die. My own mother raised you!
        Have pity on us, then, and lighten our burden.
        Enter the struggle with us—come, let me lead you in.
        You are the only one who can save us now.

                    ELECTRA *escorts* HERMIONE *to the door.*

HERMIONE Yes, yes, right away! You'll be saved
        if I can help it.

            HERMIONE *enters;* ELECTRA *pauses in the doorway.*

ELECTRA   Comrades in there!
        Here is your prey: won't you seize her now?

                                            (*from within*)

HERMIONE Help! Help! What is this?

ELECTRA   Quiet!
        You're here to save *us*, not yourself.

(to the conspirators)

Grab her, grab her! Put your swords to her throat   1380
and keep them there. Let her father see,
now that he has real men to deal with instead of
Trojan cowards, what a coward has coming to him!

> ELECTRA *goes in, shutting the doors.*
> *The chorus begins a chant.*

> *strophe*

> Make a stir, sisters,
> make a stir at the doors,
> to keep the work of murder
> from rousing the Argives, bringing them
> in arms to the royal house,
> before we can see for a fact
> Helen's red corpse in the palace,   1390
> or get the story from one of the servants!
> The disaster's in motion: How will it end?
> The gods in their justice have brought down
> judgment on Helen
> who filled Greece with tears
> for the sake of deadly Paris, murderous
> Paris of Ida, who drew all Greece to Troy.

CHORUS LEADER But quiet! Just now the bolts on the royal doors
were rattling. Yes, a Phrygian is coming out—
we'll learn from him how things are inside.   1400

> *Enter* PHRYGIAN *slave, in panic.*

PHRYGIAN I have escaped a Greek sword
running from death
in my barbarian slippers
past the cedar-timbered
Doric porticoes,
fleeing, as barbarians do,

out of the palace, out of reach—
O Earth, Mother Earth!
                                        Ai! Ai!
How, O ladies of this land,
how to leave, winging my way   1410
to the glittering sky, or to the sea
spun in the arms
of bull-horned Ocean
        as he circles the world?

CHORUS LEADER   What *is* it, servant of Helen, man of Ida?

PHRYGIAN   Ilion! Ilion!
the fruited, the sacred,
O Phrygian city and Mount Ida,
I raise this barbarian cry
in grief for you, struck down   1420
by one glance from that vision
of loveliness born of the swan,
the feathered glory, Leda's child
Helen, ruinous Helen,
avenging Fury perched
on the very battlements
        built by Apollo.
Ai! Ai!
        Lament, bewail
the shattered plain of Troy—   1430
O Ganymede, royal rider,
        lover of Zeus!

CHORUS LEADER   Man, please, *one thing at a time:* What happened in
                                                          there?

PHRYGIAN   *Ailinon! Ailinon!* wail the barbarians,
striking up the Asiatic death chant, *Aiai!*
        when the blood of kings
        shed by iron blades of Hades
                is spilled upon the earth.

There came into the palace—
        I shall now relate it, one thing at a time—   1440
           into the palace came
                two Greeks, twin lions:

one called himself son of the late generalissimo,
        the other, Strophios' son,
        dangerous like Odysseus,
        brooding and treacherous,
        sure to support his friends,
        fierce when making his move,
           cunning in battle,
           and a murderous snake.   1450
Damn him for his
        cold-blooded schemes!

Once they got inside, those two
made their way to the throne
        of Paris' bride,
        and groveled there
        with tearful faces,
        clutching at her
        this way and that,
        wrapping their hands   1460
around her knees, the two of them.

Up, up leapt her Phrygian servants
muttering one to the other,
        under the flail of terror

that foul play was afoot—
        a few still uncertain,
        others suspecting
        that the serpent who murdered
        his own mother
        was, then and there,   1470
leading the child of Tyndareos
        into the fatal
        nets of a trap!

CHORUS LEADER   And where were you? Already hiding somewhere?

PHRYGIAN   No, I happened to be standing
                     by Helen, wafting the ringlets on Helen's cheeks
                           in the Phrygian manner, with my
                     great round fan, softly fanning the air.
                           She was twirling the spindle,
                           letting the yarn fall to the floor,   1480
                                 in her wish to sew together
                           the purple draperies
                           from her Phrygian spoils, to leave
                                 as a gift at Clytemnestra's grave.

                           Orestes then addressed her:
                     "Daughter of Zeus, please, rise from your couch
                     and come across the room, to the throne
                           of Pelops our great forefather,
                           to our venerable hearth, where you'll
                           learn what I have in mind."   1490
                     He pressed and pressed her, and presently she
                           went along, unable to foresee
                           what lay ahead.

                           Meanwhile his accomplice,
                           that devil Phokian, was taking care
                                 of the rest, snarling,
                     "What? Not out of here yet, you Phrygian scum?"

                     He locked some of us in this part of the palace,
                           others in that—some in the
                           stables, some in latrines,   1500
                     one here, one there throughout the house—
                           anywhere but near our mistress!

CHORUS LEADER   And then? What happened after that?

PHRYGIAN   Mother of Ida, mighty
                                 mighty Mother,
                           what bloodshed I saw,

what crimes I witnessed
in those royal chambers!

On both sides, from the darkness
of their purple robes, they drew   1510
and held up swords, the two of them,
eyes shooting this way and that
to make sure no one was coming.

And then, like wild boars,
they squared off against
the woman, and began to close in.
"Die," they cried, "You're going to die
and it's your coward husband
who kills you, he who betrayed
to death right here in Argos   1520
his own brother's son!"
And she cried out, she shrieked,
her snowy arms beating her breasts,
her head ringing with blows—
and ran and ran, here and there,
golden sandals flashing,

but Orestes, spearing his fingers through her hair,
bracing his stance,
his Greek boot firmly planted,
and twisting her head   1530
onto her left shoulder,
was on the point of driving
deep into her gorge
the dark sword.

CHORUS LEADER   And what were you Phrygians doing to help her?
Anything?

PHRYGIAN   Screaming and shouting, we smashed our way with crowbars

through massy frames and doors

and out we came running
from here, from there,
one with stones, one with a bow,   1540
        one with sword drawn!
        But against us came Pylades
invincible, like—like Phrygian Hẹktor, or Ajax,
wearing the famed helmet of triple steel:
I saw him once, saw him at the Skaian gates.
        Then at swords' points we clashed!

        And soon we showed overwhelmingly
        how, in the heat of battle, Phrygians
        are inferior to Greeks: one ran off,
        one perished on the spot, another   1550
        fled wounded, another
        fell to his knees begging for life.

        We took cover in the shadows, or fell down dead,
                or sprawled on the floor, dying.

        Then into the palace came
        luckless Hermione, right at the moment
        her poor mother was sinking
                to the floor to perish!

And like Bacchae in unholy rage, the pair of them
        ran up to her, a fawn of the forest,   1560
        and got their hands on her.
        Then spinning around they swung back
        and went for Zeus' daughter—

                                but she was gone
        and nowhere to be seen
                throughout the palace—
Oh Zeus and Earth, and Light, and Night!—
        stolen from their clutches
        through the power of drugs, or ma-
        gicians, or thieving gods,
                who can say?   1570

What happened after that
        I don't know—I got myself
        out of there
                fast.
And so, in the end, Menelaos
who suffered so much, sweating hard at Troy
to get his wife Helen back, suffered for nothing!

CHORUS LEADER   One thing on top of another! And there seems no end—
                                                                look,
        here comes Orestes running at full tilt, sword in hand!

                        Enter ORESTES *from the palace.*

ORESTES Where's the one who got away from my sword?

                        The PHRYGIAN *falls at* ORESTES' *feet.*

PHRYGIAN I bow before you, Lord, head to the ground like a
                                                barbarian.   1580

ORESTES You're not at Troy anymore. This is Argos!

PHRYGIAN Wherever a wise man finds himself, living is sweeter than
                                                dying.

ORESTES You didn't, by any chance, shout for Menelaos, did you?

PHRYGIAN No, but to save *you*, a far greater man!

ORESTES Then even *you* think Helen perished justly?

PHRYGIAN Most justly, even if she had three throats to cut.

ORESTES You're flattering me, not saying what you feel.

PHRYGIAN Didn't she deserve it, for ruining Greece, Phrygians and all?

ORESTES Then swear you're not sweet-talking me: swear or die!

PHRYGIAN I swear by what I'd hate to lose: my very life!   1590

ORESTES *moves the sword closer to his face.*

ORESTES Were all the Phrygians as scared of steel as you are?

PHRYGIAN Take it away! Up close, it mirrors bloody murder!

ORESTES Afraid of turning to stone, as if you'd seen a Gorgon?

PHRYGIAN No, turning to a corpse. As for Gorgons, I don't know any.

ORESTES You're a slave. Why fear Hades, the great liberator?

PHRYGIAN Every man, even a slave, likes the look of daylight.

ORESTES Well said! Your wits have saved you. Back into the palace,
                                                        now.

PHRYGIAN You aren't going to kill me?

ORESTES   No.

PHRYGIAN   That's good to hear.

The PHRYGIAN *rises and makes
as if to go back into the palace.*

ORESTES Wait! I've changed my mind.

The PHRYGIAN *grovels again.*

PHRYGIAN   Sounds bad for me.

ORESTES Don't be a fool! I wouldn't stoop   1600
         to bloody your neck! Why, you're neither a man
         nor a woman! No, I came out here at first
         to put a stop to your noise—
         Argos is sharp-eared and quick to respond.
         But now, let Menelaos return—I'm not scared
         to get him back within sword range,

showing off those long blond curls of his!
For if he leads the Argives against the palace
to avenge Helen's murder, and doesn't save me, he'll see
not only his wife's dead body but his daughter's, too!   1610

Exit PHRYGIAN, *left.*
Exit ORESTES *into the palace, bolting the doors.*

CHORUS

antistrophe (*delayed*)

Disaster, sisters! Another fight
brings this family down,
another Atreid struggle!
What should we do now? Try to warn the city?
Or keep silent? . . .
Silence is safer now.
Look, on the roof of the palace, clouds of smoke
shooting to high heaven, warning everyone!
They're kindling torches, to fire the great house
of Tantalos, pressing on, on in their struggle!
The end is always in a god's hands,   1620
turned as he pleases—
but how tremendous is the power driving these avengers!
The house has plummeted in bloodshed, plunging
to ruin with Myrtilos from his chariot!

CHORUS LEADER But here comes Menelaos, making for the palace in haste—
he must have found out how things are going now.
Atreids in there! Time to bar the doors!
A man riding high will trample anyone
who's already down, as you are now, Orestes!

Enter MENELAOS *with armed men.*

MENELAOS I heard what they did, and came—   1630
the terrors, the outrages! That pair of beasts—
inhuman, that's what they are. [The tale is that Helen
has not died, no, but vanished—an empty rumor

some fellow spluttered to me in his panic.
But that's only a fabrication by the matricide,
a preposterous story.]
                              Someone open the doors!

                    (*A pause. The doors remain shut.*)
                    MENELAOS *turns to his attendants.*

All right, force them open! We must at least
save my daughter from those murderers
[and retrieve my poor, poor wife—
those who murdered Helen   1640
must die together with her, by my own hand!]

                    ORESTES *appears on the roof with his*
                    sword at HERMIONE's *throat, flanked by*
                    PYLADES *and* ELECTRA *holding torches.*

ORESTES You down there! Hands off those doors!
          Yes, I mean you, Menelaos, for all your rage. Keep it up
          and I'll tear off one of these fine old blocks
          and smash your head with it, spoiling the work
          our stonecarvers lavished on these cornices.
          Besides, the doors are bolted to keep you out.

MENELAOS What's this!? Blazing torches,
          men posted on the roof, as if under siege—
          and my daughter with a sword at her throat!   1650

ORESTES Want to go on asking questions, or hear from me?

MENELAOS Neither. But it seems I'll have to listen.

ORESTES I intend to kill your daughter, if you're interested.

[MENELAOS Murder piled on murder, now you've killed Helen?

ORESTES If only I had. The gods robbed me of the opportunity.

251

MENELAOS You kill her and then insult me by denying it?

ORESTES I hate to, but deny it I must. I only wish...

MENELAOS You only wish what? You're unnerving.

ORESTES That I'd pitched the filth of Hellas into Hades!]

MENELAOS Give me my wife's body, so I can bury her.   1660

ORESTES Ask the gods for that. I'll kill your daughter.

MENELAOS Will you? Pile corpse on corpse—the mother killer?

ORESTES The father avenger—whom you betrayed to death.

MENELAOS Wasn't your mother's blood enough for you?

ORESTES I'll never have enough of killing whores.

MENELAOS And you, Pylades, will you join him in this murder?

ORESTES His silence speaks for itself. I'll do the talking.

MENELAOS You'll regret it, too, unless you manage to fly out of here.

ORESTES We're not going anywhere. But we shall set the palace on fire.

MENELAOS What!? Destroy the house of your fathers?   1670

ORESTES Yes, so you won't get it. And then it's *her* turn, over the flames!

MENELAOS Go ahead and kill her, then! You'll have me to reckon with.

ORESTES If that's the way you want it...

ORESTES *lifts his sword.*

MENELAOS   No, no! Don't do it!

ORESTES All right, but quiet! You're getting what you deserve.

MENELAOS And you deserve to go on living?

ORESTES   Yes, *and* ruling.

MENELAOS Ruling! Where on earth?

ORESTES   Here, in the land of my fathers.

MENELAOS A fine sight, you at the lustral waters!

ORESTES   Sure—why not?

MENELAOS *You* making sacrifice before battle!

ORESTES   Are you fit for that yourself?

MENELAOS My hands are clean.

ORESTES   But not your conscience.

MENELAOS Who would ever speak to you?   1680

ORESTES   Whoever loves his father.

MENELAOS What about the one who loves his mother?

ORESTES   He's lucky.

MENELAOS That leaves you out.

ORESTES   Indeed it does: I have no taste for whores.

MENELAOS Take that sword away from my daughter!

ORESTES   Why? You're false to the core.

MENELAOS You really intend to kill her?

ORESTES   Now you're believable.

MENELAOS Wait! What do you want from me?

ORESTES   Go to the Argives, and persuade them.

MENELAOS Persuade them of what?

ORESTES   Not to kill us. Appeal to them.

MENELAOS Or you will kill my daughter?

ORESTES   That's the way it is.

MENELAOS Oh Helen, poor Helen...

ORESTES   Why not poor me?

MENELAOS I brought you back from Troy to have your throat cut!

ORESTES   If only it were so!

MENELAOS And I fought so hard.   1690

ORESTES   Yes. But not for my sake.

MENELAOS And now, this outrage...

ORESTES   For proving so useless when it counted.

MENELAOS You've pinned me.

ORESTES   You've pinned yourself, you swine.
            But come, Electra! It's time to torch the palace!

And you, Pylades, most loyal of all my friends,
set fire to the roofbeams!

MENELAOS Land of Danaos, of the founders and their horses!
Come on, Argives, bring your weapons, hurry!
He's lording it over your whole city, forcing it
to let him live—him, with his mother's blood on his hands!

MENELAOS' *men move toward the palace.*
APOLLO *appears on a platform above the roof.*

APOLLO Stop, Menelaos! Sheathe your anger: 1700
it is I, Phoibos, son of Leto,
addressing you.
                    And you, Orestes,
with your sword poised over that girl,
stop, hear what I have to say.
     As for Helen,
on whom, mistakenly, you let loose your rage
at Menelaos, I have rescued her,
snatching her from your sword at Zeus' bidding.
For the daughter of imperishable Zeus must not perish—
she's to have her throne by Castor and Polydeukes   1710
in the heavens, and bring salvation to sailors.
     So much for Helen, then. Orestes,
you must leave the country, crossing to the plains
of Parrhasia, and there live out the cycle of one year.
The Azanians and the Arcadians
will name the place Oresteion in memory of your exile.
Proceeding then to Athens, stand trial against
the three Eumenides for your mother's murder. The gods,
presiding as your judges, will determine on the Areopagos
the strict and sacred verdict of your acquittal.   1720
Then, Orestes, it will be your lot to marry the woman
at whose throat you hold that sword: Hermione.
The man who thinks he'll marry her, Neoptolemos,
never shall, for when he ventures to Delphi seeking from me
requital for the death of his father Achilles,
a Delphian sword will kill him. And give your sister,

as you once promised, to Pylades. A happy life awaits him.
   Menelaos, let Orestes reign here in Argos
and go, yourself, to rule in Sparta,
enjoying the dowry of your wife, who has given you   1730
only endless trouble until now. Find yourself
another bride, and take her into your house
now that the gods, by means of this one's beauty,

(APOLLO points to HELEN, now
joining him on the platform.)

have driven

Greeks and Trojans together in the press of war
to drain the earth of its human horde
proliferating in pride.
As for the Argives, I myself shall reconcile them
to Orestes: he is not to be held accountable
for murdering his mother. I made him kill her.

ORESTES Great Loxias! Those oracles of yours   1740
told the truth after all! And yet I kept on
shivering with fear, thinking what I heard
as your voice was really some fiend's. But no,
everything has turned out well, and I'm at your command.

He frees HERMIONE.

   Look here: I take my sword from Hermione, and
welcome marriage with her, when her father gives his blessing.

MENELAOS Helen, daughter of Zeus, farewell! I envy you
your happy home among the gods. Orestes, as Apollo
has commanded, so I obey: I give you my child in marriage.
Coming from a great house, and taking your wife
from another,   1750
may you thrive in this alliance, and I with you.

APOLLO Let each of you now go to the place I have assigned,
and cease your quarrels.

MENELAOS   I can only comply.

ORESTES I feel the same. To this new dispensation, Menelaos,
        and to your oracles, Loxias, I am reconciled.

APOLLO Go, now, each on his way,
        honoring Peace, loveliest of the gods,
        and I shall lead Helen to the halls of Zeus,
        high among the fires of heaven.
        There, by Hera and Hebe,   1760
        the wife of Herakles,
        she will be seated as goddess,
        and men will forever pour
                their offerings
        to her and the Tyndaridai,
                as she watches over
        those who go down to the sea.

CHORUS   High and holy Victory!
                        Shine on my life
                                and let me always wear the crown!   1770

NOTES

This is a translation of the Oxford text of Gilbert Murray but it also reflects work done by recent textual critics—C. W. Willink and M. L. West in particular—my indebtedness to whom is profound and extensive: I could not record it in detail without changing the nature of these notes.

I have employed brackets at a number of points in the translation, not because I am certain that all the lines in question do not belong to Euripides but because that was the simplest way of enabling readers to envision the play with and without them. My reasons for suspecting them are briefly set forth in the notes, often with reference to fuller discussion by West and Willink.

1–148 / 1–139 *Prologue*

5–16 / 4–10 Tantalos would have been familiar to the ancient audience as an abuser of the hospitality he shared with the gods. Homer (*Odyssey* 11.582–92) has him "tantalized" by food and drink forever out of reach, Pindar (*Olympian Ode* 1.56–60) has him writhing under a huge rock that ever threatens to fall on his head. In both cases he is in the underworld. Euripides chooses the rock but transfers it from the underworld to the heavens. This is a striking innovation, possibly suggesting a parallel between Tantalos, mythical sinner against the gods, and contemporary philosophers and sophists who attempted to account for reality in scientific or rational as opposed to religious or mythical terms. The "impiety" of such explanations was still keenly felt in the Athens of Euripides' day (see Aristophanes' *Clouds* and Plato's *Apology of Socrates*).

16 / 10 *he let his tongue run away with him* The exact nature of Tantalos' crime is left vague. Insofar as he incriminates himself not through action but through speech, he resembles a sophist. See previous note.

22 / 16 *what happened after that* Possibly an allusion to the incestuous union between Thyestes and his own daughter, Pelopia. Aigisthos, the son born of this union, conspired with Clytemnestra in the murder of Agamemnon.

34 / 25 *who wound her husband in an endless robe* Clytemnestra wrapped Agamemnon in a robe as he emerged from his homecoming bath, then stabbed him to death.

50 / 37–38 *the dread goddesses* The Erinyes (Furies).

59 / 46 *Here in Argos* Mycenae is the seat of Agamemnon's power in Homer, but it had been conquered by Argos in 467–66 B.C., and the tragedians tended to use the name Argos instead. Mycenae, however, belonging to epic tradition, still occurs (as at **114 / 101** and **1284 / 1246**). *they have decreed* The formulaic language would remind the Athenians of their own assembly. A body of citizens making sovereign decisions after hearing the arguments of various speakers is an anachronism in this play. Not so the issue they debate (see next note).

60–62 / 46–48 The ban against all contact with Orestes and Electra reflects their status as *polluted*. The problem how to treat polluted individuals is familiar in Homer and other literature (such as this play) set in the heroic age.

85 / 72 *still unmarried* An issue resolved at the end (**1726–27 / 1658–59**).

85 / 72 *after all these years* Roughly eighteen.

149–206 / 140–207 *Parodos* (choral entry song) in the form of a *kommos* (dialogue between Chorus and actor)

207–318 / 208–315 *First episode*

267 / 268 *the horn-tipped bow, Apollo's gift* The bow seems to exist only in Orestes' mind; at any rate, we hear nothing further of it.

302 / 301–2 *Go on into the palace, now, and get some rest* There will soon be three speaking characters present on stage at once (Orestes, Menelaos, Tyndareos), one of whom must be played by the actor now playing Electra.

319–52 / 316–47 *First stasimon*

339–40 / 337 *Some avenger / hounding the whole line* The killing of Thyestes' children by Atreus (**20–21 / 15**) produced an avenging spirit (*alastor*) who, through the agency of Clytemnestra, struck down Atreus' son Agamemnon

(Aeschylus *Agamemnon* 1501). Now a new *alastor* has arisen from Clytemnestra's blood to punish her killer, Orestes. All involved in the series of killings are either victims or embodiments of an *alastor*, or both. In this sense, "the whole line" descended from Atreus can be imagined, individually and collectively, as dogged by "some avenger."

353–846 / 348–806 Second episode

355 / 353 against Asia The Athenians of Euripides' day were in the habit of conflating the Trojans of epic poetry with contemporary Asiatics, that is, barbarians (Persians, Phrygians, etc.).

364 / 364 Glaukos Originally a fisherman who became immortal after he had eaten a magic herb. Euripides has made him the son of Nereus (the prophetic Old Man of the Sea) in order to reinforce his prophetic credentials.

386 / 383 I lack the suppliant's branches An ancient Greek suppliant carried an olive branch draped in wool.

422 / 420 Apollo takes his time. That's the way a god works The justice of the gods might take generations to reach fulfillment. So, for example, Croesus lost his throne because his ancestor Gyges had acquired it through murder five generations earlier (Herodotus 1.13).

436–40 / 432–36 Palamedes, Oiax's brother, was falsely accused of treason and put to death by the Greeks at Troy under Agamemnon. According to some sources, Oiax not only welcomed the murder of Agamemnon but also encouraged Clytemnestra to carry it out. Now that she and Aigisthos have fallen, Oiax and his allies hope to retain their influence in the city by getting rid of Orestes. The political situation briefly described by Electra (59–64 / 46–50; see note on 59 / 46) is becoming clearer. The ascription of antiwar sentiment to Palamedes in Vergil (*Aeneid* 2.84) may also be relevant: the people resent the loss of their loved ones at Troy in this play (115–16 / 102–3) as in Aeschylus' *Agamemnon* (445–51).

459 / 456–57 Here comes Tyndareos of Sparta There will now be three speaking actors on stage, representing three generations of the family.

468 / 465 their own sons Castor and Polydeukes. Only Castor fits the description exactly, Polydeukes being the son of Leda by Zeus.

480 / 476 who shared your wife with Zeus See previous note.

483 / 480 his sick eyes gleaming Tyndareos sees Orestes as *infectious*. Talking with him could be dangerous. Just such a primitive notion underlies the communal banning of murderers (59–62 / 46–48).

488 / 485 *All those years among barbarians have made you one yourself* The Trojans of Homer are not "barbarians" in the later sense of non-Greek. Another instance of the anachronism common throughout this play (see note on 355 / 353).

    The institution of blood-guilt is one of the *nomoi* (customs, laws) recognized by Greeks everywhere. To disregard it is, in Tyndareos' view, to shed one's Greekness.

490 / 487 *Yes, and not go in for lawlessness* According to Tyndareos, Menelaos takes exception to *nomoi* (see previous note) that everyone else agrees are binding.

551 / 544 *Sir* Orestes addresses his grandfather as an old man (*geron*), respectfully here, disdainfully later (596 / 585).

556 / 546 *outcast* (*anosios*), literally "unholy, unacceptable to the gods."

568 / 559 *took herself a man* In Greek a man *married* a woman, a woman *was married* to a man. Clytemnestra is thus imagined playing the man's part, Aigisthos the woman's, in a reversal of the normal roles.

582 / 568 *"pity," as you call it* Tyndareos had not in fact used this word in his indictment.

586 / 571 *my "dreadful crimes"* Again, the quoted phrase does not actually occur in Tyndareos' speech.

596 / 585 *It was you, Sir* The change in tone here marks a striking departure from defending himself to attacking his accuser (see note on 551 / 544).

600–603 / 588–90 Penelope's chastity is twice contrasted with Clytemnestra's infidelity in the *Odyssey* (11.405–61, 24.192–202). Word of it has evidently reached Argos, some three years before the return of Odysseus.

602 / 589 *husband to husband* The echo between Orestes' phrasing here and Tyndareos' at lines 513–14 / 510 ("pays murder off / with murder") is much more prominent in the Greek, where the syntax, meter, position and even syllabification of the two words involved in each case are repeated exactly, only the words themselves being different. One almost hears the taunt, "*Murder on murder* (*phonoi phonon*) is not the primary issue here: it only results from your daughter taking *husband on husband* (*posei posin*)."

604 / 591 *or maybe I shouldn't mention gods* The Furies come to mind.

619 / 598 *cleanse me of pollution* One of Apollo's major functions was to deal with pollution, both individual and collective.

634 / 612 *I'll go before them* Tyndareos, as a foreigner, has no right to address the Argive assembly. In the end, someone else presents his views (949–50 / 915–16).

650–51 / 625–26 Extremely important lines: Menelaos' self-interest is now in conflict with his duty to protect his nephew.

670 / 643 *the favor you owe my father* Agamemnon got Helen back for him.

684 / 658 *what Aulis took, also through my father* Agamemnon sacrificed his daughter Iphigeneia at Aulis. The circumlocution minimizes the horror of her death and Agamemnon's responsibility for it.

705–9 / 674–77 Highly emotional. Agamemnon's soul is in the underworld, yet it is also imagined as hovering in the air and even as delivering the words now uttered by his son.

732 / 697 *like fighting a raging fire* Here the people are a fire, at lines 733–35 / 698–700 a stormy sea, at lines 741–43 / 706–7 a ship. The confusion of imagery mirrors the discomfort Menelaos feels backing away from Orestes.

739 / 704–5 *I'll go and try to persuade* A promise not kept.

762 / 726 *running at full stride* Everything (including the meter: see next note) quickens with the arrival of Pylades.

766 / 729 The meter in the Greek text now changes from the stately iambic trimeter to the lively trochaic (literally, running) tetrameter.

771 / 733 *cousin* Pylades' father had married a sister of Agamemnon, making him and Orestes cousins.

781 / 742 *she brought him* Menelaos plays the woman's part here, like Aigisthos (see note on 568 / 559).

820 / 782 *Pray only that it seem so* This has a sophistic ring to it. Compare *Gorgias* DK82B.26: "Being is not apparent if it does not attain to seeming."

846 / 806 *no blood tie* Orestes has not forgotten that he and Pylades are cousins (771 / 733). In comparison with their devotion to each other, all else is irrelevant. This is rhetoric, not lapse of memory.

847–890 / 807–43 *Second stasimon*

854 / 812 *the golden lamb* When Atreus and Thyestes quarreled over the throne of Argos, a decision was to be made between them on the basis of who could produce a portent. Atreus hoped to win with a golden lamb that had appeared in his flocks, but Thyestes in the meantime had seduced and corrupted Atreus' wife, Aerope, who put the miraculous lamb from her husband's into her lover's possession. In this way Thyestes was proclaimed king. Zeus then intervened in Atreus' behalf, causing changes in the heavens that led to a new decision, Atreus becoming king and Thyestes going into exile.

855–56 / 814–15 *gruesome banquetings / and dismemberings of princes* The later event is placed first: Thyestes fed on the flesh of his children who had been killed and dismembered by Atreus (**20–21 / 15**).

859–60 / 818 *the divided / heirs of Atreus* Evidently, Menelaos and Orestes.

891–993 / 844–959 *Third episode*

915–16 / 872 *Danaos ... Aigyptos* Sons of Belus, descended, in the fourth generation, from the union of Zeus with Io. Danaos fled from Libya to Argos (home of his ancestress Io) and Aigyptos pursued him there. In the trial alluded to, Aigyptos was either trying to force Danaos to marry his fifty daughters to his own fifty sons or the marriage had already occurred and Aigyptos was demanding justice for the murder of the bridegrooms by their brides on the wedding night.

927 / 885 *"Who wants to speak to the issue ... ?"* This would remind the Athenians of the formula used in their own assembly (see note on **59 / 46**).

930 / 888 *Talthybios* In the *Iliad*, one of Agamemnon's messengers.

939 / 898 *Lord Diomedes* An important hero in the *Iliad*, where he is referred to as "Lord over Argos."

964–65 / 931 *And then / not a soul spoke up in support* The silence of Menelaos at this point is deafening (see note on **739 / 704–5**).

967–80 / 932–42 I agree with Willink (pp. 236–37) that the bracketed lines quoting what Orestes said in the assembly are likely to be the work of someone other than Euripides. We have already heard what Orestes has to say in his defense (**551–623 / 544–604**). What he is quoted as saying here is anticlimactic (picking up the misogynistic theme developed by the previous speaker, **957–62 / 923–29**), repetitive ("as good as dead ... as good as dead" [**973 / 936–37 ... 979 / 941**]), and not particularly clear ("doing / the opposite" [974–75 / 938]). It may also be relevant that the entire speech can be deleted without disrupting the flow of thought ("Your brother came forward / But he didn't sway the crowd" [966 / 931, 981 / 943]).

992–93 / 955–56 The messenger's parting words suggest that he heard Orestes plead Apollo's complicity before the assembly (as before Tyndareos at 612–21 / 591–99); it is the argument's failure to move the people, not Apollo's failure to appear at Orestes' side, that is likely to be on his mind. This is the last reference to Apollo's complicity until the climax of the play.

993 / 956 *but rather your destroyer* Plays (as often) on the similarity in Greek between the name Apollo and the verb *apollunai* ("to destroy").

994–1062 / 960–1012 *Kommos*, in place of a stasimon.

1001–2 / 965 *this land walled in / by giants* Literally Cyclopean land. The gigantic Cyclopes built the walls of Mycenae/Argos and Tiryns.

1024–25 / 982–83 *the rock / hanging in the sky* For Tantalos and his punishment see note on 5–16 / 4–10.

1027 / 983–84 *spinning there* Electra's language suggests familiarity with the Anaxagorean view of the heavenly bodies held in place by centrifugal forces.

1033–35 / 987–90 Poseidon had given Pelops a chariot drawn by winged horses.

1036 / 990 *over the sea* Pelops is imagined driving from the island of Lesbos (home, in the version Euripides is apparently following, of Pelops' bride, Hippodameia) to Greece.

1037 / 990 *Myrtilos* The charioteer of Oinomaos, father of Hippodameia. Oinomaos refused to allow his daughter to marry anyone but the man who could defeat him in a chariot race, the losers forfeiting their lives. When Pelops came to compete for Hippodameia's hand, Myrtilos agreed to help in return for enjoying first night with the bride. He then removed the linchpin from Oinomaos' chariot, replacing it with one of wax. Oinomaos perished in the race and Hippodameia married Pelops, who rewarded Myrtilos for his treachery by casting him into the sea.

1038 / 993 *Geraistos* In southern Euboea, on the coast of the Myrtoan Sea, so named for Myrtilos who met his death there.

1041 / 996 *the curse* Myrtilos, falling to his death, cursed Pelops and his descendants.

1043 / 997 *Hermes* Father of Myrtilos, an appropriate avenger.

1044 / 998 *that fleece-gold lamb's back* See note on line 854 / 812.

1049–50 / 1003–4 *on its lonely road to dawn / and evening both at once* A complex blend of mythological and scientific elements, typical of Electra's language here and elsewhere (see notes on **5–16** / 4–10, **1027** / 983–84). "Dawn" and "evening" stand poetically for east and west. The opposite motions can occur simultaneously because they involve different perspectives: the sun travels east with respect to the stars in the zodiac (a recent discovery at the time of the play's production), west with respect to the earth. Presumably, it used to travel in the same direction as the other stars; now it is alone, not only in its journey across the daytime sky but also in its journey through the heavens ("its lonely road").

According to the traditional account, Zeus, taking Atreus' side in the dispute with Thyestes (see note on **854** / 812), caused the sun to set in the east. This was a portent superior to the golden lamb produced by Thyestes, and so it confirmed Atreus in his possession of the throne. Euripides has made the astronomical change associated with the crimes of Pelops' descendants permanent instead of temporary (the portent described above occurs but once). An original harmony, in which sun and heavenly bodies moved in concert, has been forever disrupted as a result of human wickedness.

1051–52 / 1005 *the seven / Pleiades* The constellation of the Pleiades does duty for all the stars.

1063–1283 /1013–1245 *Fourth episode*

1099–1100 / 1049–51 The sentiment expressed is not perverse: Greek epitaphs for those who have died young often lament the failure to marry and have children.

1125 / 1075 *Go back to your father* Evidently Orestes views the alienation of Pylades and Strophios (**804–6** / 765–67) as temporary.

1151 / 1101 *that sword* That is, the sword you were talking about (see **1112** / 1063). It is clear from line **1175** / 1125 that they have not yet procured the swords they will need.

1154 / 1104 *these women are here as our friends* The complicity of the Chorus is required for dramatic plausibility. It is also conventional in Greek tragedy.

1160–65 / 1110–15 These lines, together with lines **1176–78** / 1126–28, prepare for the appearance of the Phrygian later (**1399–1599** / 1367–1526).

1160 / 1110 *entourage* Barbarian attendants in the Greek (see notes on 355 / 353 and 488 / 485).

1161 / 1111 *Phrygians* Allies of the Trojans in Homer, often used of the Trojans themselves in later literature, as here.

1267–83 / 1225–45 The act culminates in a brief evocation by all three characters of Agamemnon's ghost, surely intended to recall the elaborate scene in Aeschylus' *Libation Bearers* (306–509) in which Electra and Orestes and the Chorus (Pylades is present but silent in that scene) form a similar trio calling on the ghost of Agamemnon for assistance in the killing of Clytemnestra. Here Helen is the intended victim.

1284–1342 / 1246–1310 *Kommos*, in place of a stasimon

1285 / 1247–48 *first rank of Pelasgia's first city* The women of the Chorus belong to the noblest families of Argos, just beneath Electra herself in social standing. This makes the Chorus' complicity with the royal pair natural as well as conventional (see note on 1154 / 1104).

1319–21 / 1286–88 Electra's fear that Orestes and Pylades have been so stunned by the sight of Helen's beauty that they cannot carry out their intention of killing her recalls how Menelaos after the fall of Troy approached Helen with the intention of punishing her for her adultery, only to drop his sword at the sight of her breast. This, the most famous illustration of his uxoriousness, was depicted in art and mentioned in earlier and in contemporary poetry (*Little Iliad*; Ibycus; Euripides *Andromache*, 627–31; Aristophanes *Lysistrata*, 155–56).

1328 / 1296 *Argos! Argos! Treachery! Murder!* The attempt on Helen's life occurs (in accordance with tragic convention) off stage during this scene, to be described on stage in the next scene.

1333 / 1301 *Menelaos, I'm dying!* From here on to the moment Apollo appears with the deified Helen at the end of the play, every reference to what is occurring at this moment *could* be taken to mean that she has perished.

1341 / 1310 *Skamander* The famous river at Troy.

1343–1624 / 1311–1548 *Fifth episode*, with *kommos* and divided choral ode. This is one of Euripides' most daring and surprising formal experiments, and it cannot be accommodated within the traditional divisions of the Aristotelian tragic structure. Beginning as a spoken episode (1343–83 / 1311–52), it soon changes to a vast *kommos* between the Chorus and a Phrygian slave fleeing the palace (1401–1576 / 1369–1502), which becomes in effect a monody (a solo song) for the Phrygian, a weird and unprecedented lyrical messenger speech (see further the final section of the Introduction), interrupted only by occasional prompts from the Chorus. This is followed by an agitated but inconsequential dialogue beween the Phrygian and Orestes (1579–1610 / 1506–36). The scene comes to a lyric end with the antistrophe (1611–24 / 1537–49) of an ode whose strophe was sung and danced two hundred lines earlier (1384–97 / 1353–65), at the beginning of the lyric sequence.

1389–90 / 1357–58 *before we can see . . . / Helen's red corpse* The display of the corpse will convince Menelaos that the conspirators mean business (see 1241 / 1196).

1391 / 1359 *or get the story from one of the servants* Anticipating what occurs in the next scene. Ordinarily the palace doors would open and the killers themselves emerge, showing their handiwork. Here the killing itself fits into a larger scheme: the corpse is meant for Menelaos' eyes, and he has yet to return. The Chorus hopes either to dash in and catch a glimpse before he comes or to hear what has happened from a witness.

1393–94 / 1361–62 *The gods in their justice have brought down / judgment on Helen* Serves to reinforce the impression that Helen has met her fate (an impossible outcome as far as the audience is concerned). The antistrophe answering this strophe does not occur until 1611 / 1537.

1399 / 1367 *a Phrygian* The Phrygian who now emerges from the palace is one of Helen's household slaves. As such, he would have reminded the Athenians of the Phrygian slaves in their own households. He has, however, a number of more exotic features. He is not necessarily a eunuch, though Orestes' characterization of him as "neither a man / nor a woman" (1601–2 / 1528) and his employment in the women's quarters suggests as much. At times in his aria and in the interchange between him and Orestes, he stands for the Trojans familiar in Homer (see note on 1161 / 1111), at other times, especially when his effeminacy and cowardice come to the fore, he brings to mind Persians or Asiatics in general, the "barbarians" as the Athenians tended to see them. He is both the sort of enemy conquered by Menelaos and the sort of ally currently assisting the Spartans in their struggle with Athens (see Introduction VII). He is, finally, the only singing messenger in Greek tragedy. His song, as West (p. 277) describes it, is "articulate, high-flown, typical of late Euripidean lyric. Its incongruity in the mouth of such a character is part of the humour of this delectable scene."

1422 / 1385–86 *loveliness born of the swan* Zeus came to Leda (see notes on 468 / 465 and 480 / 476) in the form of a swan; Helen was born of their union.

1425 / 1389 *avenging Fury* For all his franticness, the Phrygian here sees things correctly: Helen *was* an instrument of the gods. See lines **91 / 79**, **1733–36 / 1662–63**.

1426–27 / 1388 *the very battlements / built by Apollo* The walls of Troy.

1431 / 1391 *Ganymede* A Trojan prince, son of Tros. Zeus fell in love with him and took him off to Olympus.

1486 / 1439 *"Daughter of Zeus ..."* See note on line **1422 / 1385–86**.

1578 / 1505 *running at full tilt* Orestes enters at a run, and the meter, appropriately, becomes trochaic when he speaks (see notes on **762 / 726** and **766 / 729**) and stays trochaic throughout his conversation with the Phrygian. The interchange between Orestes and the Phrygian is indeed lively: an ancient commentator condemned lines **1585 / 1512** and **1594 / 1521** as "too comic" and West remarked, "There is no funnier scene in Greek tragedy."

1585 / 1512 *Then even you think Helen perished justly?* Here and again at lines **1609–10 / 1534–36** Orestes is clearly under the impression that he has killed Helen. West (p. 284), citing line **1689 / 1614** as evidence that Orestes knows he has *not* killed her, remarked that we must either change the text of line **1585 / 1512** or "convict Euripides of carelessness."

1585–86 / 1512–13 The echo "justly? / Most justly" is reminiscent of similar interchanges between the braggart warriors and clever servants familiar on the comic stage. An ancient scholiast censured the interchange here as "unworthy of the tragedy and of Orestes' plight."

1594 / 1521 The Scythian policeman in Aristophanes' *Women at the Thesmophoria* (1101–4) also does not know what a Gorgon is. Euripides adds a pun on the two meanings of Greek *kara* ("head" and "person"). An ancient critic called the line "too comic" (see previous note).

1609–10 / 1534–36 *he'll see / ... his wife's dead body* Orestes is evidently confident of being able to locate Helen though she was not there when he and Pylades went for her after seizing Hermione (**1559–70 / 1493–97**).

1615 / 1540 *Silence is safer now* The Chorus is traditionally passive: it can only react to what the characters do.

1622 / 1546 *these avengers (alastores).* See note on lines **339–40 / 337**.

1623–24 / 1547–48 *plunging / to ruin with Myrtilos from his chariot* The calamity threatening the house now is the direct consequence of what happened in the remote past: the descendants of Pelops were doomed from the moment Myrtilos uttered his curse (see notes on 1037 / 990, 1038 / 993, and 1041 / 996).

1625–1770 / 1549–1693 *Exodos*

1632–36 / 1556–60 [*The tale is . . . a preposterous story*] The only identifiable source of Menelaos' information at this point is the Phrygian, whom Orestes let go just prior to boasting that he was not afraid of meeting Menelaos face to face (**1605–6 / 1531–32**). It is unclear whether the gods (or some other mysterious agency) whisked Helen away alive or dead (**1562–70 / 1493–97**). To represent Menelaos as convinced that Helen vanished *after* she was killed would spoil the calculated ambiguity of lines **1555–58 / 1490–92**. Apart from this, Willink (p. 340) points to a number of flaws in the portion of Menelaos' utterance bracketed here. The lines in question may well have been interpolated.

1639–41 / 1564–66 The preceding expression, "We must at least save my daughter" (**1637–38 / 1562–63**), makes the addition of Helen (**1639 / 1564**) illogical (West, p. 288). This is another possible interpolation.

1654–59 / 1579–84 Orestes himself is under the impression that Helen has perished (**1585 / 1512** and **1609–10 / 1534–36**). Why he should now disabuse Menelaos of the same impression is puzzling, for it is precisely what he would want Menelaos to think at this moment, even if he himself did not.

Electra's plan envisions displaying Helen's body to convince Menelaos that the conspirators are serious in their threat to murder Hermione if he does not cooperate (**1237–49 / 1191–1203**). Now that the body, or Helen herself, has disappeared, it would be just as easy for Orestes to claim that the gods robbed him of her corpse as it would be to claim that they rescued her alive, especially when Menelaos himself is certain she is dead.

Willink (pp. 342–43) draws attention to a number of problems in phrasing. It is perhaps also relevant that the line in which Orestes first denies having killed Helen (**1655 / 1580**: "If only I had. The gods robbed me of the opportunity") opens with the same phrase as his reply to Menelaos' lament at line **1689 / 1614** ("If only it were so"), a reply that could easily have given the cue to an interpolator here. (See note on **1689 / 1614**.)

1661 / 1586 *Ask the gods for that* The words may be taken literally or figuratively: the gods know where Helen's body is because they have taken it away (the literal reading) or simply because they know everything (the figurative one). The figurative sense is the one intended by Orestes, but it is the literal that turns out to be the case (with the qualification that Apollo has taken Helen away alive, not dead).

1666 / 1591 *And you, Pylades, will you join him in this murder?* The actor playing Pylades cannot answer this question. There are two speaking actors on stage now and a third (Apollo) about to arrive. The futility of the question is not apparent, however, until Orestes answers for Pylades. (See next note.)

1667 / 1592 *His silence speaks for itself. I'll do the talking* The silencing of Pylades (loquacious until now) would have hinted at the arrival of another character (played by the third available speaking actor), possibly also at the impending resolution of the drama by divine intervention. Of equal importance, it draws attention to Orestes' independence: he is finally acting on his own initiative.

1683–84 / 1608–9 These are extremely difficult lines to render without some awkwardness in English. In response to Menelaos' request to remove the sword, Orestes simply says literally "You are false." In response to the question Menelaos asks next, whether he intends to kill Hermione, Orestes answers, echoing his previous utterance, "There you are not false" (i.e., you hit the truth that time). The train of thought is as follows: Orestes would consent to remove the sword if he believed Menelaos capable of keeping his word, but he cannot believe him because he is, in his very nature (the Greek verb here emphasizes this), "false." When Menelaos then asks if he really intends to kill Hermione, Orestes cannot resist using the word "false" again, this time ironically. We have brought out what is implicit by adding the interrogative "Why" (i.e., Why should I let her go, since I cannot believe any promises you might make in return for her release?).

1689 / 1614 *If only it were so!* To be taken as a reply to Menelaos' lament *in its entirety* (that he has brought Helen back only to see her slaughtered). It has been interpreted, however, as if it referred to the slaughter alone. West (p. 284) and, possibly, the ancient interpolator (see note on **1654–59** / 1579–84), understood it in this way. The slaughter of Helen, however, *and* Menelaos' efforts to bring her back mean one thing to Menelaos, quite another to Orestes, and the difference is crucial.

The phrasing of Menelaos' lament (compare **1574–76** / 1500–1502) gives Orestes (and Euripides) the opportunity of calling to mind the episode described in the note to lines **1319–21** / 1286–88: if Menelaos were man enough, he would have gotten Helen back not to enjoy her again but to punish her for her adultery. "If only it were so!" means, then,

"If only you had gone to all that trouble *in order to kill her*, but everyone knows why you took the trouble, being the sort of man you are." The subtlety of this retort may have opened the way first to misunderstanding, then to changes in the text, especially at lines 1654–59 / 1579–84.

1692–99 / 1616–24 The most suspenseful moment in the play: Menelaos seems to surrender, and Orestes to accept it with another insult (1692 / 1616). As Menelaos makes no further effort after line 1692 / 1616, Orestes presses on, giving the command to fire the palace but not, yet, moving to carry out his threat against Hermione. Menelaos, instead of capitulating before the palace is torched, and possibly because he senses Orestes' reluctance to kill Hermione, orders his men to advance against it. Everything is about to collapse, leaving Helen apparently and Orestes certainly dead in Argos (contrary to both their traditional fates) when Apollo appears above the palace. A spectacular finale, to say the least.

1694 / 1619 *most loyal of all my friends* The compliment to the loyalty of Pylades is doubly appropriate: (a) Menelaos' treachery stands out in stark contrast against it; (b) Orestes' last words to his friend in the play remind us of what he said when he first saw him enter. The contrast with Menelaos is implicit in the earlier passage, too (758–65 / 722–28).

1696 / 1621 *Land of Danaos, of the founders and their horses!* Not necessarily a sign that Argive troops are approaching: Helen had called on Argos from within the palace (1328 / 1296), so, too, Electra at the start of her lament (994 / 960).

1697 / 1622 *Come on, Argives, bring your weapons, hurry!* The men who respond to this exhortation are most likely the men ordered to attack the doors at line 1637 / 1562. See previous note.

1709 / 1635 *For the daughter of imperishable Zeus must not perish* Helen's status as daughter of Zeus first appears at line 1422 / 1385–86. It emerges at key points twice in the Phrygian episode (1486 / 1439, 1563 / 1493), where the form employed for Zeus' name is Dios. Here Euripides employs the dialectal form Zenos in order to make a pun between the root of the name (Zen-) and the infinitive (*zen*, "to live"). Helen owes her salvation from death directly to her connection with Zeus, indirectly to the coincidental resemblance between the root of Zeus' name and the word for life.

The similarity between *zen* ("to live") and Zen- in Zenos ("of Zeus") is purely fortuitous from an etymological point of view, but such chance resemblances between words were taken seriously by the ancients. For another example in this play, see note on line 993 / 956.

1714 / 1645 *Parrhasia* In southern Arcadia.

1719 / 1651 *the Areopagos* The hill of Ares in Athens, site of the court for the trial of homicides.

1721–27 / 1653–59 Electra's marriage to Pylades has been well prepared (**1129–31** / 1078–79, **1141–43** / 1091–93, **1252–55** / 1207–10); the match between Orestes and Hermione would not have troubled the original audience (it would have been familiar from Euripides' *Andromache,* if not from other sources as well). Of greater importance, Euripides has portrayed Orestes at the apparent nadir of his fortunes as a youth tragically deprived of the opportunity to experience the joys of marriage and children (**1079–100** / 1029–51). Marriage is the logical culmination of a play that ends positively for an adolescent hero, especially one who has suffered so much in his encounter with the female sex (see Introduction VI).

1723–26 / 1654–57 Neoptolemos, the son of Achilles, is depicted as betrothed to Hermione in Homer's *Odyssey* (4.5–9). After the Trojan War, however, Neoptolemos went to Delphi to take Apollo to task for bringing about the death of Achilles, and there he perished, evidently before he could marry Hermione.

1728 / 1660 *Menelaos, let Orestes reign here in Argos* Confirms the suspicion, expressed by Orestes at **1107–8** / 1058–59, that Menelaos has had designs on the throne of Argos.

1733–36 / 1662–63 According to the *Kypria,* one of the "cyclic" epic poems rounding out the story of the Trojan War, Zeus decides to relieve the earth of its excessive population. The war occasioned by Helen's elopement with Paris is the means employed.

1733 / 1662 *the gods, by means of this one's beauty* As Helen herself implies at line **91** / 79, she has been an instrument of divine intention all along (see note on **1425** / 1389).

1737–39 / 1664–65 Orestes' strongest point in his self-defense (**612–21** / 591–99) is the only one Apollo advances. Menelaos had criticized it (**418–19** / 416–17) and the Argive assembly, to judge from the messenger's last utterance (see note on **992–93** / 955–56), had not been persuaded by it. Now both are compelled to admit its truth and to accept its exculpatory value.

1742–43 / 1668–69 *thinking what I heard / as your voice was really some fiend's* A new disclosure, not to be taken ironically (see Introduction XI).

1755 / 1681 *Loxias* Another name for Apollo.

1757 / 1682–83 *honoring Peace, loveliest of the gods* That is, getting along with one another: the strife that has been the play has come to an end. Perhaps also the poet's implicit advice to his fellow citizens: they had rejected peace on favorable terms with Sparta two years before, after the victory at Kyzikos.

1760–61 / 1686–87 *Hebe, / the wife of Herakles* Hebe is the daughter of Zeus and Hera. Her name means Youth. Herakles is the son of Zeus and the mortal Alkmene, famed for his Twelve Labors and rewarded for them with exaltation to divine status after his death. Euripides is careful to escort the deified Helen into an Olympus peopled with former mortals: Herakles here and her own brothers at lines 1710 / 1636 and 1765 / 1689.

1768–70 / 1691–93 The Chorus has the last word, a prayer that the play now over will find favor with the judges. We do not know how *Orestes* fared with the judges at its original performance. On its popularity afterwards, see Introduction v.

IPHIGENIA AT AULIS

Translated by

W. S. MERWIN

and

GEORGE E. DIMOCK, JR.

INTRODUCTION

Euripides' *Iphigenia at Aulis* was not produced until after the author's death, and it is generally thought to be, to some degree at least, unfinished. Many passages, particularly the end, are either unusually corrupted by time and interpolation, or did not receive the master's final touch, or both. Because the text is in this unsatisfactory state, it is natural that scholars should take the play as we have it less seriously than Euripides' other plays and should have dismissed as interpolations those parts of it which they did not like. They do this at their peril, however.

For one thing, Bernard Knox in an important article has effectively removed the only compelling grounds for suspecting major interpolations or serious incompleteness.[1] For another, the more we consider the manifest intent of the suspected passages, the more we seem to see not the banalities and cheap effects characteristic of interpolators, but the daring yet inevitable inventions of a writer who can be only Euripides. Who but Euripides could have ended this play with Clytemnestra denouncing the messenger's account of Iphigeneia's miraculous preservation? Clytemnestra considers that Agamemnon has fabricated it to forestall her wrath over her daughter's sacrifice, and no wonder, for we remember Agamemnon's lying tale which brought her to Aulis in the first place. Earlier in the play the Chorus has wondered whether such stories as that of Leda and the Swan have not been foisted on men "in the tablets of the Muses," as though Euripides were preparing us specifically for the doubt cast on the myth here. Thus the "happy" ending is

1. Bernard M. W. Knox, "Euripides' *Iphigeneia in Aulide* 1–163 (in that order)," Yale Classical Studies 22 (1972): 239–62.

undercut in typically Euripidean fashion, even though this is done in a suspected, obviously unmetrical passage. The truth seems to be that the final page of the manuscript from which our extant copies derive was not so much incomplete as partly illegible,[2] and that even where our copies have not preserved the exact language that Euripides wrote or would have written, they have faithfully kept his conception. It is a brilliant one.

In Greek tragedy the figure of Iphigeneia embodies the question, "Why would anyone sacrifice his daughter's life as the price of waging a punitive war?" And, thanks to Aeschylus' treatment of Iphigeneia in his Agamemnon, right behind that question stands another: "What sort of military victory is worth the destruction of youth, of progeny, of the future of the race, which such a war as the Trojan War brings upon both victors and vanquished?" For Euripides the Trojan War was not worth the life of even one girl; and by the same token neither was the Peloponnesian War which Athens was losing even as Euripides was writing this play. Yet, during the last twenty-five years of Euripides' career, most of the Greek states had in fact been sacrificing their youth and future to the Peloponnesian War, just as in the myth Agamemnon showed himself willing to sacrifice his daughter for the privilege of taking revenge on the Trojans. We shall see that *Iphigenia at Aulis* is Euripides' last attempt to confront his fellow-Greeks with a picture of their tragic folly.

So tragic in fact was the Peloponnesian War felt to be that the great sophist Gorgias proposed a remedy for it in a famous speech given at the Olympic games, probably in 408 B.C., two years before Euripides' death.[3] The remedy, however, must have seemed to Euripides worse than the disease: Gorgias recommended that the warring Greeks submerge their differences in a common crusade against the "barbarian" Persians, a second Trojan War as it were. Our play is among other things a response to this proposal of Gorgias', as its caricature of pro-Hellenic, anti barbarian chauvinism shows. In it Euripides makes clear to his fellow Greeks how reasonable human beings, all of whom know better, consent to their own destruction in disastrous wars of aggression like the Trojan War, the Peloponnesian War, or the war against the Persians recommended by Gorgias. Doubtless, Euripides had lived too long and seen too much to hope that his play could prevent such insanity. Certainly his *Trojan Women* had not stopped the Athenian invasion of Sicily. But at least he could expose such adventures for what in his opinion they really were.

---

2. Sir Denys Page, *Actors' Interpolations in Greek Tragedy* (Oxford, 1934), 196.
3. Ulrich von Wilamowitz-Moellendorf, *Aristoteles und Athen* (Berlin, 1893), 1:172.

Iphigenia at Aulis is a tragedy because it demonstrates inexorably how human character, with its itch to be admired (*philotimia* in Greek), combines with the malice of heaven to produce wars which no one in his right mind would want and which turn out to be utterly disastrous for everybody. In this play we shall see no tragic hero or heroine confronting some abyss in the universe, nor even a group of villains who do in the fair young maiden in spite of all her mother can do to prevent it; we simply shall see ordinary humanity acquiescing in its own destruction; but before we are finished we may agree with the author's evident feeling that few things can be more tragic than that.

As the play presents it, the situation is this: having got as far as Aulis on the east coast of Greece, the Greek expedition against Troy is held up for want of a wind. Kalchas the soothsayer has privately assured Agamemnon, Menelaos, and Odysseus that if Agamemnon will sacrifice his daughter Iphigeneia to the goddess Artemis, the winds will blow and Troy will be taken; if they do not, they will never reach Troy. Agamemnon has consented and has already sent for his daughter under the pretext of marrying her to Achilles, but as the play opens, he has had a change of heart. We see him, although he is still in a torment of indecision, send off a letter countermanding his instructions that Iphigeneia be brought to Aulis. In this way the conflict of the play is opened: whether or not it is worth even one human life to fight the Trojan War. At this stage nobody really doubts that the right thing to do is to save Iphigeneia. Agamemnon himself says, "What I have done / is wrong, and I want to undo it" (**143–44** / 107–8). In spite of his vacillation, he shows that he is as appalled at his previous actions as the old man who will bear his letter:

> I have lost the use of my reason! My ruin
> is straight ahead of me. No. Go. Start.
> Run. Never mind the age in your legs.
> (**173–75** / 135–39)

From now on we experience the play as an agonizing effort to save the life of Iphigeneia, an effort which turns out to be doomed. Our horror mounts as we watch door after door close upon her escape and, when finally she is led offstage to be sacrificed, even she now consenting to her own destruction, our dismay is complete.

Her ensuing miraculous "salvation" by the goddess, even if we choose to believe in it, is no help at all. Clytemnestra has lost her daughter as surely as though she had died; the only difference is that in this case she is not even allowed to mourn for her (**1953–58** / 1441–44). And nothing has affected the demonstration that perfectly "nice" people, when the moment comes, will sacrifice children for the sake of military victory, no matter how unnecessary and damaging to the victors themselves such a victory may be.

What makes the play especially devastating is that in the beginning it seems, against all expectation, that Iphigeneia may be saved. What could be more gratifying than to see even the shameless politician Agamemnon come to the conclusion that he cannot after all kill his own daughter? Then, to our delight, in spite of his propensity to weakness and vacillation, he stands firm against the importunities of his brother Menelaos, infatuated with the idea of getting back Helen. When, after this, Menelaos, too, comes round, we can scarcely contain our hopeful enthusiasm for Iphigeneia's salvation. It will be the reversal of this tide of feeling, as Iphigeneia nevertheless comes to be sacrificed, which will produce the play's peculiarly powerful effect.

Gradually, inexorably, our hope is destroyed. Even after fate has taken a hand and the letter has proved to be too late, even after Iphigeneia has arrived and Agamemnon and Menelaos have decided that there is no way to keep the common soldiers from hearing about the oracle and compelling their leaders to sacrifice the girl, there still seems to be a chance. Clytemnestra has accompanied her daughter to Aulis. Surely she can think of something? Admittedly before she discovers the truth we experience the almost unbearable scene in which Agamemnon, while concealing it from his wife and daughter, makes it only too plain to the audience that the proposed wedding means Iphigeneia's death; but will not Clytemnestra eventually find this out? She does find it out and she does think of something: she obtains an unconditional promise of protection from the man who is traditionally the greatest hero of them all, the supposedly incomparable Achilles. She and he concert a double plan: first, she and Iphigeneia are to plead with Agamemnon to see if he will not relent. If he does, an appeal to the army can at least be attempted. If he does not, or if the army is implacably set on the sacrifice, recourse can still be had to the supposedly invincible arms of Achilles.

As we might expect, the appeal to Agamemnon is a scene of extraordinary power. The women's case seems irresistible, and yet it fails. Agamemnon is sure that the army will kill him and the rest of his family and sacrifice Iphigeneia themselves if he fails to go through with the outrage. Pleading this compulsion, he goes offstage to make the final preparations for the ceremony himself.

It is at this point, really, that all is lost. Iphigeneia herself feels the trap closing, even though Achilles has not yet failed her, and sings a lament complaining of fate and the role of the gods. Apparently she has understood, as the audience soon will also, that only in legend can a hero, however great, prevail over a whole army by force. As if to make this point, Achilles enters to tell how the army has threatened to stone him to death. To be sure, he has brought his weapons and says that he is willing to undertake the battle in Iphigeneia's defense as he promised; but only a brief interrogation by Clytemnestra is needed to make it obvious that he cannot possibly succeed. It will be one man against thousands.

With the last door closed upon her escape, Iphigeneia decides to make a virtue of necessity, as Achilles indeed remarks afterwards. Her announcement of her decision begins as follows:

> Mother, both of you, listen to me.
> I see now that you are wrong
> to be angry with your husband.
> It is hard to hold out against the inevitable.
> (1836–39 / 1368–70)

Accordingly she decides to die willingly "for Greece," and "with glory." Evidently a major part of her purpose is to prevent the loss of any more lives than her own, particularly the life of Achilles; but in this of course, she will be unsuccessful. As the whole audience knows, he will be killed in the war. As she leaves the stage singing a hymn to Artemis in which she pictures herself as Troy's sacker and the preserver of the freedom of Hellas from barbarian rape, we are left desolate. If even under such circumstances as we have witnessed, Iphigeneia cannot be saved, and if youthful idealism such as hers can be made to accept, as it only too evidently can, such crude jingoism as her hymn implies, hope for mankind is dim indeed.

True, the play has often been read quite differently, as though Iphigeneia's unselfish adoption of her father's belated attempts to justify the war against Troy suddenly made it legitimate. But a closer look makes it hard to see how this can be. How can we forget what we so gladly welcomed in Agamemnon at the beginning of the play: his perception that it is wrong to kill his daughter in order to win a war over a worthless woman? He and his daughter have both submitted to the sacrifice on the assumption that it is a bowing to necessity, a poor second choice compared with what they know to be most desirable. What that is has seldom been put better than by Iphigeneia herself in her plea to her father:

> ... In three words I can say it all:
> the sweetest thing
> we ever see is this daylight. Under the ground
> there is nothing.
> Only the mad choose to be dead. The meanest life
> is better than the most glorious death.
> (1674–79 / 1249–52)

When all is lost and she chooses not to struggle for her life any longer or to imperil Achilles, Achilles unintentionally reveals to us what she is really doing:

> ... What you have said
> is beautiful, and worthy
> of your country. You are no match
> for the gods, and you have given up
> the struggle against them. You have reconciled
> what should be with what must be.
> (1904–9 / 1407–9)

The idea that Iphigeneia's sacrifice is inevitable is based first and foremost on the alleged lust for conquest of the mass of the Greek army. No doubt this lust is real enough once Agamemnon has spread abroad the oracle that Iphigeneia's sacrifice means certain victory. Without such encouragement, the army is obviously eager to go home because of the contrary winds at Aulis. According to Menelaos, "The Danaans / clamored for the ships to be sent home / and an end to these senseless efforts"; and Achilles speaks of the same feeling as persisting among his Myrmidons (1087–97 / 812–18) at the very time when, we realize, Agamemnon is arranging with Kalchas for his daughter's immolation (1015–18 / 746–48). Agamemnon publishes the oracle and arranges the sacrifice because he is sure Odysseus or Kalchas will do it if he doesn't (684–713 / 518–33), but how can he be sure? We have first seen him persuade Menelaos, its chief proponent, that the sacrifice is a crime against human nature; why can he not persuade Odysseus and Kalchas?[4] It is at least worth a try and, if that fails, even an attempt to persuade the army would be worth it. But Agamemnon is too much in the habit of bowing to what he assumes is the will of his constituency (29–31 / 25–27) to make any further effort to save his daughter; he ensures her death instead.

The rest is sheer excuse. Agamemnon had no difficulty in resisting the alleged obligation to Hellas as long as Menelaos was urging it (529–32 / 410–11); he pointed out that the gods had done his brother a favor in

---

4. I thank the General Editor for this insight.

relieving him of a worthless wife (490–91 / 389–90). It is only some time after he feels his hand forced (720 / 537) that he says, "I owe it to Greece" (1019 / 748), and only for his daughter's benefit that he develops the finer flowers of his false patriotism. Indeed the speech in which he does this gives itself away. It begins with the truth, a vivid evocation of a war-crazed army, and manages only by the most violent illogic to end on a note of high-sounding morality:

> ... Look: how many ships,
> the war fleet, assembled here, the proud men of Greece
> and their bronze battle-gear, and they
> cannot sail to the towers
> of Ilion, and seize
> the famous citadel, Troy,
> according to Kalchas the prophet, unless I
> sacrifice you.
> Some strange Aphrodite has crazed
> the whole Greek army with a passion to sail at once
> to the barbarians' own country
> and end this piracy of Greek marriage.
> If I disobey the goddess, if I ignore
> the oracle, then the army will sail to Argos,
> they will kill you and me, and your sisters
> who are still at home. I have not become
> Menelaos' creature. I am not guided by him.
> It is *Greece* that compels me
> to sacrifice you, whatever I wish.
> We are in stronger hands than our own.
> *Greece* must be free
> if you and I can make her so. Being Greeks,
> we must not be subject to barbarians
> we must not let them carry off our wives.
> (1689–1712 / 1259–75)

The reference to Aphrodite in this speech by itself condemns the expedition: what moral difference is there between the Aphrodite who sent Paris to rape Helen out of Greece, and the Aphrodite who is sending the Greeks to rape Troy? As for the freedom of Greece,[5] what can it be worth when Greece's leaders are so evidently the slaves of what they take to be the passions of the mob? Finally, who are the real barbarians: the Greeks who will sacrifice their own children, or the Trojans who want to keep for themselves the most beautiful woman in the world? As we suggested earlier, the last four lines of the speech are nothing less than a patent caricature of Greek chauvinism. These motives, which

---

5. This and the following point I owe also to the General Editor.

Iphigeneia innocently adopts, can never convince us of the substantive value of her action, noble and beautiful though we feel it to be.

Nowhere in Euripides, I think, is the conquest of Troy presented unequivocally as a good thing; in at least the great majority of instances it is a terrible example of man's inhumanity to man, and our play is no exception. To be convinced of this we have only to read what the Chorus sings at lines 1022–72 / 751–800, as though to warn us against Agamemnon's "I owe it to Greece" speech which I have just referred to. They describe the coming sack of Troy in terms completely sympathetic to the Trojans, and they are appalled at the destruction Helen will cause. Later, having weighed the marriage of Peleus and Thetis and the prediction that the fruit of it, Achilles, will destroy Troy against Iphigeneia's coming death at the altar, they conclude with the following question:

> Oh where is the noble face
> of modesty, or the strength of virtue, now
> that blasphemy is in power
> and men have put justice
> behind them, and there is no law but lawlessness,
> and none join in fear of the gods?
> (1468–73 / 1090–97)

Even though they are Greeks, they see in the destruction of Troy no justification for Iphigeneia's sacrifice, whether that sacrifice is voluntary or not. When Iphigeneia does volunteer, they praise her nobility, but add,

> It is the role of destiny, in this,
> and the role of the goddess,
> that are sick.
> (1896–99 / 1402–3)

Thus neither the content of Iphigeneia's patriotism, nor its source, nor the Chorus' judgment of it, shows us anything in which we may take comfort.

Most of all it is Iphigeneia herself who convinces us that her gesture, for all its selfless nobility, is tragically mistaken. The name of Helen echoes through the play as that of the one person most responsible for the horror we are witnessing, and we are not surprised when Iphigeneia nobly refuses to play Helen's role. In rejecting Achilles' offer to fight for her and consenting to her own death, she gives the following as her ultimate justification:

> I say what I am about to say
> with no regard for anyone.
> Tyndareos' daughter,
> Helen, will bring on enough fighting, enough
> death, for the sake of her body. As for you, stranger,
> do not die for me,
> and do not kill.
> Let me save Greece if that is what I can do.
> (1919–26 / 1416–20)

She wishes not to add to the bloodshed; but the terrible irony of it all is that in consenting to the sacrifice she is consenting to the whole Trojan War and the deaths of all the thousands who will be killed in it. Achilles will be killing and dying on her account at least as much as he will be killing and dying for Helen, since without Iphigeneia's sacrifice neither he nor the rest of the army can even sail to Troy, much less commit the horrors the Chorus has been reminding us they will commit.

> In the end Iphigeneia walks offstage to be sacrificed singing,
> I who will conquer Troy
> and bring down the city of Ilion.
> (2006–7 / 1475–76)

In these lines Euripides forces us to identify her with Helen. By the date of Euripides' play, the audience knew Aeschylus' famous *Oresteia* practically by heart. In *Agamemnon*, the first play of that trilogy, the Chorus sang (689) of the fatal name of Helen, "death of ships, death of men, death of the city"—*helenas, helandros, heleptolis*—and here in our play Iphigeneia both calls herself *heleptolis* in the lines we quoted above and is so called by the Chorus in its answer to her song. She has become as responsible as Helen for the expedition to Troy, for the fall of the city, and for the miserable homecoming of the Achaians.

She is, of course, though unwittingly, also responsible for Clytemnestra's murder of Agamemnon and Orestes' murder of Clytemnestra. In spite of what she thinks, she is hardly "bringing salvation for Greece" (2004 / 1472–73). In fact, the direct results of her consenting to be sacrificed are worse than resistance would have been. If, as Agamemnon feared, the army kills Achilles and the Atreidai and sacrifices Iphigeneia against her will, at the least there will be no matricide, and without Achilles to contend with, Troy may well survive. All in all, it does not seem as though we can regard Iphigeneia's noble gesture with satisfaction.

Nor is Artemis' alleged rescue of Iphigeneia in the play's epilogue a sign of moral approval on the playwright's part. As we have already noticed, it may be a hoax, and even if it is not, it does nothing to mitigate either Clytemnestra's bereavement or Agamemnon's and the Achaians' guilt. Kalchas' words hailing the miracle, as reported by the messenger, demonstrate its moral emptiness:

> ...Commanders
> of the assembled armies of Greece, look:
> the goddess has placed this victim
> on her altar, a deer from the mountains,
> and she accepts this instead of the girl,
> rather than stain her altar with noble blood.
> With this she is happy, and now she blesses
> our voyage to attack Ilion.
> (2135–41 / 1591–97)

Kalchas has not been presented in this play in such a way as to inspire confidence in his interpretation of divine phenomena. If, on the other hand, Artemis really "now...blesses this voyage to attack Ilion" as he says, we can only see the goddess as corrupt; that is, if we regard the Trojan War in the light in which the Chorus and the goddess' own demand for Iphigeneia's sacrifice have taught us to regard it. In Aeschylus, Artemis demanded as the price of going to Troy that Agamemnon act out against his own progeny the destruction of the young which the war would bring. That at least was just and moral. Kalchas' Artemis by contrast refuses "to stain her altar with noble blood" at the very moment that she is "blessing" the voyage which will end in the death of Achilles and the decapitation of Priam, not to mention the destruction of the flower of Greece and the whole life of Troy.

Evidently Euripides included the rescue of Iphigeneia in his play partly at least in order to demonstrate its irrelevance from a moral point of view. He would be the more inclined to do so if it was, as seems likely, an original part of the story of Iphigeneia. The story may belong, like the story of Abraham and Isaac, to a type in which a divinity first demands the sacrifice of a human and then, for whatever reason, allows the substitution of an animal. Both Aeschylus in his *Oresteia* and Euripides in *Iphigeneia at Aulis* wanted to make a point not present in the original version, namely, the cruelty and callousness of a parent and an army who would sacrifice a child for the sake of military conquest. Aeschylus solved the problem of the substituted animal by omitting it and giving the impression that Iphigeneia was actually sacrificed, although it is interesting that not even he was completely unequivocal about this. Arrived in their narrative at the point where the knife must finally strike, Aeschylus' Chorus sings (*Agamemnon* 248–49, Lattimore),

> What happened next I saw not, neither speak it.
> The crafts of Kalchas fail not of outcome.

Theoretically even on this occasion Iphigeneia may have been saved. In *Iphigeneia at Aulis* on the contrary, Euripides has his messenger tell us specifically that the goddess substituted a deer for the girl; but, as we have already seen, this information is presented in a way and in a context which only deepen the negative implications of the sacrifice, indicting gods as well as men for the insanity of aggressive war.

In our play Euripides identifies the essential cause of aggressive war as *philotimia*, the urge to be thought superior. Agamemnon even suggests that prophets make predictions like the one concerning Iphigeneia because they "want only to be important," or, to put it as the Greek has it, because they are *philotimon* (687 / 520). Though startling at first, such an idea seems less surprising when we remember that at the beginning of the Peloponnesian War the priests who managed the oracle of Delphi had predicted victory for the Peloponnesians "if they did their best."[6] Euripides, who was no friend of the oracle, evidently felt that that prediction had done much both to encourage the outbreak of the war and to raise Peloponnesian hopes once they were in it, thus making peace between Athens and Sparta more difficult. Such a feeling on Euripides' part would explain the assumption in the play that it is the oracle that makes the army deaf to reason or pity or longing for home. Under the circumstances it would be natural for the poet to attribute the giving of such a response as Delphi's to irresponsible self-importance. Whether or not the Delphic institution believed that the prophecy itself was true, it would manifestly have been better for Greece if it had been suppressed. In like fashion the lust for war of the army in the play is the more convincing when we recall the passion for victory which infected the Athenians and prevented peace on various occasions during the Peloponnesian War. This, too, is *philotimia*. In fact, the measure of *philotimia*'s virulence is its universality. Iphigeneia's death at the altar, and thus the Trojan War, is the work of the *philotimia* of everyone concerned.

In Agamemnon we see an individual in whom love of place conquers his honesty in spite of his clear perception of the counterfeit nature of rank and position. It is true that his better feelings prevail briefly over his *philotimia*, but he seems almost relieved to find his hand forced, and,

6. Thucydides 2.54.

unlike Clytemnestra, he is only too proud and pleased at the thought that his daughter has been taken away to dwell among the gods.

Menelaos is able to rise above his craving for Helen, but not above his enjoyment of powerful connections. Agamemnon's tears bring him over to his brother's side in the matter of saving Iphigeneia, but when his brother changes back, he changes, too.

Clytemnestra would clearly be willing to die for her child many times over, but she is over impressed with the social superiority of good form and Achilles' "greatness," indeed with the whole aristocratic mystique. She consents too easily to the decorous restraints with which Achilles hobbles the defense of Iphigeneia, and she ought to know better than to submit so tamely to her daughter's misapplied patriotism.

Achilles in some ways is the most interesting case of all because he is an example of a whole theory of education whose goal is outlined by the Chorus (746–62 / 558–72). Everyone knows what is right, they sing, and training in humility and self-control can teach men to practice virtue. Achilles has been reared by the centaur Cheiron to protect him from the evil propensities of men (956–59 / 708–9), and if there is one thing he has learned, it is the ability to control himself by the use of reason (1266–72 / 920–25). In this, it is suggested, he is the opposite of Paris (763–79 / 573–89). We become aware almost instantly, however, that his education is vitiated by his sense of the importance of the heroic ideal and of himself as an epic hero. He vows magniloquently and often to save Iphigeneia's life, but entirely as a matter of honor, mostly his own, though he cares for hers as well. The one thing that his speeches do not contain is simple human feeling such as Paris might entertain: it does not seem to have occurred to him that a young girl is about to die. The epic *philotimia* of this most priggish young man ruins the effort to save Iphigeneia in at least four different ways. First, in the name of aristocratic decorum, he prevents Clytemnestra from making any of the emotional displays which might have moved the troops to pity. Second, out of social tact and not to risk his friendship with Agamemnon unnecessarily, he disassociates himself from the attempt to convince Agamemnon by argument. Third, when it finally becomes a question of his own action, he so lacks the common touch that he does not realize that the army will merely be infuriated and call him a slave to sex when he pleads that Iphigeneia is *his* bride (1800–1810 / 1352–57). Instead, he ought to try to convince them that no victory is worth what this one will cost. But that is not an idea which he himself could understand. He proclaims that for the sake of the expedition, he would have let Agamemnon use his name to trap Iphigeneia if Agamemnon had only asked him first (1321–31 / 961–67) and this is not the attitude of one who knows the value of human life. Fourth, his *philotimia* shows itself at perhaps its worst when, having bungled the defense of Iphigeneia in debate, he does not counsel flight but instead offers to defend her at the same time that he makes it absolutely clear that thousands of men are coming to drag her off by the hair. In that context, his pointing to his armor, his vows to protect her and "stop Odysseus" are merely ludicrous. No wonder Iphigeneia bows to the supposed inevitable. When Achilles takes his leave, followed by his now demonstrably useless weapons, we are reminded of nothing so much as of Agamemnon's desertion of his daughter at the end of the previous scene. Achilles will lay his arms near the altar, he says, in case Iphigeneia should change her mind when the knife is at her throat; yet how little he really expects to use those weapons is shown by the sequel, in which not Agamemnon but he leads the sacrificial procession and makes the prayer dedicating Iphigeneia to Artemis. The arms which were to protect her may be lying close at hand, but the knife which will kill her, hidden under the sacred barley in the basket, is the most important object in the procession itself.[7] This Achilles, who makes not even the mildest protest to Agamemnon and does nothing of any practical value to save the girl in spite of all his promises, is at most a caricature of the Achilles of the *Iliad*. The generosity of Homer's figure and his understanding of the meaning of death is not there. Instead we feel that Euripides' Achilles is more than content that Iphigeneia should die—voluntarily, splendid creature!—and that he should live to go to Troy and wear the golden armor of Hephaistos (1446–51 / 1067–73). Our final image of him as he leads the procession around the altar is not so much a picture of treachery as of the impenetrability of heroic self-esteem.

Even Iphigeneia is infected with *philotimia*; she, too, has been brought up under the heroic code. That is what induces even her, who knew so well that the meanest life is better than the most glorious death, to think of the tragic sacrifice which will send the ships to Troy as her monument, her wedding, her children, the meaning of her life. Was innocence ever so abused?

There remain the Old Man and the Chorus. The Old Man staunchly supports Clytemnestra, but it is clear that this is an old retainer's proud loyalty to his original mistress rather than recognition that the war is not worth it. He, too, has had his speech to make in praise of

7. A brilliant discussion of this type of sacrifice and its connection with tragedy is contained in Walter Burkert, "Greek Tragedy and Sacrificial Ritual," *Greek, Roman, and Byzantine Studies* 7 (1966): 87–121.

"greatness" (32–37 / 28–32). The Chorus knows that Agamemnon is wrong to sacrifice his daughter, that "refusing to harm a child" is better. Contrasting Iphigeneia's sacrifice with the marriage of Peleus and Thetis, the Chorus denounces the whole expedition against Troy as criminal. Yet even it has its passion for the men, the ships, and the armor, as we see in its entrance-song, and at the end, like everyone else, the Chorus "reconcile[s] what should be with what [in its opinion] must be." The words with which the Chorus closes the play are shocking:

> Son of Atreus, sail
> with a light heart to the land of Phrygia,
> and return with a light heart
> and heavy spoils
> from Troy.
> (2180–84 / 1627–29)

The Chorus' worst lapse, however, occurs at the moment of Clytemnestra's and Iphigeneia's arrival in the camp. The Chorus knows what is in store for Iphigeneia but, warned to keep silent by Agamemnon, it does not tell. Under the circumstances its concern not to frighten the tender "bride" is grisly.

The Chorus in fact affects us as though it had a peculiar kind of double vision. Its instincts in general are good; it knows what is right, but at the same time it knows what is supposed to happen, and that deprives its good words of much of their force. It has heard of the prophecy made at Peleus' marriage that Achilles would win glory at Troy (1440–52 / 1062–75), and therefore even as it begs Agamemnon to listen to his wife's plea or applauds Achilles' promise to save Iphigeneia's life, it must feel fairly sure that there is no hope. When at the end of the play its hopelessness is not only proved correct, but apparently given heaven's seal of approval, it is not surprising that the Chorus, too, lapses into the old *philotimia* and "reconciles what should be with what must be."

This idea of "what must be" is contributed to by the "destiny" and the "role of the goddess" which the Chorus finds "sick" (1897–99 / 1403). Iphigeneia makes her own comment on this sort of destiny when, after she has traced her own fate all the way back to Hecuba's dream and the "Judgment of Paris," she sings of the winds of Zeus which bring happiness to some and despair to others (1716–68 / 1279–1332). Why must the winds which will bear the fleet to Troy involve her death? It is all so arbitrary. Can this really be the "what must be" with which "what should be" must be reconciled? If this were all, our world would be dark indeed;

but actually Euripides' play offers us an escape from the clutches of *philotimia* and fate.

The Chorus' belief in the prophecy of Achilles' future, like Iphigeneia's belief in the prophecy of Paris' future, suggests how *philotimia* and belief in destiny are related. Both are rooted in acceptance of the truth of the Greek myths. In them "greatness," that is, the world's regard, is what men desire above all, and it is won almost exclusively by military success. Military success, in turn, is administered arbitrarily by fate and the gods. In other words, it is tragic. This state of affairs leaves men nothing to do but to fight and accept their fate. The struggle for military superiority is everything, and realizing this we can better understand the war-madness of the rank and file of the army in the play. On the assumptions of the myths, *philotimia* is the only alternative. As for belief in fate, it is for obvious reasons peculiarly a soldier's attitude, and the myths reinforce the tendency to entertain it. In the old tales, the end is always known, and the habit which this inculcates of looking for the fulfillment of a known outcome encourages regarding any human situation as one whose issue is determined by fate and the gods. This known outcome is the "what must be" against which the characters in the myths struggle in vain, just as Iphigeneia and the Chorus do in our play.

But what if the old tales are not true, as our play has at least suggested? Then greatness may not be all in all for men, and no end is necessarily inevitable. Necessity, destiny, the gods even, may not exist and need not be served. By questioning the myths our play potentially destroys the basis both for *philotimia* and for belief in destiny.

Even when the myths are largely accepted, *Iphigeneia at Aulis* shows us that their influence can be resisted. It shows us how even in such indifferently endowed characters as Agamemnon and Menelaos, brought up though they have been to the heroic way of life, human feeling can prevail over the mystique of greatness, at least for a while. Furthermore, when they succumb, they succumb to a presumed political necessity rather than to the mythological one. It is true that the political necessity is the result of the army's acceptance of the values and world-view of the myths, but we now see that that view, some day perhaps can be overcome: if, for example, enough people ponder deeply plays like this one.

In *Iphigeneia at Aulis* Agamemnon and Menelaos encourage us to resist not only the supremacy of *philotimia*, but the idea of mythological necessity as well. They do this by casting doubts on the skill of prophets and the efficacy of prophecy. Their strictures against Kalchas cause us, observing the fact that he is the lone authority for the demands of Artemis, to be filled with questions like, Why believe Kalchas? Who knows whether Iphigeneia's death will make the wind blow? Why does not someone ask the Greeks these questions in the effort to save her? Such questioning on the part of the play's audience can only make it less willing to accept the authority in the play of the mythological ideas of "what must be" and of *philotimia* alike.

More than all this, the play encourages us to fight against what seems necessity in the most drastic way of all, absolutely, even without hope. It does this by making us recoil so violently at the spectacle of a man giving in to necessity in so extreme a situation: a father deliberately arranging to have his daughter's throat cut. Most of us, less subject to *philotimia* than Agamemnon, would risk our own deaths and those of our whole family before we would in person arrange for the sacrifice of our child. Again, questions crowd upon us: What would have happened if Agamemnon and Menelaos, even without hope, had undertaken to win Odysseus' and Kalchas' silence by force or persuasion? Or, when that failed, what if they had made supplication together with Clytemnestra and the children before the whole army? What if they had fled to Mycenae with what followers they could muster and had attempted to defend "the walls the Cyclopes built?" The play demands that we ask these questions by its very emphasis on the fact that these things were *not* done. Clytemnestra and Iphigeneia failed to supplicate Achilles in public before the army, and Clytemnestra failed to seek Achilles through the host, all from a false sense of decorum and *noblesse oblige*. What would have happened if they had? Or, finally, what would have happened if Iphigeneia had let Achilles fight for her, and Clytemnestra had clung to her daughter and made Odysseus drag her off by the hair? At the very least there would have been the satisfaction of not submitting tamely to a personal outrage; nor would Iphigeneia and her mother have been led to accept the false and in this play's terms degrading notion that the Trojan War was a patriotic duty for all Greeks. Let us suppose that none of these things would have been enough to save Iphigeneia, and that any or all of them might have caused the deaths of Agamemnon, Menelaos, Clytemnestra, Orestes, and Agamemnon's other daughters into the bargain. Even so, it would have been both a more edifying human spectacle and less destructive in the end. And if others should be led by such an example to refuse in the same way to play the game of heroic superiority, who would say that the tyranny of tragic Necessity might not in time be broken?

Best of all, we can see that *Iphigeneia at Aulis* shows us how to be free of necessity not just in the distant future but at any time, and that this

was a demonstration of which the contemporary audience stood in
desperate need. In the play Agamemnon has said, in effect, "I must
kill you, my dear daughter, for if I do not, we shall all die and our
country will lose its freedom." In Euripides' last years precisely the same
argument was undoubtedly being used to persuade the citizens of
Athens to continue their by then hopeless war against the Peloponnesians. Looking at the play in the way we have been doing, we can see that
through it Euripides was saying to the Athenians something like the
following:

> You fear for your freedom. What slavery could be so terrible as the things
> this war is forcing you to do? You are already slaves many times over.
> You fear for your lives; yet like Iphigeneia you are willing to sacrifice
> yourselves, or like Agamemnon to sacrifice your children, in order to
> fight a war you cannot win. Why will you not instead, by making peace,
> by surrendering even, risk your lives and your freedom for the sake of
> peace? Even if it should mean the end of Athens, as it almost surely will
> not, there will be other men, other cities, and Athens, instead of destroy-
> ing herself body and soul as she is now doing, will be remembered by
> men of understanding as a city which came to an end more noble than
> even Iphigeneia's. For those who know when and how and for what to
> die, "necessity" holds no terrors.

Athens surrendered in 404 B.C., two years after Euripides' death and
not until she had lost her last fleet and suffered the starvation attendant
on a four months' siege. As we suggested at the beginning, even so
eloquent a play as *Iphigeneia at Aulis* does not stop wars by itself. Yet
in the end the Athenians did give evidence that they had understood
what Euripides was saying. One of the terms of the surrender, when it
came, was that the Athenians should destroy that part of their walls on
which their power at sea depended. Xenophon tells us that they did so
(*Hellenica* 2.2.23), "to the music of flute girls and with great rejoicing, for
they considered that that day was the beginning of freedom for Greece."

Evidently Euripides was not the only Athenian happy to turn his back
on *philotimia* and surrender his city's dominance in exchange for a more
equitable and equable world.

GEORGE E. DIMOCK, JR.

IPHIGENIA AT AULIS

Translated by

W. S. MERWIN

and

GEORGE E. DIMOCK, JR.

CHARACTERS

refer back to this ✱ *(handwritten)*

AGAMEMNON   King of Mycenae, leader of the Greek —look up family *(handwritten)* expedition against Troy

OLD MAN   Clytemnestra's slave, attendant on Agamemnon

CHORUS   of young women of Chalkis

MENELAOS   brother of Agamemnon, husband of Helen of Troy

FIRST
MESSENGER   leader of Clytemnestra's escort

SUPERNUMERARY
CHORUS   of Clytemnestra's attendants

CLYTEMNESTRA   Queen of Mycenae

IPHIGENEIA   daughter of Agamemnon and Clytemnestra

ORESTES   infant son of Agamemnon and Clytemnestra

ACHILLES   hero-to-be of the Trojan War

SECOND
MESSENGER

Line numbers in the right-hand margin of the text refer to the English translation only, and the Notes beginning at page 369 are keyed to these lines. The bracketed line numbers in the running heads refer to the Greek text.

Scene: In front of Agamemnon's tent, in the camp of the Greek armies by the bay at Aulis, where the ships are waiting. It is some time before dawn. As the light rises it will be perceived that the tent has a main entrance flanked by two side doors. AGAMEMNON enters through the main door, a waxed tablet in his hand. He paces up and down before the tent in great indecision, then turns and calls in at the main door.

AGAMEMNON   Come here, old man. In front of my tent.

OLD MAN   (*inside*) I'm coming. Is there something new,
        King Agamemnon?

AGAMEMNON   Be quick about it!

OLD MAN   (*entering*) I am quick. There's no sleep in me.
My eyes won't stay shut now they're old.

AGAMEMNON   What star is that, what time
crossing heaven?

OLD MAN   Sirius, pursuing the seven Pleiades,
still traveling high at this hour.

AGAMEMNON   No bird-sound, no murmur from the sea.   10
The winds are silent along these
straits of Euripos.

OLD MAN   Then why are you up
pacing outside your tent, King Agamemnon?
There's not a voice stirring yet in Aulis.
The watch is quiet
up on the walls.
Might we not go in?

AGAMEMNON   I envy you, old man. I envy any man
whose life passes quietly, unnoticed by fame.   20
I do not envy those in authority.

297

OLD MAN   But it is they who have the good of life.

AGAMEMNON   You call that good? It's a trap. Great honors
taste sweet
but they come bringing pain.
Something goes wrong
between a man and the gods
and his whole life is overturned.
At other times the notions of men, all
different and all insatiable,   30
grate it away by themselves.

OLD MAN   I don't like it, hearing a king
talk that way. Atreus did not
sire you, Agamemnon, into a world
of pure happiness. You must expect
to suffer as well as rejoice,
since you're a man.
And the gods will see to that, whether
you like it or not.
But you've lit your lamp. You've written   40
some message. That's what you have in your hand.
You keep putting on
the seal and taking it off again.
You write and then you
rub out what you've written.
You drop it to the ground, and tears
stream down your face.
From what I can see
despair appears to be driving you
out of your reason. Oh my king,   50
Agamemnon, tell me what it is.
I am a man of good will. I am
loyal to you, you can trust me with it.
I was in your
wedding procession, don't you remember,
back at the start. Tyndareos gave me
to your wife as part of the dowry,
because I could be trusted.

298

AGAMEMNON Leda, the daughter of Thestios, had three
           girls of her own: 60
           Phoibe, and my wife Clytemnestra,
           and Helen.
           And the highest-born young men in Greece came
           asking to marry
           Helen.   *fight for
           And threatened each other,   Helen*
           looking for blood. Each of them said
           that if he himself did not get to marry her
           he would murder whoever did.
           So her father Tyndareos   70
           could not think what he should do to avoid disaster.
           Should he give her to one of them
           or not let her marry at all?
           Then he thought of a way.
           The suitors would have to take an oath, all of them
           together, a solemn oath, sealed   *oath to
           with a burnt offering,   marry &
           swearing to defend whichever of them   any interfere
           should win Helen, Tyndareos' daughter, for his wife.
           And if anyone   80
           should ever carry her off, and keep   *causes*
           her husband from her bed, whether   *war*
           he came from Greece or somewhere else, they would all
           make war on his city and bring it to the ground.
           So they swore. Old Tyndareos
           was sharper than they were:
           when it was over he left the choice to his daughter.
           He said, "Now why shouldn't she marry
           as the sweet breath of Aphrodite directs her?"
           And her love fell—that's the pity of it—   90
           on Menelaos.
           It was later
           that this Paris, who judged
           the beauty of goddesses,
           as the Argives tell it,
           came from Phrygia to Sparta. There were gold flowers
           stitched onto his clothes,

299

he glittered with barbarian jewels,
he loved her.
She returned it. While Menelaos was away   100
he carried her off with him
to the summer pastures of Ida.
Menelaos, stung by his fate, raged
through all Greece, reminding
everyone who had sworn that oath
that they were bound to come to his help now.
And the Greeks rushed to arms. And they have come
to the straits of Aulis
with their fighting gear, their ships, their shields,
their chariots, their horses,   110
And because Menelaos is my brother, they chose
me to be their general.
I wish they had saved the honor for someone else.
And when the whole army had mustered
here at Aulis,
the wind died. Calm. We still cannot sail.
There is only one hope of our going,
according to Kalchas,
the prophet. Iphigeneia, my daughter,
must be sacrificed to Artemis,   120
the deity of this place.
Then the wind will take us to Troy,
and the city will fall to us.
When I heard this I called Talthybios the herald
and said, "Sound the trumpet, sound it,
and tell them all to go home. I could never
make myself kill my own daughter."
But at that my brother started reasoning with me,
arguing, urging me
to commit this horror,   130
till I wrote a letter telling my wife
to send our daughter here
to be married to Achilles.
I told her
what a great man he is, and I said

300

he would not sail with us until a bride
from our own family
had been sent to his home in Phthia.
A story I made up   he lied
so that my wife would send the girl.   140
Among the Achaians the only ones who know
are Kalchas, Odysseus, and Menelaos.
And what I have done
is wrong, and I want to undo it. That is why
I wrote this second letter that you found me
sealing and unsealing. Take it. Go to Argos.
I will tell you what it says
since you are loyal to my wife and my house. (*Reads.*)
"Clytemnestra, daughter of Leda,
I mean this letter to rule out the first one." (*Pauses.*)   150

OLD MAN Tell me the rest. Read it. Then I will be able
to repeat the message myself
as it is in the letter.

AGAMEMNON (*reads*) "Do not send your daughter
to this folded harbor of Euboia,
Aulis,
a shore where no waves come in.
We will find some other time for her marriage."

OLD MAN But Achilles, when he learns
there's no bride for him after all,   wife   160
will he not blaze up
raging against you and your wife? That
frightens me. How will you deal with that?

AGAMEMNON Only his name has been used. Achilles himself
knows nothing
of our plans, the marriage,
what I said about giving him my daughter
as his bride.

OLD MAN Then you promised her to the son of a goddess
         simply to fetch her here   170
         to be a victim for the Argives! King Agamemnon,
         your daring appalls me.

AGAMEMNON I have lost the use of my reason! My ruin
           is straight ahead of me. No. Go. Start.
           Run. Never mind the age in your legs.

OLD MAN I will lose no time, my lord.

AGAMEMNON Do not pause at the springs in the shade,
           nor stop to sleep.

OLD MAN The gods keep me from it!

AGAMEMNON When you get to where roads fork, take a sharp look   180
           down all of them. Make sure
           no chariot slips past you,
           too fast or not noticed,
           bringing my daughter here to the Greek ships.

OLD MAN It shall be done.

AGAMEMNON If she has left the palace
           and you meet her and her escort
           make them turn back. Take
           the reins yourself and shake them loose
           and urge on the horses to Mycenae   190
           where the Cyclopes built the walls.

OLD MAN One thing. What will make your wife
         and your daughter trust me
         when I tell them the message?

AGAMEMNON This seal, on the letter.
           Take it, and go now. Day
           is breaking. Already the sun's

Trust within a seal?

chariot of fire has sent
brightness into the sky. Go. Take up
your task. We must all suffer.   200

> *The* OLD MAN *goes off right*

similar to
pre-destination?

No mortal
ever knows happiness and good fortune all
the way to the end.
Each one is born with his bitterness waiting for him.

> *He goes in through the main door. The* CHORUS *of young*
> *Chalkidian women enters left.*

CHORUS I have crossed the narrows
of Euripos, I came sailing and I beached
at Aulis, on the sands. I left
Chalkis, my city, where the spring
of Arethousa wells up and runs flashing
down to the sea. I came   210
to see for myself this army of the Achaians,
the oar-winged ships of the heroes,
the thousand galleys
which blond Menelaos and Agamemnon of the same
great lineage sent,
as our husbands tell us,
to fetch Helen again:
Helen.
Whom Paris the herdsman seized
from the reedy bank of the river Eurotas   220
where Aphrodite had led her for him, after
the goddess had bathed in the dewy fountain
and taken her place beside
Hera and Pallas Athene
for her beauty to be judged.
Through the grove
where the victims die on the altar
of Artemis I came

running, and I blushed for shyness
at my fever to see   230
the pitched strength of the Danaans, the tents
hung with weapons, the clanging
press of armed horsemen.
Now I set eyes
on the two that are named Aias, I see
Oïleus' son and that son of Telamon
who is the hope of Salamis,
and with them Protesilaos,
and Palamedes, child of Poseidon's son,
hunched down, weaving   240
their cunning into a game of draughts.
Near them is Diomedes
delighting in throwing the discus,
and Meriones, scion of Ares,
wonder of men. Laërtes' son
has come there from his craggy island,
and Nireus, most handsome of the Achaians.
I have seen wind-footed Achilles
in full armor racing over the sands:
Thetis' son, whom Cheiron reared,   250
and he was racing against horses,
four of them, and a chariot, on the curved track.
I saw the beauty of those horses, gold
worked into their bits and bridles,
the yoke pair dappled
gray with white in their manes, the trace horses
bays with dappled white fetlocks;
and Eumelos, the grandson of Pheres,
driving them, shouting,
goading them on faster, and they   260
hugged the turns, but Peleus' son
in all his armor stayed with them the whole way,
never falling behind the chariot rail and the axle,
and won.
And I came to where the ships lie. Even a god
would find no words for the way that sight

stirs a woman's eyes. Pleasure took my breath away.
The fleet of the Myrmidons from Phthia, fifty
lean vessels, lay to the right
bearing statues   270
of the sea-god's daughters, the Nereids, in gold,
high on their sterns,
to show that those ships were Achilles'.
Next to them lay the galleys of the Argives,
their admiral
Mekisteus' son, whom Talaos
brought up to manhood;
and Sthenelos, Kapaneus' son, was there.
Then the sixty ships from Attica; the son
of Theseus is their commander, and their ensign   280
is Pallas Athene with her winged chariot
and its horses, a sign which lightens the hearts
of mariners.
Then the flotilla of fifty ships
from Boiotia with their ensign rising
from each of the sterns: Kadmos
holding a dragon of gold. Leïtos,
born of the earth,
is their admiral. And the same number
of ships from Lokris, commanded by the son   290
of Oïleus, who had come
from the famous city of Thronion
to moor beside them.
The son of Atreus had brought a hundred vessels
from Mycenae
where the Cyclopes built the walls. The king,
his brother and companion-in-command,
sailed with him to bring vengeance
on the bride who had abandoned his house
to lie with a barbarian. I saw the ships   300
from Pylos, that Gerenian Nestor brought,
and their sign is the river
Alpheios, that flows
by his country, shown on his sterns

in the form of a bull. Then the twelve
Ainian vessels that obey King Gouneus,
and near them the lords of Elis, who are called
the Epeians: Eurytos commands
the ships that came with them.
And the white-oared Taphian galleys followed   310
King Meges, Phyleus' son, from the rocky islands
of Echinai that frighten sailors.
To the left
the twelve sleek galleys of Aias of Salamis
made up the end of the line
that ran back down the beach
without a break, beside the army. The barbarian
who joins battle with these should not
cling to his hopes of sailing home.
I have seen the whole fleet,   320
and when it is famous and they
tell of it where I live
I will remember.

        MENELAOS *and the* OLD MAN *enter right, quarreling.*

OLD MAN Menelaos, you have no right to do this!

MENELAOS Get away! You are too loyal to your master.

OLD MAN Your reproach does me honor.

MENELAOS You'll be sorry if you go on meddling.

OLD MAN You had no right
to open the letter I was carrying.

MENELAOS And you had no right to carry a letter   330
that would harm the Greek cause.

OLD MAN Argue with others about that.
Give me the letter.

MENELAOS I will not.

OLD MAN *(seizes him)* Then I won't let go.

MENELAOS I'll bloody your head with my scepter.

OLD MAN What greater glory than to die for my master?

MENELAOS Let go! Your words are too big for a slave.

OLD MAN *(calling in at the main door of the tent)* Master! Help!
This man
snatched your letter out of my hand,   340
Agamemnon! Mutiny!

AGAMEMNON *enters from the main door.*

AGAMEMNON What is this? Brawling and arguing
outside my tent door?

MENELAOS My voice takes precedence here, I believe.
At a sign from AGAMEMNON, *the* OLD MAN *goes in at the
right-hand side door.*

AGAMEMNON How did you come to quarrel
with this old man, Menelaos?
And why were you so violent with him?

MENELAOS Look at me, Agamemnon. Then I will
start to tell you.

AGAMEMNON Do you think I'm afraid   Status   350
to look you in the eye, Menelaos?
I am a son of Atreus.

MENELAOS Do you see this letter? It was meant
to betray all of us.

AGAMEMNON That letter—in the first place
give it back to me.

307

MENELAOS Not until I have told the Greeks what it says.

AGAMEMNON You mean you broke the seal. So you know
What you have no business knowing.

MENELAOS Yes, I broke the seal. And it's you   360
who will suffer as a result, for acting
behind our backs.

AGAMEMNON How did you come to find him? Oh gods
what shamelessness!

MENELAOS I was watching for the arrival
of your daughter from Argos.

AGAMEMNON You see? Shameless again! What right have you
to spy on what concerns me?

MENELAOS I chose to. I'm not your slave.

AGAMEMNON This is beyond endurance! Am I not to be allowed   370
to govern in my own house?

MENELAOS No, because you're not to be trusted.
You never were, you aren't to be trusted now,
you never will be.

AGAMEMNON How smooth you are with your slanders. *smart mouth*
I despise a nimble tongue.

MENELAOS How do you feel about a mind
true to nothing and no one? It is you
who must answer for yourself. And don't try
to shout down the truth   380
just because you're angry.
I won't be too harsh with you.
Have you forgotten the fever
of your ambition at the first thought

of leading an army against Troy?
You pretended
not to want the command but really
you'd have paid anything to be general.
You know how you humbled yourself
at the time. Touching hands,   390
keeping open house to the whole
citizenry,
making them all speak to you, one by one,
whether they wanted to or not.
Anything
to entice preferment out of the crowd.
But once you'd been chosen to command, all that changed.
You dropped the friends you didn't need any more.
It was hard to get to talk with you, you shut
yourself in.   400
Is one to admire a man
who changes as soon as he gets what he wants
and turns from friends
the moment he's in a position to help them?
That's the first point
in which I found you wanting, Agamemnon.
Next, you led the combined armies
of the Hellenes here to Aulis
and then at one stroke all your importance
collapsed   410
just because the wind fell.
You were nothing
if the gods would not fill your sails. And the Danaans
clamored for the ships to be sent home
and an end to these senseless efforts.
I haven't forgotten the sight
of your face when you heard that. What anguish,
what gloom at the thought
that you might not sail in, after all,
lord   420
of a thousand ships
flooding Priam's beach with arms. Then you asked me

to help you. "What shall I do? Isn't there
something I can do?" Anything
rather than lose the command
and the glory.
Then when Kalchas said, "Yes:
sacrifice your daughter to Artemis
and the Greek ships
will be able to sail,"   430
how happy you were to promise.
And no one—admit it—forced you
to write to your wife
and tell her to send the girl here,
pretending that she would marry Achilles.
Then you change your mind,
you unburden yourself of a different message
and it's discovered.
At this point you'd never murder your daughter.
Well. This same sky   440
watched you speak otherwise. It's true
men find this happening to them
all the time. They sweat and clamber
for power until it's theirs,
then all at once they
fall back and amount to nothing again.
Sometimes it's the fault of the populace,
too stupid to know who's talking sense.
Other times it's richly deserved: the leaders
turn out not to be able   450
to keep the city safe.
I grieve above all
for Greece and her mortification.
She had set her heart on glory. Now
she will have nothing to answer
when the barbarian trash laugh at her,
thanks to you and your daughter.
Oh I would never put a man at the head
of a country or an army
just because of his connections.   460
A general needs to have a mind.

contradicted

CHORUS It is terrible when discord
divides brothers
and they fight each other with words.

AGAMEMNON It's my turn now. And I'll keep my
reproach dignified: brief,
restrained.
Not staring wide, shamelessly, but with
modesty, remembering that you
are my brother. No man who amounts to anything   470
is without a sense of shame. You
come to me in a passion,
breathing hard, eyes
suffused with blood. Tell me, who
has wronged you? What do you want? Are you pining
for a virtuous wife? I'm afraid
I can't do much for you there. The one you had
is no credit to your government.
Am I, then, supposed to suffer
for your shortcomings   480
when they're no fault of mine? It's not
my ambition that is biting you.
You care about nothing,
nothing but holding a beautiful woman in your arms.
You've abandoned all decency, all sense.
The passions of a degraded man are degraded.
And if I was mistaken to start with, and later
was wise enough to change my mind,
is that madness? No, you're the one who's mad.
The gods in their kindness took a bad wife off your
hands   490
and you're trying to get her back.
The suitors, it's true,
were so misguided
as to swear an oath to Tyndareos
while the lust was on them. In my view
some goddess—Hope, I imagine—accomplished that.
Not you in any case.
Still, lead them, by all means

to fight your war for you. They're foolish enough
to stick to their oaths. But the gods   500
will not be fooled. They can recognize
oaths that were set up as traps, and sworn to
under duress.
I will not kill my children.
There's no justice in things turning out
precisely the way you want them to—you get
your vengeance on a worthless wife—
while my days and nights melt
in tears, at the unholy
crimes I've committed against my own children.   510
These are the few things
I wanted to say to you once and for all.
You should be able to understand them.
You can refuse
to be sensible if you want to. But for my part
I will set straight my own affairs.

CHORUS This is not what was said before.
        But the change
        is for the better:
        refusing to harm a child.   520

MENELAOS Oh misery! Then I see I have no friends.

AGAMEMNON When you have friends you try to destroy them.

MENELAOS Is there no way that you will show
          that you are my father's son?

AGAMEMNON I will share your reason, not your madness.

MENELAOS You would share my troubles, if you were a brother and
                                                    a friend.

AGAMEMNON Say that when you have behaved like a brother and
                                            a friend to me,
           not when you are doing me harm.

312

MENELAOS   And Greece—you mean you'll abandon her now
           to her struggle?   530

AGAMEMNON Greece has been driven mad by the same god
           who drove you out of your senses.

MENELAOS   Congratulate yourself on your scepter
           now that you've betrayed your own brother.
           I'll find some other way, other friends—

                              Enter a MESSENGER *right.*

MESSENGER Commander of all the armies of Greece, King
           Agamemnon, I have brought you,
           from home, your daughter
           whom you called Iphigeneia.
           And her mother, your Clytemnestra, is with her,   540
           and the boy Orestes. You've been away from home
           a long time, and the sight of them
           will be a joy to you.
           It's been a tiring journey, and they are resting
           now, bathing their soft feet
           at the flowing spring,
           and the horses are resting, too;
           we turned them loose to graze there in the good pasture.
           I came on ahead to tell you,
           so that you would be ready. But rumor   550
           travels faster. The army knows
           your daughter is here. And they are running
           and crowding to get a look at the girl;
           everyone wants to catch a glimpse
           of those whom fortune has blessed.
           They say, "Is there going to be a wedding,   } gossip
           or did King Agamemnon miss the child
           so much that he sent for her" Others say,
           "Offerings are being made
           consecrating the child to Artemis,   560
           goddess of Aulis,

313

as though for a wedding, but who
will be the bridegroom?" Come. Do
what comes next, Agamemnon. Bring the sacrificial
basket, and lead the procession
around the altar. Set the garlands on your heads.
King Menelaos, prepare
the marriage feast. Let the flute
trill within doors and the floor
resound with the dancing, for this is the day   570
that dawned to see your child made happy.

AGAMEMNON Thank you. You may go inside. What is left to do
no doubt will turn out well, in the course of fate.

The MESSENGER *goes in at the right-hand door.*

Oh miserable creature that I am,
now what can I say? Where
can I begin in the face of this misery?
I have fallen into the snare of fate.
I laid my plan, but I was outwitted
from the start by the cunning of destiny.
How fortunate are the humbly born.   580
They can shed tears when they need to, they can tell
all their grief. But those of our station
are not allowed to appear
undignified. We are the slaves of the mob we lead,
molded by the pomp we must show in public.
I am ashamed
of my tears. But in the presence of this
enormity I am ashamed not to weep.
And my wife—
what words can I find, when I see her? How   590
will I greet her? With what eyes
will I welcome her? It was terrible
enough. Why did she have to come here, too,
when I never sent for her? But it is natural
for her to come here with her daughter,
to be present, the bride's mother,

to give her child in marriage.
And that's how she will learn of my treachery.
But the unhappy
girl. Girl? Why do I call her a girl?   600
When it seems that Hades
is about to make her his wife. ~~Oh I~~
~~pity her~~. I can hear her
calling out to me, "Father!
Are you going to kill me? I hope that you
and everyone you love are married like this."
And Orestes will be there, too, scarcely
old enough to walk, and he will
scream cries without words,
but my heart will know what they mean.   610
Oh what ruin Priam's son
Paris has brought me! All this he called down
by winning the love of Helen.

CHORUS   Grief lays hands on me, too,
         though I am a stranger, and a woman, and these
         are a king's troubles.

MENELAOS Brother, give me your hand.

AGAMEMNON Here is my hand. ~~You have won~~. I must bear
          ~~the loss~~.

MENELAOS I swear by Pelops, whom our father   620
         called "Father," and by Atreus himself
         who sired us both, that I will
         speak to you now openly, as I feel,
         without any hidden object in mind,
         but speaking from my heart. When I saw the tears
         running from your eyes
         I felt tears of my own
         and pity. I will not set myself against you
         any longer. I call back what I said before.
         I am with you now, and I add my voice   630

315

to yours: do not
kill your child, not for my sake.
It cannot be just for you to suffer
so that I can be satisfied,
nor for your children to die
while mine fill their eyes with the light.
What do I need after all? Could I not find
a wife who would do me credit
if I chose to marry again? Am I to lose
a brother, whom I should treasure, merely to win back   640
Helen,
buying evil with good?
I was rash. I behaved like a child, until
I came close to the thing itself
and saw what it means, to kill one's own child.
Then pity overcame me. For the girl
from my own family who was going to lose her life
because of my marriage. What has your daughter
to do with Helen? Let the army
break up and leave Aulis. Brother,   650
no more tears, now. Yours are the cause of mine.
Whatever the oracles say of your daughter,
from now on it concerns you, not me.
I give you my share in it. You can see how long
my threats lasted. I admit
I changed my mind. But that's
natural if a man loves his brother.
At every step I've tried to see
the right way to act.
That's not the vacillation of a weakling.   660

CHORUS Your words are noble. They are worthy
         of your ancestors.
         Tantalos himself, the son of Zeus,
         might well have been proud of them.

AGAMEMNON Menelaos, thank you. I never could have hoped
            that you would speak as you have spoken now.

316

But what you have said is right
and worthy of you. Discord
flares up between brothers
over love or the family estate.   670
It is poisonous to both sides. I hate it.
But I have reached a point where circumstances
leave me no choice. I shall be
forced to shed her blood,
to kill my daughter.

MENELAOS Forced? Who can make you kill the girl?

AGAMEMNON The combined armies of the Achaians.

MENELAOS Not if you've sent her home
to Argos.

AGAMEMNON I might be able to do that   680
without anyone knowing. But afterward—

MENELAOS What? You're wrong
to go in such dread of the mob.

AGAMEMNON Kalchas will tell the whole army
what was prophesied.

MENELAOS Not if he's dead. And that's a simple matter.

AGAMEMNON The tribe of prophets wants only to be important,
the whole rotten crowd of them.

MENELAOS When they don't prophesy
they're useless, and when they do   690
it does no good.

AGAMEMNON But aren't you afraid of something,
something I've just remembered?

MENELAOS Not unless you tell me what it is.

AGAMEMNON Someone else
knows everything. The son of Sisyphos,
Odysseus.

MENELAOS There's no reason for Odysseus
to do anything to injure you or me.

AGAMEMNON He's cunning, and it always turns out   700
that he and the crowd are on the same side.

MENELAOS He loves power. A terrible love.

AGAMEMNON Can't you see him rising
to his feet in the middle of the Argives
and repeating
the oracles that Kalchas spelled out to us,
telling how I promised
the sacrifice to Artemis
and then failed to keep my promise?
Can't you see   710
his words sweeping the whole army along with him
when he tells them
to kill you, kill me, and then sacrifice the girl them-
                                                             selves?
Even if I
could escape to Argos, they would follow me there.
They'd tear the city to the ground,
even the great walls that the Cyclopes built.
You see why I'm in despair. Almighty gods, how helpless
you have made me now!
There is nothing I can do. But you, Menelaos,   720
when you go back to the camp,
save me from one thing at least.
Take care that Clytemnestra
learns nothing of all this,
until I take my child and give her to Hades.

Let me suffer my ordeal
with as few tears as possible.
And you, women of Chalkis,
you will do well to say nothing.

      MENELAOS *goes off left.* AGAMEMNON *goes in at the*
                            central door.

CHORUS Blessed are they   730
      who share the delights of Aphrodite
      and are not burned alive by them, moderate
      and happy,
      whom the passion has not stung into madness, at
                                   whom

      the archer with the golden hair,
      Eros, has not aimed
      desire in his two arrows, the one
      striking rapture, the other
      devastation. Oh Cyprian,
      most beautiful of the goddesses, keep   740
      such wild flights from me.
      Let me know love
      within reason, and desire within
      marriage, and feel your presence,
      not your rage.
      The natures of humans
      are various, and human ways of acting
      are different,
      but everyone knows what is right,
      and teaching   750
      inclines them at last to virtue.
      Humility is wisdom,
      making us see the right way
      as something beautiful.
      And from this beauty honor is born
      and life earns immortal fame.
      It is a great thing, the pursuit of virtue:
      in women it is a stillness

in their love;
among men, multiplied   760
ten thousand times among citizens,
it makes a city great.
Oh Paris, they took you as a baby
to grow up herding white heifers on Mount Ida,
making on reeds a barbarous
music, a thin echo
of the Phrygian pipes of Olympos.
The milk-laden cattle
never stopped grazing when the goddesses
stood forth for you to judge their beauty.   770
You chose
madness, and madness brought you
here to Greece, to the palace
inlaid with ivory,
and to the eyes of Helen
that took your gaze full of love and returned it.
And from that rose the dispute that sends
the armed Greeks in their ships
to sack Troy.

>   CLYTEMNESTRA, IPHIGENEIA, *and* ORESTES *enter in a*
>   *chariot escorted by the* CHORUS OF ATTENDANTS.

CHORUS OF   Oh great is the fortune   780
ATTENDANTS of the great!
            See, the king's daughter, Iphigeneia,
            my queen.
            And Tyndareos' daughter, Clytemnestra. How great
            were their ancestors! How momentous
            the occasion that brings them here!
            Those who excel in power and in wealth
            are gods, in the eyes
            of mortals less favored by fortune.

CHORUS OF   (moving to the chariot) Let us stand here, women of
WOMEN   Chalkis,   790

320

and hand the queen down from her chariot.
Make sure she does not stumble.
Gently, carefully, help with our hands,
let us help Agamemnon's
noble child to
descend unafraid for her first steps in Aulis.
(*to the occupants of the chariot*) We, too, are strangers
                                    here. Gently, quietly,
we welcome the strangers from Argos.

CLYTEMNESTRA I think your kind greeting is a good omen.
I have come here bringing   800
this girl, as I hope, to a happy marriage.

                    To the ATTENDANTS.

Take from the chariot
the gifts I brought with her, her dowry.
Carry them in and set them down carefully.

            The ATTENDANTS *carry the gifts into the tent.*

Daughter, come from the chariot, alight
on your delicate feet. And you,
young women, give her your arms, help her down.
Someone do the same for me,
as I step from the chariot. Someone stand
in front of the horses' yoke.   810
A colt's eye takes fright
if there is no one to reassure it.
This is Agamemnon's son. The baby
Orestes. Take him.
Are you still asleep, my child,
lulled by the rocking of the chariot?
When you wake, wake happily. This is your sister's
wedding day. You had
noble forebears, you will have

a noble kinsman: the sea-nymph's son   820
who is like his ancestors the gods.

CLYTEMNESTRA *hands* ORESTES *to a member of the
Chorus, descends, takes* ORESTES *again, and sets him
down at her feet. As she speaks the next lines* AGAMEMNON
enters through the main door.

Sit here by my feet, child. Iphigeneia,
come to your mother. Stand close
and show these strangers
what reason I have to be happy. Now
here comes your dear father. Greet him.

IPHIGENEIA (*starts to run to* AGAMEMNON, *then turns to* CLYTEMNESTRA)
Mother, don't be angry
if I run from you
to be the first to embrace him.

CLYTEMNESTRA (*speaking at the same time*)
Oh most revered in my eyes, Agamemnon, King,   830
you commanded us to come, and we are here.

IPHIGENEIA (*running to* AGAMEMNON)
I want to run and put my arms around you,
Father, after such a long time!
How I have missed your face! Don't be angry!

CLYTEMNESTRA It's as it should be, child. You were always,
of all the children I bore him, the one
who loved your father most.

IPHIGENEIA Father, how happy I am to see you.
It has been so long.

AGAMEMNON And I am happy to see you, Iphigeneia.   840
The same words rise to my lips.

IPHIGENEIA   Oh, if you could be as happy as I am! Father,
             what a wonderful thing
             to have brought me here to you.

AGAMEMNON   Perhaps my child. Perhaps.

IPHIGENEIA   How troubled your eyes look, yet you say
             you are happy to see me.

AGAMEMNON   A king and a general
             has many burdens.

IPHIGENEIA   Oh forget them, forget them for now. I am here.   850
             Put them aside and be with me.

AGAMEMNON   I am with you. I am nowhere else.

IPHIGENEIA   Then don't frown anymore.
             I want those lines to leave your face.

AGAMEMNON   See, How happy I am to look at you.

IPHIGENEIA   But your eyes are overflowing with tears.

AGAMEMNON   We will be separated
             for so long.

IPHIGENEIA   I don't understand what you mean.
             Dear father, I don't understand.   860

AGAMEMNON   If you understood I would feel even worse.

IPHIGENEIA   Then we'll talk and I won't understand,
             if that will make you happier.

AGAMEMNON   Oh! (aside) I can't contain my suffering!
             (aloud) Thank you.

IPHIGENEIA Stay home, Father. Stay with your children.

AGAMEMNON I want to. But I can't do what I
                       want to
                       and it makes me unhappy.

IPHIGENEIA Oh I wish there were no more   870
                      spears, no more
                      of this grievance that's come to Menelaos!

AGAMEMNON Before they are done
                       they will destroy others as they have me.

IPHIGENEIA Father, how long you've been
                      shut away in Aulis!

AGAMEMNON And even now something
                       prevents me from sending the army on its way.

IPHIGENEIA Where do they say
                      the Trojans live, Father?   880

AGAMEMNON In the country where Priam has a son,
                       a son named Paris
                       who I wish had never been born.

IPHIGENEIA You are going all that way, Father,
                      leaving me behind.

AGAMEMNON Now you see
                       what you did not understand before.

IPHIGENEIA Oh if only it were proper for me to go with you!

AGAMEMNON You will think of your father
                       on your own long voyage.   890

IPHIGENEIA Will my mother come with me
                      or will I be alone?

AGAMEMNON Neither father nor mother. Alone.

IPHIGENEIA You won't make me live
somewhere else, will you, Father?

AGAMEMNON I have said enough. Too much. Girls
are not meant to know about such things.

IPHIGENEIA When you have finished what you have to do
at Troy, Father,
sail straight home to me.   900

AGAMEMNON Before that
I must make a sacrifice. Here in Aulis.

IPHIGENEIA Sacrifices are to find out
how we may please the gods.

AGAMEMNON You will see. You will stand by the font
of purifying water.

IPHIGENEIA Will we dance around the altar?

AGAMEMNON How I envy you, knowing nothing!
Now go in. It's better
for young girls not to be seen.   910
Give me a kiss, and your right hand.
You will soon be far away from your father,
and for a long time.
Oh breast, cheeks, oh blonde head,
what a crushing weight
Helen and the Trojan city
have called down upon you!
I must not touch you any more.
It sets the tears flowing. Go in.

                    IPHIGENEIA *goes in at the left-hand door.*

          Daughter of Leda, forgive me   920

for this access of grief
at giving my child in marriage to Achilles.
Partings such as these are happy, of course,
but when a father must send
his daughter to the house of another
after all his years of watching over her
it cuts into the heart.

CLYTEMNESTRA I feel it, too. I'm not so foolish as to reproach you
for grieving. I will feel just the same,
you know, when I lead the child   930
out into the marriage hymns,
so I don't blame you.
But time will heal the sadness. It's the custom and
we will get used to it. Tell me
about his ancestors, and where he was born.
All I know is his name.

AGAMEMNON To Asopos
a daughter was born, named Aigina.

CLYTEMNESTRA Who married her? A mortal, a god?

AGAMEMNON Zeus himself. And she bore him a son,   940
Aiakos, king of the island of Oinone.

CLYTEMNESTRA And which of his children succeeded him?

AGAMEMNON Peleus. He married one of the daughters
of Nereus, the sea-god.

CLYTEMNESTRA With her father's blessings, or did Peleus
take her in defiance of the gods?

AGAMEMNON Zeus made the betrothal, and gave her in marriage.
He has the authority.

CLYTEMNESTRA Where were they married?
Under the waves of the ocean?   950

AGAMEMNON At the foot of Pelion,
the sacred mountain where Cheiron lives.

CLYTEMNESTRA In the country where they say the centaurs live?

AGAMEMNON There all the gods came to the marriage of Peleus
and the wedding feast.

CLYTEMNESTRA And was it Thetis or his father Peleus
who brought Achilles up?

AGAMEMNON It was Cheiron,
to keep him from learning the evil ways of men.

CLYTEMNESTRA Wise teacher! And Peleus was wiser still,   960
sending the boy to him.

AGAMEMNON Such is the man who will be your daughter's husband.

CLYTEMNESTRA He sounds acceptable. Where in Greece is he from?

AGAMEMNON From Phthia, on the river Apidanos.

CLYTEMNESTRA And that is where he will take our daughter?

AGAMEMNON That is for him to decide.

CLYTEMNESTRA May it be a happy marriage!
When will it take place?

AGAMEMNON At the full moon.
That is the most propitious time.   970

CLYTEMNESTRA Have you made our daughter's
sacrifice to the goddess?

AGAMEMNON I will. We had just come to that.

CLYTEMNESTRA And afterwards you will have the marriage feast?

AGAMEMNON   When I have offered the gods
            the sacrifice they require of me.

CLYTEMNESTRA   And where shall I prepare the women's banquet?

AGAMEMNON   Here. By the high sterns of the ships from Argos.

CLYTEMNESTRA   Here? Well, there is no choice. I hope
               good fortune comes of it.   980

AGAMEMNON   Do you know what you should do?
            Please do it.

CLYTEMNESTRA   What do you want? You know I'm not in the habit
               of disobeying you.

AGAMEMNON   Then here, in the presence of the bridegroom,
            we men will—

CLYTEMNESTRA   You? Will I not be there
               for the things a bride's mother must do?

AGAMEMNON   I will give away your child. The army and I.

CLYTEMNESTRA   And where will I be when that happens?   990

AGAMEMNON   In Argos, taking care of your daughters.

CLYTEMNESTRA   Leaving my child here? And who
               will raise the bridal torch?

AGAMEMNON   I will provide the light, all the light
            proper for the bridal pair.

CLYTEMNESTRA   That is wrong, wrong. And such things are important.

AGAMEMNON   It is not right for you to stay here
            jostling among the soldiers.

328

CLYTEMNESTRA It is right that I should give
my children in marriage. I am their mother. 1000

AGAMEMNON It is not right for our daughters at home
to be left alone.

CLYTEMNESTRA They are well looked after,
safe in their part of the palace.

AGAMEMNON Please do it.

CLYTEMNESTRA No, by the goddess who reigns in Argos.
You see to the things outside
that concern you. I'll go in
and see to the preparations for my daughter's wedding.

She goes in at the left-hand door.

AGAMEMNON Oh, it was no use. I tried but I failed 1010
to send my wife out of my sight.
I contrive plots, I lay plans to deceive
those dearest to me
and it all comes to nothing.
Now I must arrange with Kalchas, who performs
our sacrifices,
the thing which the goddess demands
and I hate the thought of.
I owe it to Greece.
A wise man supports in his house 1020
a good and faithful wife. Or no wife at all.

He goes off left.

CHORUS Now they will sail
to Simois where the waters spin silver,
the Greeks in pride of numbers,
of ships, of weapons. They will come
to Ilion, to the plains below Troy
shining in the blessing of Apollo,

where Kassandra, they say, flings
like sunlight the blonde falls of her hair
from under the green laurel when the god   1030
grips her and she shakes
and sees what is to come.
At Troy on the ramparts, on the circling
walls, drawn up,
the Trojans will be waiting
as Ares in his bronze battle gear
comes nearer with the falling oars,
the hanging prows riffling the estuary mouths
of Simoïs. What he will want
is Helen, the sister   1040
of the twin sons of Zeus, the Dioskouroi,
who are stars in heaven.
To possess her again out of Priam's kingdom,
the prize
of the Achaians' spears, shields, labors in battle,
and bring her once more into Greece.
The god will girdle with slaughter
the stone-cased stronghold
of Pergamos, the Phrygians' city. He will see
Priam's head hewn from its shoulders   1050
and every house in Troy
smashed and rummaged. Then what a crying
from the girls and from Priam's queen.
And Helen herself, the daughter of Zeus,
will taste tears for the day she left her husband.
Oh may such anguish never befall us,
women of Chalkis, nor our children's children,
as shall then work through the Lydian women
for all their gold,
and through the wives of Phrygia so that they   1060
stand by the looms saying, "Who now
will wrap his wrist in my swaying hair and uproot me
out of my ruined home,
dragging me through my tears?
It is all thanks to you, daughter

of the swan with the sinuous neck, whose wings
hid Zeus from Leda,
if that is true.
It is still you
even if that is no more than a story   1070
out of the books of the Muses,
with no meaning."

Enter ACHILLES *left, unarmed and dressed with ostenta-*
tious simplicity. He looks about twenty-five years old.

ACHILLES Where is the commander of the Achaians?
Will one of his servants tell him that Peleus' son
Achilles is standing at his door?
It is not the same for all of us
having to wait here
by the straits. Some of us,
who have no wives, sit here by the shore, having left
empty houses at home. Others, who are married,   1080
still have no children.
Such is the frenzy that has seized Greece
for this war,
not without the consent of the gods.
With things at this pass, let me say,
what is due to me. Anyone else who wants to
may speak in his own behalf. I came away
from Pharsalia, I left Peleus,
to be kept waiting for
a wind, beside the straits,   1090
trying to keep my men quiet, my Myrmidons:
day after day they come up to me and say, "Achilles,
what is keeping us here? How much more
time must we waste on this expedition to Troy?
Do what you came here to do
or else lead the army home.
Don't wait for the sons of Atreus."

CLYTEMNESTRA *enters from the left-hand door.*

CLYTEMNESTRA Son of the Nereïd, I heard your voice
                          and came out to greet you.

ACHILLES Oh sacred modesty, who   1100
                   is this beautiful woman?

CLYTEMNESTRA You could hardly expect to recognize me
                          since you never saw me before,
                          but your regard for modesty is commendable.

ACHILLES Who are you? And why have you come
                   to the camp of the Greek army,
                   you a woman, here among the shields?

CLYTEMNESTRA I am the daughter of Leda,
                          Clytemnestra. Agamemnon is my husband.

ACHILLES Brief and to the point.   1110
                   But it is not seemly for me
                   to be seen talking with women.

                                                      He starts to go off left.

CLYTEMNESTRA Wait. Why do you run away? (*following him*)
                          Give me your right hand—here is mine:
                          a happy beginning to this betrothal of ours!

ACHILLES (*turns politely, then recoils in horror*) Do you know
                                  what you are saying? Touch
                   your hand? How could I face Agamemnon
                   if I touch what heaven forbids me to touch?

CLYTEMNESTRA Why do you say heaven forbids it,
                          son of Thetis the sea-nymph,   1120
                          when you are about to marry my daughter?

ACHILLES Marry? Lady, what do you mean?
                   I am left with no answer. Has some delusion
                   led your mind astray?

332

CLYTEMNESTRA I know it is natural
for men to be shy, faced with new kin
and the talk of marriage.

ACHILLES Lady, I have never courted your daughter,
and the sons of Atreus have not spoken
one word to me about marriage. 1130

CLYTEMNESTRA What does this mean?
Indeed my words must be as shocking to you
as your words are shocking to me.

ACHILLES We must both find the explanation. There must be
some truth under what we both said.

CLYTEMNESTRA I have been deceived. It seems
I have been preparing a marriage
that exists only in my mind.
I am filled with shame.

ACHILLES Perhaps someone is amusing himself 1140
with both of us.
Ignore it. It doesn't matter.

CLYTEMNESTRA I will take my leave. I am humiliated.
I have been made to lie.
I can no longer look you in the face.

She starts to go in at the left-hand door.

ACHILLES Lady, good-bye. I shall go in
to see your husband.

*He starts to go in at the main entrance, then pauses as he
hears the* OLD MAN *call through the right-hand door.*
CLYTEMNESTRA *pauses also.*

OLD MAN (*off*) Wait, stranger! Grandson of Aiakos,
son of the goddess, you
I'm calling, and you, daughter of Leda. 1150

ACHILLES Who is that, shouting through the doorway?
How shaken he sounds!

OLD MAN I am a slave. That's the truth, why not say it?
Fate has given me no choice.

ACHILLES Whose slave? Not mine, certainly, here
among Agamemnon's possessions.

OLD MAN That lady's, in front of the tent.
I was given to her by Tyndareos, her father.

ACHILLES Well, here I am. Why did you want me to stay?

OLD MAN Is there no one else here   1160
besides you and her?

ACHILLES We are alone. Come out from the king's tent. Speak.

OLD MAN What I most feared has come to pass. Oh destiny,
(*entering*) spare those I pray for!

ACHILLES Your words sound ominous,
and the message, it seems, is important.

CLYTEMNESTRA Don't wait to kiss my hand. What did you want to
tell me?

OLD MAN You know me, lady. You know my
devotion to you and your children.

CLYTEMNESTRA I know you've been a servant in the palace   1170
for a long time.

OLD MAN I came to King Agamemnon
as part of your dowry.

CLYTEMNESTRA Yes, you came with us to Argos
and you've always belonged to me.

334

OLD MAN I have. And I put your interests
　　　　　ahead of your husband's.

CLYTEMNESTRA Now tell us. What is your secret?

OLD MAN Your daughter. Her father
　　　　　is going to kill her.   1180
　　　　　With his own hand.

CLYTEMNESTRA What? I spit against what you say, old man!
　　　　　　　You're out of your senses!

OLD MAN He will plunge a blade into her white throat.

CLYTEMNESTRA Oh, torment! Has he gone mad?

OLD MAN No, he is sane about everything except you
　　　　　and your child. There he's lost his reason.

CLYTEMNESTRA Why? What demon could prompt him to such a
　　　　　　　　　　　　　　　　　　　　　　　　　thing?

OLD MAN The oracle. According to Kalchas. Saying
　　　　　what must happen before the fleet can sail.   1190

CLYTEMNESTRA What horror is coming to me, and the child
　　　　　　　whose father will kill her! Sail where?

OLD MAN To the country of Dardanos, for Menelaos
　　　　　to bring back Helen.

CLYTEMNESTRA So the fates have woven Iphigeneia's death
　　　　　　　into Helen's homecoming?

OLD MAN Now you know it all. He intends
　　　　　to sacrifice your daughter to Artemis.

CLYTEMNESTRA And the talk of marriage, which brought me here?

335

OLD MAN   The king knew you would bring her, and gladly,   1200
          to marry Achilles.

CLYTEMNESTRA   Oh daughter, you have come here
               to your death, and your mother with you.

OLD MAN   The child's fate is terrible. So is yours.
          It is a monstrous decision, Agamemnon's.

CLYTEMNESTRA   I am helpless. I am lost. Whatever I do
               the tears come.

OLD MAN   If losing a child is painful, you have
          reason for tears.

CLYTEMNESTRA   But where did you learn all this, old man?   1210
               How did it come to your ears?

OLD MAN   I was sent to you with a second letter
          about the first one.

CLYTEMNESTRA   Telling me again to bring the girl here
               to die, or warning me not to?

OLD MAN   Warning you not to. At that moment
          your husband was in his right mind.

CLYTEMNESTRA   If you had such a letter for me
               why was it not delivered?

OLD MAN   Menelaos took it from me.   1220
          All your troubles come from him.

CLYTEMNESTRA   Son of Thetis and Peleus,
               have you heard this?

ACHILLES   I have heard the cause of your grief,
           and I do not take lightly
           the way I have been involved in the matter.

CLYTEMNESTRA They are going to kill my child.
They tricked her with this talk of marrying you.

ACHILLES I, too, blame Agamemnon,
and not only for the reasons you speak of.   1230

CLYTEMNESTRA (*dropping to her knees and embracing* ACHILLES' *legs*)
Son of a goddess, I, a mortal,
am not ashamed to clasp your knees. What good
would pride do me now? What matters more to me
than my daughter's life?
Son of a goddess, save us: me
in my wretchedness,
and Iphigeneia, who they said was your betrothed,
even though it was not true.
I myself put the bridal wreath on her head for you,
I brought her here to be married,   1240
and now I am leading her to her death.
You will be blamed if you do nothing to defend her.

She rises, puts her left hand to ACHILLES' *cheek and takes
his right hand in her own.*

Even though you were never married to her
you were called her husband.
I implore you by your beard, by your right hand,
by your own mother. Your name, Achilles,
destroyed me; now you must clear it.

Kneels and takes his knees again.

There is no altar where I can take refuge,
none except your knees.
No friend smiles on me here. You have heard   1250
of Agamemnon's raw heartlessness.
Nothing is sacred to him.
And I am a woman, come
into a camp of sailors, hard to control

and ripe for any crime—though they can be
useful enough when they want to be.
If you can bring yourself to stretch out
your hand over me, we are saved.
If not, we are lost.

CHORUS   Giving birth is a mystery. It casts   1260
          a powerful spell over mothers. All, all of them
          without exception
          will risk any suffering
          for the sake of one of their children.

ACHILLES Pride rises up in me
          and draws me on. But I have learned
          to curb my grief in adversity, and my joy
          in triumph.
          Mortals who have learned this
          can hope to live by reason. There are moments   1270
          when it is good not to be too wise,
          but there are times, too, when taking thought is useful.
          I was brought up in the house of Cheiron,
          the most righteous of men,
          and he taught me to act from a simple heart.
          If the commands of the sons of Atreus
          are just, I will obey them. If not,
          I will refuse. But whether here
          or in Troy, I will remain free,
          and in my fighting will bring credit on the war god   1280
          with my whole strength. As for you,
          you have been treated cruelly
          by those closest to you,
          and as far as is proper for me, I shall extend
          my pity to cover you. Never shall your daughter,
          who has been called my betrothed,
          be slaughtered by her father. He shall not use
          me in his manipulations.
          That way my name would be her butcher
          as surely as if it had drawn the sword.   1290

Your husband is the cause of this, but my own
body would be defiled
if through me that girl were to die,
horribly, brutally used, as she
has been. It fills me with rage
to think how she has been treated. I would be
the lowest of the Argives, a nothing,
and Menelaos a hero,
I would be no son of Peleus, but some
demon's offspring, if I   1300
let my name do your husband's killing for him.
I swear by Nereus, whom the waves cradled, father
of Thetis who gave me birth,
King Agamemnon shall not touch your daughter
nor so much as graze her gown
with his finger-tips,
or that barbarous settlement in Lydia,
Sipylos, where his sires
first saw the light,
is a Grecian city,   1310
and no one has heard of Phthia.
This Kalchas, their prophet, will find
a bitter taste in the barley
and the lustral water before that sacrifice.
What is a prophet? Someone
who utters one truth in a flock of lies,
if he's lucky, and if he's not
everybody forgets.
I'm not saying this to earn a bride.
There are thousands I could marry.   1320
But I will not suffer this insult from King Agamemnon.
He should have asked my permission
if he wanted to use me to lure the girl here
into his snare,
since it was to see her married to me
that Clytemnestra would have brought her most will-
                                                      ingly.
I would have lent the use of my name

339

to the Greeks,
so that the ships could sail to Ilion.
I am here with the others. It is the same war.   1330
I would not have refused to help.
But I have been treated by these commanders
as though I were nobody. They accord me their
honor or they ignore me as they please.
My sword may decide that. Blood will color it
before we sail to Phrygia
if anyone thinks to take your daughter from me.
Be calm. In your time of danger, suddenly
I appeared to you as if I were some great god.
I am not. But to save the girl,   1340
I will be.

CHORUS   Son of Peleus, what you have said is worthy
of you, worthy of the proud sea-goddess
and her son.

CLYTEMNESTRA   How can I find the right praise,
neither cloying with flattery, nor so meager
that it offends you? Men of worth
have a way of hating those who praise them too much.
I am ashamed to enlarge on my sufferings.
They are mine, they do not concern you. Still,   1350
even if their afflictions are not his, a good man
may help those in trouble. Take pity on us.
Our plight deserves it. First I thought
you would be my son—an empty hope, as I learned.
Now my child is threatened with death:
a bad augury for your marriage one day,
unless you take steps to protect yourself.
But why do I urge you? From beginning to end
you have spoken nobly. My child
will be saved, if you can save her. Would it please you   1360
if she came and embraced your knees as a suppliant?
True, it is not seemly for a girl to do so,
but if you wished she would come

with dignity, and eyes cast down. And yet
if my supplication alone
can move you
I would rather she were not called.
She is over-timid, perhaps. But all forms
of modesty
are worth respecting.   1370

ACHILLES Do not bring your daughter
here for me to see. Why should we incur
the comments of the ignorant?
An army crowded together, loosed from work at home,
will gossip and spread foul stories.
Whether you supplicate me or not, you come
to the same end. For me
the one thing of importance
is to save you from disaster.
And this you may count on: I never lie.   1380
May I die if I deceive you. And live
only if she does.

CLYTEMNESTRA May you be blessed all your days
for helping those who are unhappy.

ACHILLES We must lay plans. Listen.

CLYTEMNESTRA Go on. I need no urging to listen to you.

ACHILLES Let us try to make her father see reason.

CLYTEMNESTRA He is too cowardly. He is afraid of the army.

ACHILLES Arguments can beat down arguments.

CLYTEMNESTRA A cold hope. But what do you want me to do?   1390

ACHILLES First, plead with him not to kill his daughter.
If he refuses you, then you can come to me,

but you may persuade him
by yourself.
Then there would be no need for my help.
You are safe, in any case. And there would be
no breach, then, in my friendship with Agamemnon,
no cause for the army to reproach me,
no weapon used to bring it about,
only reason. So it would turn out well for you   1400
and those dear to you
and I would not be forced to act.

CLYTEMNESTRA How wise you are! I will do as you say. But suppose
                        something goes wrong: where
                        and how will I see you again?
                        Shall I come, in my misery, searching
                        for your hand to rescue us?

ACHILLES I will be watching, in the right place.
                You will not have to be stared at
                hunting through the troops to find me. Do nothing   1410
                that would disgrace your fathers.
                Tyndareos should not suffer shame.
                He was a great man in Greece.

CLYTEMNESTRA You are right. Lead me. I ask only
                        to be your slave.
                        If there are gods the gods will reward your goodness.
                        If there are none what does anything matter?

                        CLYTEMNESTRA *goes in at the left door, the* OLD MAN
                                        at the right. ACHILLES *goes off left.*

CHORUS Oh what a sound of Libyan flutes,
                of lyres leading the dance, of reeling
                reeds raised the marriage hymn   1420
                on Pelion, when the Muses
                came robed in their bright hair to the banquet
                with the gods, and their gold

sandals stamped the ground
on the way to the marriage of Peleus,
and their voices
carried over the centaurs' slopes, and through
the woods of Pelion, praise
of Thetis and Aiakos' son.
There Dardanos' child,   1430
Trojan Ganymede, the darling of Zeus, poured out
mixed wine from the deep bowls of gold,
and in celebration the fifty
daughters of Nereus turned
their braided dance on the white sand
of the shore.
And the centaurs came
riding, with pine spears and crowned with leaves,
to the feast of the gods, and the bowl
that Bakchos filled, and they cried, "Daughter   1440
of Nereus, great
is the son you will bear:
a light and a splendor to Thessaly,
as Cheiron, who knows
the oracles of Apollo, foretells,
saying that your child will sail with an army
of Myrmidons, and their spears, to the land of Troy
to burn King Priam's glorious city,
his limbs traced
in gold armor wrought for him   1450
by the god Hephaistos,
the gift of his mother Thetis, the sea-goddess."
So the gods celebrated the marriage of Peleus
and the first-born of the Nereids.
But you, Iphigeneia, on your
lovely hair the Argives will set
a wreath, as on the brows
of a spotted heifer, led down
from caves in the mountains
to the sacrifice,   1460
and the knife will open the throat

and let the blood of a girl.
And you were not
brought up to the sound of the shepherd's pipe
and the cries of the herdsmen,
but nurtured by your mother
to be a bride for one of great Inachos' sons.
Oh where is the noble face
of modesty, or the strength of virtue, now
that blasphemy is in power   1470
and men have put justice
behind them, and there is no law but lawlessness,
and none join in fear of the gods?

CLYTEMNESTRA *enters from the left-hand door.*

CLYTEMNESTRA I have come out looking for my husband.
He has been away from here for some time. My
                                                  daughter,
poor child, has learned
of the death her father plans for her.
One minute she is shaken with sobbing
and the next the tears
flow almost in silence.   1480
But it was Agamemnon I named: here he is.
He will soon stand convicted
of planning a crime against his own child.

AGAMEMNON *enters left, alone.*

AGAMEMNON Daughter of Leda, I am glad
that we meet out here,
for I must speak to you now of things that a bride
should not hear.

CLYTEMNESTRA It's a good moment for that.

AGAMEMNON Call the child out to her father.
The libations are ready, and the barley grains   1490

ready to be thrown into the purifying flame,
and the calves that must loose
to Artemis their dark blood
to bless the marriage.

CLYTEMNESTRA You find innocent words to describe it
but there are no words
for what you have decided. (*She calls in at the left
door.*) Come, child.
You know what your father means to do.
Wrap the baby Orestes
in your robe and bring him with you.   1500

IPHIGENEIA *enters from the left door, carrying* ORESTES.
With her free hand she covers her face with her robe.
CLYTEMNESTRA, *too, keeps her face turned from*
AGAMEMNON.

Here she is, obedient to your command.
For the rest,
I will answer for us both.

AGAMEMNON Why are you crying, child? Aren't you still happy
to see me? Why are you holding your robe
in front of your eyes,
with your face turned to the ground?

CLYTEMNESTRA I cannot think where
to start my bitter story,
for its beginning is grief,   1510
its middle is grief,
its end
is grief.

AGAMEMNON What is it? Why are all three of you
afraid to look at me?

CLYTEMNESTRA My husband,

find the honesty of a man
and answer me with it.

AGAMEMNON There is no need for you to speak that way.
Ask me your question.   1520

CLYTEMNESTRA Do you intend to kill your daughter?

AGAMEMNON What a horrible thing to ask! What a vile suspicion!

CLYTEMNESTRA Simply answer the question.

AGAMEMNON Any reasonable question I would answer.

CLYTEMNESTRA This question. This is the only one I care about.

AGAMEMNON Oh immovable law of heaven! Oh my
anguish, my relentless fate!

CLYTEMNESTRA Yours? Mine. Hers. No relenting for any of us.

AGAMEMNON How have you been wronged?

CLYTEMNESTRA How can you ask? What a question   1530
for a man of sense!

AGAMEMNON (to himself) I am lost. Someone has betrayed me.

CLYTEMNESTRA I know the whole story. I have found out
what you mean to do to me.
Your silence itself is a confession.
So is your sighing. No need to waste words.

AGAMEMNON Then I will say nothing. What good would it do
to lie, and add shamelessness to my troubles?

CLYTEMNESTRA Listen to me, then. I will use plain words, and not
talk in riddles. In the first place   1540

you took me by force, you married me
against my will.
You killed the husband I had, Tantalos.
You ripped from my breast
my baby, still
living, you smashed it on the ground.
Then when my brothers, the sons
of Zeus, on their shining horses,
bore down on you bringing war,
you came on your knees to my old father   1550
Tyndareos, and he saved you.
So you got me for your wife, again.
I came to love you. Admit
that as your wife I have deserved no reproach.
My demands in love have been modest. I have done
what I could to increase your house
so that you would be glad to come home, and you
                                           went out
proud and at peace. It is not often
that a man acquires a good wife.
There is no end of the other kind. And I bore you   1560
this son, and three daughters, and now
you have the cruelty
to take one of these from me.
And if anyone asks you
why you intend to kill her, what will you say?
Shall I answer for you? So that Menelaos
can have Helen back. Strange
bargain: you'll pay your child's life
as the price of a worthless woman.
We'll buy back our own harm   1570
with what is most dear to us.
Now I want you to think of this. You'll sail
to the war, and I'll be left in the house.
You may be gone for years. There I'll be.
And with what heart, do you imagine, I will pass
my days in those halls, finding
all her places empty,

347

her girl's room empty of her forever, and
finding myself alone
with nothing but my tears and the endless   1580
grieving at her fate: "My child,
it was your own father who killed you.
No one else. That was his hand,
no one else's. That was his reward for love.
And after that, he will come home again."
Then almost any occasion
would serve, for my other children and me
to give you the welcome you will have earned.
In the name of the gods, don't force me to turn
against you. Don't wrong me yourself.   1590
As you kill our child what prayers will you be saying?
What blessing can you ask
as you have cut her throat? A bad voyage home,
since your setting out was the consequence of a crime?
And in justice, could I give you my blessing?
We would have to think the gods had no minds,
to pray for murderers.
And when you come back to Argos
will you kiss your children? It will be forbidden
by the gods. And which of the children   1600
will dare even to look at you? They will be afraid
that you will kiss them only to kill them.
Did any of that ever cross your mind? Or do you
think of nothing but waving scepters
and leading armies? Would it not have been fair
to say to the Achaians, "Men of Argos,
you want to sail to Troy. Draw lots. Let us see
whose daughter will die." That way would have had
its justice. There is none
in your offering up your daughter   1610
as a victim for the army. Or let Menelaos,
to whom it matters most, after all, cut his own
daughter's throat: Hermione's, for the sake
of her mother. But it is my own child
who is to be torn from me, when I have been

faithful to you,
while she who dishonored her husband's bed will find
her daughter safe at home, in Sparta,
and be happy. Now answer me,
tell me if one thing I've said is not true.   1620
But if there is justice and truth
in what I say, do not kill your daughter and mine.
Turn back, be wise.

CHORUS   Do as she asks, Agamemnon.
It is good when people help each other,
to save children. Who can deny that?

IPHIGENEIA *hands* ORESTES *to her mother, then kneels*
and clasps AGAMEMNON'S *knees.*

IPHIGENEIA   If I had the tongue of Orpheus, Father, whose song
could charm stones so that they followed after him,
if my words could persuade
whoever I wished to whatever I wished, I would use   1630
all my arts now. But all that I know how to do
at this moment is cry. I offer you my tears.
I press against your knees
like a suppliant's torn branch, my body
which my mother bore you. Do not send me
into death before my time. It is sweet to see
the light. Do not make me look
at what is under the earth.
I was the first who called you father, the first
you called your child,   1640
the first to climb on your knees, and we
held each other, we loved each other. You said,
"Will I see you living in your husband's house,
enjoying the happiness that is my daughter's right?"
And I answered, touching your beard, as I do now—
but now as the gesture
of a suppliant—, "And what will I do for you
then, Father? When you are old

349

will you come to live with me,
and let me nurse your age, in return   1650
for what you have done for me?"
I remember what we said, but you have forgotten.
And now you want to kill me. Oh, in the name
of Pelops, of your father
Atreus, of my mother, suffering here
again as at my birth, do not let it happen.
What have I to do with Paris
and Helen, and what they have done?
Why should Paris' coming to Argos mean that I
must die? Look at me. In my eyes. Kiss me,   1660
so that at least I may remember that
when I am dying,
if you will not listen to what I say.

AGAMEMNON *and* IPHIGENEIA *kiss. As she speaks the follow-*
ing lines, IPHIGENEIA *takes* ORESTES *from* CLYTEMNESTRA
and holds him up to AGAMEMNON.

My brother, you are so small
to have to help your friends. But cry
with me, cry to your father, beg him
not to kill your sister. See,
even babies sense the dread of evil to come.
Even without being able to speak, he cries to you,
begging. Take pity on me.   1670
Respect your daughter's life. Both of us,
your own blood, touch your beard,
imploring you: a baby,
a grown girl. In three words I can say it all:
the sweetest thing
we ever see is this daylight. Under the ground
there is nothing.
Only the mad choose to be dead. The meanest life
is better than the most glorious death.

She hands ORESTES *to* CLYTEMNESTRA.

CHORUS Oh reckless Helen, now from you 1680
and your marriage
a deadly struggle begins
between the sons of Atreus and their children.

AGAMEMNON I know when pity is due, and when it is not.
I love my children. Only the mad do not.
Wife, it is terrible to me
to bring myself to do this,
and terrible if I do not.
For I am forced to do it. (*to* IPHIGENEIA) Look: how
many ships,
the war fleet, assembled here, the proud men of Greece 1690
and their bronze battle-gear, and they
cannot sail to the towers
of Ilion, and seize
the famous citadel, Troy,
according to Kalchas the prophet, unless I
sacrifice you.
Some strange Aphrodite has crazed
the whole Greek army with a passion to sail at once
to the barbarians' own country
and end this piracy of Greek marriage. 1700
If I disobey the goddess, if I ignore
the oracle, then the army will sail to Argos,
they will kill you and me, and your sisters
who are still at home. I have not become
Menelaos' creature. I am not guided by him.
It is *Greece* that compels me
to sacrifice you, whatever I wish.
We are in stronger hands than our own.
Greece must be free
if you and I can make her so. Being Greeks, 1710
we must not be subject to barbarians,
we must not let them carry off our wives.

He goes off left.

351

CLYTEMNESTRA Oh strangers, oh my daughter, now I see
              your death! Your father is running away from you,
              after giving you up to Hades.

IPHIGENEIA   Oh mother, how can I bear it?
              The same lamenting song
              falls to us both, our fate.
              I must say good-bye to the light. I will not
              see the sun anymore. Oh unlucky   1720
              valley of Phrygia, filled with snow,
              oh high slopes of Ida where Priam
              once left a baby, torn from its mother,
              to die: Paris, his own child, known
              in time as the son of Ida,
              Paris of Ida,
              among the Phrygians. If only the herdsman
              had not brought him up with the flocks,
              not reared him, Paris, Alexander,
              to watch his flock by the clear   1730
              springs where the nymphs rise,
              and the rich pastures starred
              with roses and hyacinths
              for the goddesses to gather.
              It was there that Pallas came,
              and seductive Cypris, and Hera, and with them
              Hermes, the gods' messenger:
              Cypris proud of the desires she wakens,
              Pallas proud of her spear,
              Hera proud of the bed of Zeus,   1740
              came for the fatal judgment, vying in beauty,
              whose issue is my death,
              oh my friends,
              whatever glory it brings to the Argives.
              For I am to be the first sacrifice
              to Artemis for the passage to Ilion.
              And he who begot me has betrayed me and left me,
              and I curse in my despair,
              I curse the day that ever I saw you, Helen,   1750

352

for I am to be murdered, I am to fall
to my ungodly father's
ungodly knife. Oh if only
Aulis had never opened
her folded bay to the bronze-beaked galleys,
the fir keels that will ferry them to Troy,
or the breath of Zeus had not blown fair up the current
of Euripos. Sweetly he blows
on this man's sails and on that man's, making those
men

happy. To others he brings   1760
bad luck, bitter compulsion.
Some can set out on voyages, and some
can make port. Others must wait. Truly
we are creatures
of labor and suffering, and nothing for long.
Labor and suffering,
and the plain sight
of our destiny is the cruelest thing of all.

CHORUS Oh daughter of Tyndareos, what anguish,
what bitter sorrows   1770
you have called down on Greece!

(*to* IPHIGENEIA)

I pity you. You do not deserve your fate.

IPHIGENEIA (*looking offstage, left*) Mother, mother! I see men
coming.

CLYTEMNESTRA (*looking in the same direction*) Achilles, too, child,
the son of the goddess,
in whose name you were brought here.

IPHIGENEIA (*running to the left door and calling to the servants
inside*) Women, open the doors so that I can hide.

CLYTEMNESTRA Why, child?

IPHIGENEIA I would be ashamed to see him.

CLYTEMNESTRA Why?

IPHIGENEIA I am ashamed of my unlucky marriage.   1780

CLYTEMNESTRA There is no time now for delicacy. Stay here.
Do not be shy. We must do what we can.

> *Enter* ACHILLES *left, followed by attendants bearing his
> shield, spears, sword, breastplate, greaves, and helmet.*

ACHILLES Unhappy daughter of Leda.

CLYTEMNESTRA Unhappy is what I am.

> *Noise of shouting offstage.*

ACHILLES The Argives are shouting.
They want a terrible thing.

CLYTEMNESTRA What are they shouting?

ACHILLES About your daughter.

CLYTEMNESTRA Your words have an unhappy beginning.

ACHILLES They say she must be sacrificed.   1790

CLYTEMNESTRA And will no one speak against them?

ACHILLES They shouted about me, too.

CLYTEMNESTRA What did they say?

ACHILLES "Stone him to death!"

CLYTEMNESTRA For trying to save my daughter?

ACHILLES For that.

CLYTEMNESTRA Who would have dared
to raise a hand against you?

ACHILLES Every Greek there.

CLYTEMNESTRA But your own army of Myrmidons,   1800
surely they took your side?

ACHILLES They were the first to threaten me.

CLYTEMNESTRA Oh my child, we are lost.

ACHILLES They said I was foolish about this marriage.

CLYTEMNESTRA What did you answer?

ACHILLES That they were not to kill my bride.

CLYTEMNESTRA Good.

ACHILLES Whom her father had promised to me.

CLYTEMNESTRA And brought here from Argos.

More shouting offstage, left.

ACHILLES Their voices drowned me out.   1810

CLYTEMNESTRA The mob. An infernal thing!

ACHILLES But I will defend you.

CLYTEMNESTRA You alone? Against the whole army?

ACHILLES *points to the armor-bearers.*

ACHILLES See. These men are carrying my armor.

CLYTEMNESTRA May heaven reward your courage.

ACHILLES Heaven will.

CLYTEMNESTRA And my daughter will not be sacrificed?

ACHILLES Not if I can stop it.

CLYTEMNESTRA Will they come here to take the girl?

ACHILLES Thousands of them,   1820
led by Odysseus.

CLYTEMNESTRA The son of Sisyphos?

ACHILLES That one.

CLYTEMNESTRA Did he offer to do it, or did the army choose him?

ACHILLES They chose him, but the choice pleased him.

CLYTEMNESTRA A vile choice: to be the accomplice
in a murder.

ACHILLES I will stop him.

CLYTEMNESTRA Is he going to drag her away against her will?

ACHILLES By her blonde hair.   1830

CLYTEMNESTRA And what should I do then?

ACHILLES Hold on to her.

CLYTEMNESTRA You mean that will stop them
from killing her?

ACHILLES That is what it will come to.

IPHIGENEIA Mother, both of you, listen to me.
I see now that you are wrong
to be angry with your husband.
It is hard to hold out against the inevitable.
The stranger deserves to be thanked   1840
for being willing to help us, but on no account
must we let the army be stirred up against him.
It would not help us, and he might come to harm.
Now mother, listen to the conclusion
that I have reached. I have made up my mind to die.
I want to come to it
with glory, I want to have thrown off
all weak and base thoughts. Mother,
look at it with my eyes,
and see how right I am.   1850
All the people, all the strength of Greece
have turned to me. All those ships,
whether they sail, whether Troy falls,
depend on me. I will be the one
to protect our women, in the future,
if ever the barbarians dare to come near.
When they have paid for the ruin
of Helen, whom Paris carried away,
they will never again be so bold as to ravish
well-born wives out of Greece.
All these good things I can win by dying.
Because of me, Greece   1860
will be free, and my name will be blessed there.
I must not cling to life too dearly.
You brought me into the world for the sake
of everyone in my country,
and not just for your own.
Thousands of men have slung shield on shoulder,
                                        thousands
have taken hold of the oars
when they saw their country wronged.   1870

And each of them will strike and, if need be, die
for Greece. And shall my one life
stand in the way of it all?
What justice would there be in that? What answer
could I make to those who are ready to die?
There is another thing. It would not
be right for this man
to join battle with the whole of the army
and die for the sake of a woman.
If it means that one man can see the sunlight   1880
what are the lives of thousands of women
in the balance? And if Artemis
demands the offering of my body,
I am a mortal: who am I
to oppose the goddess? It is not to be
considered. I give my life to Greece.
Take me, kill me,
and bring down Troy. That will be my monument
for ages to come. That will be my wedding,
my children, the meaning of my life.   1890
Mother, it is the Greeks
who must rule the barbarians,
not the barbarians the Greeks.
They are born to be slaves; we
to be free.

CHORUS   Young woman, what you have said is noble.
          It is the role of destiny, in this,
          and the role of the goddess,
          that are sick.

ACHILLES Daughter of Agamemnon, if I could win you   1900
          for my wife, it would prove that some god
          wanted to make me happy. I envy
          Greece because you are hers, and you
          because she is yours. What you have said
          is beautiful, and worthy
          of your country. You are no match

for the gods, and you have given up
the struggle against them. You have reconciled
what should be with what must be.
But as for me, the more clearly I see your spirit   1910
the more I long to have
so noble a woman for my bride. Look. I want
to save you. To take you home with me.
I call Thetis my mother to witness: now more
than anything it would grieve me
not to pit myself against all the Danaans
and save you.
Think. Death is awesome. Something terrible.

IPHIGENEIA   I say what I am about to say
with no regard for anyone.   1920
Tyndareos' daughter,
Helen, will bring on enough fighting, enough
death, for the sake of her body. As for you, stranger,
do not die for me,
and do not kill.
Let me save Greece if that is what I can do.

ACHILLES   Oh noble spirit! After that
what is there for me to say? You have chosen.
A splendor in your soul has led you—
why should a man not say it?   1930
But later you may think differently. I want you
to know how I keep my word. I will have these arms
lying by the altar, ready
not to join in your death but to prevent it.
Even when the knife is almost at your neck
it will not be too late to accept my offer.
Turn, and I will not let you die
because of a moment's recklessness.
I will go now to the goddess's temple, with these arms,
and wait there until you come.   1940

ACHILLES *goes off, left, followed by his armor-bearers.*

IPHIGENEIA You are silent. But the tears keep falling.
Mother, why these tears for me?

CLYTEMNESTRA I have reason enough, with this ache in my heart.

IPHIGENEIA No more of that. Do not take
my own courage from me.
Will you do one thing for me?

CLYTEMNESTRA Speak. How could I fail you in anything, child?

IPHIGENEIA Do not cut off a lock of your hair
as is done for the dead.
Put on no mourning for me.   1950

CLYTEMNESTRA What do you mean, child? I am losing you ...

IPHIGENEIA No. I am saved. My name will be your glory.

CLYTEMNESTRA I don't understand. I am not to mourn for you?

IPHIGENEIA No. I shall have no grave.

CLYTEMNESTRA What of that? It is not the grave we mourn,
but the dead.

IPHIGENEIA The altar of the goddess, the daughter of Zeus,
will be my grave. Tears are forbidden there.

CLYTEMNESTRA My daughter, what you say is true.
I will obey you.   1960

IPHIGENEIA For I am blessed by fortune. It was I
who could bring help to Greece.

CLYTEMNESTRA And what shall I say to your sisters?

IPHIGENEIA Do not dress them in mourning either.

CLYTEMNESTRA Have you some message of love to send them?

IPHIGENEIA Say good-bye to them for me. And bring up
Orestes to be a man
for my sake.

CLYTEMNESTRA (*holding* ORESTES *up to* IPHIGENEIA) Put your arms
around him
since you are looking at him for the last time.   1970

IPHIGENEIA (*hugging him*) Dear child, you did what you could
for those you love.

CLYTEMNESTRA Is there something I can do in Argos,
something that would give you pleasure?

IPHIGENEIA Don't hate my father. He is your husband.

CLYTEMNESTRA He will not like the course he must face because of you.

IPHIGENEIA He destroyed me for the sake of Greece
against his will.

CLYTEMNESTRA But he used lies,
low schemes unworthy of Atreus.

IPHIGENEIA Who will lead me to the place   1980
so that they don't need to touch my hair?

CLYTEMNESTRA I will go with you...

IPHIGENEIA (*interrupting*) No. That would not be right.

CLYTEMNESTRA ...holding on to your gown.

IPHIGENEIA Mother, listen to me. It is better for both of us
if you stay here. One of my father's
servants here can lead me to the meadow
where I am to be killed.

An attendant comes forward and takes IPHIGENEIA's
hand.

CLYTEMNESTRA My child, you are going...

IPHIGENEIA And I shall never come back.   1990

CLYTEMNESTRA Leaving your mother.

IPHIGENEIA As you see. Not because I deserve it.

CLYTEMNESTRA Wait. Do not leave me...

IPHIGENEIA Now there must be no tears.
And you, young women,
join in my hymn to Artemis the virgin,
and celebrate my fate.
Let silence
descend on the army of the Argives.
Let the basket be brought,   2000
light the fire of purification,
bring the barley. Father
must lead the procession around the altar.
I am coming bringing salvation for Greece,
and victory. Lead me.

The attendant begins to lead IPHIGENEIA *offstage left
while she sings her triumphant lament.*

I who will conquer Troy
and bring down the city of Ilion.
Set the wreath on my head.
Bring the purifying waters.
Around the temple of Artemis, around   2010
the altar of blessed Artemis,
in honor of the goddess begin
the dance. I will wash away
with my own blood the spell
that the oracle revealed.

CHORUS Oh noble and revered mother,
we may not shed our tears for you.
The gods are not worshipped that way.

IPHIGENEIA Young women, sing with me now
glory to Artemis the goddess   2020
whose temple faces Chalkis
where the ships wait, and
the passion for war is burning,
here in the narrows of Aulis,
because of me. Oh Pelasgia where I was born,
Mycenae,
home!

CHORUS Are you invoking the city of Perseus
which the Cyclopes built?

IPHIGENEIA You brought me up   2030
to be the light of Greece.
Dying, I can say it.

CHORUS Your glory will not die.

IPHIGENEIA Oh light that brings the day, splendor
of Zeus, I am going
from this world to another destiny,
another home. Good-bye
light that I love.

                    She goes out left, singing. CLYTEMNESTRA *carries*
                    ORESTES *inside the left door of the tent.*

CHORUS See, she is going. She who will conquer
Troy and bring down the city of Ilion.   2040
She leans her head for the victim's garland,
for the sacred water. She goes
to drench with her blood the altar
of the divine goddess,

to the sword that will cut
her lovely throat. Your father is waiting
with the pure libations, and the Achaians
are waiting to sail to Troy.
But let us raise our voices to Artemis, daughter
of Zeus, to ask   2050
for a happy destiny. Awesome goddess,
pleased by this human sacrifice, send now
to Phrygia, to the land of deceitful Troy,
the armies of Greece.
There let Agamemnon
wreathe the Achaian weapons with garlands
of victory, and himself win
a crown of unfading glory.

MESSENGER *(enters left and calls at the left door)* Daughter of
                    Tyndareos, Clytemnestra,
          come out and hear my message.   2060

CLYTEMNESTRA *(enters, carrying* ORESTES*)* I heard your voice.
                    Here I am,
          distraught, shaking with terror,
          for fear that you have brought some new disaster
          to add to the grief I have.

MESSENGER It is about your daughter. I have
          something miraculous to tell.

CLYTEMNESTRA Tell me, tell me at once.

MESSENGER Beloved mistress, you shall hear everything
          as it happened, from the beginning,
          unless the seething of my mind   2070
          confuses my words. When we had come to the grove
          sacred to the daughter of Zeus,
          and the flowered meadow of Artemis,
          leading your child
          to the place where the army

364

was ordered to assemble,
the Argives ran, all crowding to the spot.
And King Agamemnon, when he saw his daughter
coming through the grove to the place of sacrifice,
groaned aloud and turned his head, hiding   2080
his eyes and their tears with his robe.
But she came up to her father and said, "Father,
here I am. And I give my body
willingly as a sacrifice
for my country, for all of Greece.
Lead me to the altar
if this is what destiny has decreed.
For my part, I hope
it turns out well for all of you.
May the spoils of victory be yours,   2090
and then the sight of your homes again.
Let none of the Argives lay hands on me.
I will offer my neck in silence,
I will not flinch." That is what she said,
and everyone who heard marveled
at the girl's bravery and nobility.
Then the herald Talthybios, whose office it was,
called out from among them, to the army,
for the sacred silence,
and the prophet Kalchas drew from its sheath   2100
the whetted knife, and laid it
in the basket worked with gold,
and set the crown upon her head. And Peleus' son
took the basket and the lustral water
and circled the altar, calling out,
"Daughter of Zeus, who bring death
to the wild creatures, who turn
your gleaming star through the darkness, accept
this sacrifice offered to you by us, the army
of the Achaians, and King Agamemnon,   2110
this pure blood
from the throat of a beautiful girl. Now let our
war fleet embark on a smooth voyage

and our weapons bring down the walls of Troy."
Then the sons of Atreus and the whole army stood
with their eyes fixed on the ground, and the priest
took up the knife,
praying, and looked for the place
to plunge it. Pain welled up in me
at that, and I dropped my eyes.   2120
And the miracle happened. Everyone
distinctly heard the sound of the knife
striking, but no one could see
the girl. She had vanished.
The priest cried out, and the whole army
echoed him, seeing
what some god had sent, a thing
nobody could have prophesied. There it was,
we could see it, but we could scarcely
believe it: a deer   2130
lay there gasping, a large
beautiful animal, and its blood ran
streaming over the altar of the goddess.
Then Kalchas, with
such joy as you can imagine, shouted, "Commanders
of the assembled armies of Greece, look:
the goddess has placed this victim
on her altar, a deer from the mountains,
and she accepts this instead of the girl,
rather than stain her altar with noble blood.   2140
With this she is happy, and now she blesses
our voyage to attack Ilion.
Therefore let everyone who is to sail
take heart and go down to his ship,
for today we must leave the hollow gulf of Aulis,
and cross the Aegean Sea."
Then when Hephaistos' flame had left nothing
of the victim but ashes, he offered
the customary prayer for the army's safe return.
Agamemnon sent me to say this,   2150
to tell you of this

destiny which the gods have sent
and of the glory which he has won
among the Greeks. I saw it myself. I was there.
It is plain that your daughter
has been taken up into heaven.
Let this quiet your grief
and put an end to your anger against your husband.
No man living can tell what the gods will do,
but they save those whom they love.   2160
This same day has seen
your daughter dead and brought to life again.

CHORUS   With what joy for your sake
          I hear the messenger's words! Showing
          how the girl is alive in heaven with the gods.

CLYTEMNESTRA   Oh child, what deity has carried you off?
          How may I address you? How can I be sure,
          how can I know,
          that this is not all a lie, made up
          to silence my bitter grieving?   2170

CHORUS   Here comes King Agamemnon. He will tell you
          the same thing.

          AGAMEMNON *enters left, attended by generals, priests with
          the paraphernalia of sacrifice, soldiers, camp-followers,
          sailors, and others taking part in the expedition to
          Troy.*

AGAMEMNON   Lady, as for your daughter,
          we have reason to be happy. For truly
          she has the gods for company.
          Now you must take this young calf here
                    (*indicates* ORESTES)
          and travel home. The army is preparing to sail.
          Good-bye. My greetings will be slow
          in reaching you from Troy. May you be happy.

CHORUS Son of Atreus, sail   2180
        with a light heart to the land of Phrygia,
        and return with a light heart
        and heavy spoils
        from Troy.

        AGAMEMNON, *generals, etc., go off left, followed by the*
        CHORUS. CLYTEMNESTRA, *carrying* ORESTES, *goes in the*
        main door of the tent. She does not look back.

NOTES

1–204 / 1–163 *Prologue*

103 / 76 *stung by his fate . . .* Editors are wrong to be suspicious of Agamemnon's use of the word *morōi* to mean "fate" here rather than "death." Compare Homer, *Odyssey* 1.34, 35; Aeschylus *Agamemnon* 1146.

151 / 117 *Tell me the rest* Editors sometimes rearrange the order of the lines in the MSS. in order to make the Old Man's speech precede the entire letter; but this is incorrect, as Gilbert Murray saw. Even now that Agamemnon has admitted that to sacrifice Iphigeneia would be a horrible wrong, he is uncertain about his decision to send the letter and pauses while reading it.

190–91 / 152 *Mycenae / where the Cyclopes built the walls* In Euripides' day, as in modern times, the walls of Mycenae and Tiryns were remarkable for being built of huge boulders in the style of the long-past Mycenaean age. Such stonework was popularly ascribed to a race of giants, the one-eyed Cyclopes. Euripides repeatedly calls attention to this feature of Agamemnon's capital city (296 / 265, 717 / 534, 2029 / 1501), probably to suggest the fundamental cruelty and barbarism of the principles by which its people live. We will not be wrong to think of the savage Cyclopes of Homer's *Odyssey*. See note on 2028–29 / 1500–1501.

205–323 / 164–302 *Parodos* (Choral entry song) This choral song is suggestive of Homer's famous Catalogue of Ships, from which most of its names and many of its details are taken. The ostensible point is the splendor and magnitude of the host and the greatness of its undertaking. By his arrangement and selection of detail, however, Euripides exposes this effect to ironic contemplation.

369

208–10 / 168–70 *Chalkis ... where the spring / of Arethousa wells up and runs flashing / down to the sea* This somewhat gratuitous mention of Chalkis' fountain seems intended to remind an Athenian audience of the much more famous fountain of Arethousa on the island of Ortygia in the harbor of Syracuse. It was there that Athenian sea power some seven years previously had received the blow which caused Athens to lose the Peloponnesian War. The parallel between the Athenians' attempt on Syracuse and the Greeks' attempt on Troy is not to be missed.

235–37 / 192–94 *the two that are named Aias ... Oïleus' son and that son of Telamon / who is the hope of Salamis ...* Aias son of Oïleus at the sack of Troy raped Kassandra in Athene's temple. For this crime the goddess brought storm and shipwreck upon the Achaians on their homeward way and Aias himself was drowned.

Aias son of Telamon, the famous bearer of the seven-oxhide shield, also failed to return home. When the arms of Achilles, which had been offered as the prize for being the most effective fighter at Troy, were awarded to Odysseus rather than to Aias, he set out to kill the Greek generals in the night. Athene balked him of his revenge by driving him mad, so that he vented his rage on captured cattle instead. When he came to his senses he killed himself from disappointment and chagrin. The name Aias was associated by Sophocles and others with the cry of grief *aiai*.

238 / 194–95 *and with them Protesilaos ...* Protesilaos was the first Greek to set foot on the beach at Troy. He was instantly killed, "leaving behind," Homer says, "in Phylake his wife with nail-scored cheeks, and his house half-built." *Iliad* 2.698–702.

239 / 198–99 *Palamedes, child of Poseidon's son ...* In revenge for Odysseus' treacherous murder of Palamedes at Troy, Poseidon's son Nauplios set false beacons on the rocks of Euboia's Cape Kaphareus and wrecked many of the Greeks on their way home.

242 / 199 *Diomedes ...* In the fighting at Troy, Diomedes wounded both the goddess Aphrodite and the god Ares. Together with Odysseus he stole the statue of Athene from her temple inside the city. Although he survived the war, he returned home to find his wife unfaithful and his kingdom usurped. He ended his days in Italy after founding one or more cities there.

244 / 201–2 *scion of Ares ...* an honorific epithet for a warrior, rather than a genealogical statement.

258 / 217 *Eumelos, the grandson of Pheres* ... Eumelos' father Admetos had the honor of having Apollo for his herdsman when that god was expiating his murder of the Cyclopes. Naturally the horses here being driven by Eumelos turned out well, since Apollo raised them. There was a less happy result of Apollo's visit, however. In his gratitude for Admetos' kind treatment, Apollo tricked the Fates into allowing Admetos to survive his appointed death-day, provided he could get some one else to die in his place. As Euripides presents the story in his play *Alcestis*, Admetos was not slow to ask that either his father or his mother take his place in Hades' house. To his chagrin both refused him. He then applied to his wife, Alcestis, who proved more generous, but her consent turned out much worse than his parents' rebuff. After she died he realized that he would have done much better to die himself. As he puts it (*Alcestis* 937–40), "Sorrow will never come to her again. She died in glory, freed from all life's trouble. But I, who should not now be living, have missed my chance to die. I shall lead a life of misery. I see it now."

Partly from grief and partly because she had a right to ask these things, since she was giving her life for his, he swore to her on her deathbed that he would mourn for her perpetually and never take another woman into his house. This left him very little life at all, particularly since he had already disowned his parents for what he regarded as their selfish cruelty towards himself. At the end of the play his friend Herakles brings Alcestis back to him from the dead, but the grisly joke of it is that he makes him accept her *before* he knows who she is. In doing so Admetos breaks his promise to Alcestis on the same day that he made it, with the result that whatever respect he may still deserve from us after he has showed his willingness to let his wife die for him, lies in ruins. That he is not named here in the normal way as Eumelos' father suggests his disgrace. As alluded to here in our play, however lightly, the story of Admetos is obviously relevant both to Agamemnon's refusal to sacrifice himself for his daughter and to Iphigeneia's willingness to sacrifice herself for him, for Achilles, and for the rest of the Greeks.

279–80 / 248–49 *the son / of Theseus* ... It is not known whether Akamas or Demophon is meant. In Homer the leader of the Athenians is Menestheus, no relation to Theseus.

286–88 / 256–59 *Kadmos / holding a dragon of gold. Leitos, / born of the earth* ... Kadmos founded the Boiotian capital city of Thebes in the following manner: killing the dragon which guarded a spring on the city's site, he sowed its teeth in the earth. Armed men sprang up and, at the instigation of Kadmos, fought together. The five survivors became the founders of the leading families of Thebes. "Leïtos, born of the earth" is a member of one of these families. Since the father of the dragon was Ares, all five families were in a manner descended from the god of war, and strife was seldom absent from the early history of the city. Most notably, the unwitting crimes of Oedipūs were followed by the feud between his sons who, having first banished their father, killed one another in their insane contention for the throne. This occurred when one brother brought an Argive army against his own city in the expedition known as "the Seven Against Thebes."

290–91 / 263 *the son / of Oileus* ... Aias the Less, see note on 235–37 / 192–94.

324–729 / 303–542 *First episode*

350–52 / 321 *Do you think I am afraid / to look you in the eye, Menelaos? / I am a son of Atreus* By a plausible etymology "Atreus" may be taken to mean "The Unflinching."

531–32 / 411 *the same god / who drove you out of your senses* Aphrodite, see 481–86 / 385–87, 1084 / 809, 1697–1700 / 1264–66.

620–21 / 473–74 *Pelops, whom our father / called "Father"* ... Pelops, who gave his name to the Peloponnesos, was commonly thought of as the originator of the curse on the house of Atreus because of the violence and trickery with which he won his bride, Hippodameia. Her father, Oinomaos of Olympia, used to test her suitors' worthiness by letting them take her off with them in their chariots and then setting out in pursuit in his. When he caught them, as he invariably did, he speared the young man from behind. Pelops bribed Oinomaos' charioteer to pull out Oinomaos' linchpin and replace it with a wax dummy. Oinomaos was killed in the resulting wreck, whereupon Pelops, instead of paying off the charioteer, broke his oath and pushed him off a cliff into the sea. The trickiness of the Peloponnesian nobles is kept in view throughout the play (e.g. 85–86 / 66–67, 372–74 / 332, 620–25 / 473–76, 686 / 519, 1012–14 / 744–45, 1978–79 / 1457, 2053 / 1527 "deceitful Troy" after all this! 2167–69 / 1616–17, and see the note on 663 / 504).

658–59 / 503 *At every step I've tried to see / the right way to act* We have given Menelaos the benefit of the doubt here, but in Greek his words express an unmistakable ambiguity. They mean, "I have always cultivated the best people," just as clearly as they do what we have translated, and Menelaos has just pointed out that Agamemnon is a more valuable connection than Helen.

663 / 504 *Tantalos himself, the son of Zeus* ... The respect that the Chorus shows for the house of Tantalos creates great ironic tension. Tantalos tried to deceive the gods by serving them the flesh of his son Pelops at a banquet. The gods detected the ruse and restored Pelops to life. Altogether, the Atreïds had a bad record where their children were concerned. Pelops' son Atreus in anger at his brother Thyestes killed his own nephews and at a feast of pretended reconciliation fed them to their unsuspecting father. If the line of Tantalos is representative, the great families of Greece, so envied in this play, are families of monsters.

698–99 / 525 *There's no reason for Odysseus / to do anything to injure you or me* Odysseus' name is explained in the *Odyssey* as meaning "man of hostility," so that actually he is an injurer by nature.

730–798 / 543–606 *First stasimon*

767 / 576–77 *Phrygian pipes* ... Mount Ida was in Phrygia; hence Paris' music was composed in the Phrygian mode. Euripides' contemporaries considered "music," by which they meant both what we call music and the words set to it, to be half of education. It was thought to train the soul as "gymnastic" (the other half) trained the body. The Chorus implies that so much music in the Phrygian mode had corrupted Paris' character.

799–1021 / 607–750 *Second episode*

1006 / 739 *the goddess who reigns in Argos* Hera, queen of the Olympian divinities. Her temple near Mycenae was one of the oldest and most famous in Greece; in fact she was for the Argives what Athene was for the Athenians. As Zeus' consort she was in particular goddess of the rights of wives and mothers.

1020–21 / 749–50 *A wise man supports in his house / a good and faithful wife. Or no wife at all* Distaste for his task makes Agamemnon think of its ultimate cause. He holds that wives like Helen are not worth room and board.

1022- 72 / 751–800 *Second stasimon*

1041–42 / 768–69 *the Dioskouroi, / who are stars in heaven* They were identified with the constellation Gemini and brought safety to sailors at sea, often appearing as the static-electrical phenomenon known as St. Elmo's fire.

1050 / 777 *Priam's head hewn from its shoulders* ... In its present incomplete state the text does not tell us who it is that is beheaded, but compare Virgil *Aeneid* 2.554–58.

1066–67 / 793–96 *the swan with the sinuous neck, whose wings / hid Zeus from Leda* ... Zeus was said to have visited Leda in the form of a swan when he engendered Helen and the Dioskouroi.

1073–1417 / 801–1035 *Third episode*

1110 / 829 *Brief and to the point* The people of Laconia (Sparta) were notoriously "laconic."

1155–56 / 859 *Whose slave? Not mine, certainly, here / among Agamemnon's possessions* Ironic reference is made to Agamemnon's later appropriation of Achilles' slave-girl Briseïs, the cause of the "Wrath of Achilles" which became the subject of Homer's *Iliad*.

1418–73 /1036–97 *Third stasimon*

1474–2005 / 1098–1474 *Fourth episode* (including sung dialogue, 1714–72 / 1276–1335)

1501 / 1120 *Here she is, obedient to your command* Obedience was especially cultivated among the Spartans, with whom Agamemnon and Clytemnestra are associated. Compare **831 / 634, 983–84 / 726**, and the epitaph for the Spartan dead at Thermopylai. Euripides is treating Spartan virtue with irony.

1682–83 / 1254 *a deadly struggle begins / between the sons of Atreus and their children* ... Iphigeneia's resistance to being sacrificed by her father is a premonition of her father's death at Clytemnestra's hands, sacrificed, as Clytemnestra will say, to Iphigeneia's Fury. From this murder, in turn, will spring Orestes' murder of his mother.

1722–23 / 1284–85 *oh high slopes of Ida where Priam / once left a baby* ... Priam's queen Hecuba dreamed that she gave birth to a burning torch, and the soothsayers proclaimed that the child with which she was then pregnant would destroy his city. Priam exposed the baby on Mount Ida, but a bear found it and suckled it, and it lived to be brought up by shepherds. As it grew to manhood so great was the child's prowess that the shepherds called it Alexandros, which means "Protector." Alexandros soon found his way to the city of Troy, where he was recognized as Paris, the prince who had been exposed.

1833–34 / 1367 *You mean that will stop them / from killing her?* Reading a question mark at the end of 1367 in the Greek.

1923–25 / 1418–19 *As for you, stranger, / do not die for me, / and do not kill* ... As it turns out of course, Achilles will both kill and die because of Iphigeneia, for only if she is sacrificed can the war take place in which he will both kill many and be killed himself. Iphigeneia's allowing herself to be slaughtered will cost more lives than resistance would.

1966–68 / 1450 *And bring up / Orestes to be a man / for my sake* Orestes' "manhood" turned out to mean that he must kill his mother.

1979 / 1457 *low schemes unworthy of Atreus* It was Atreus who revenged himself on his brother Thyestes by murdering Thyestes' children. He then invited him to a banquet and served him his sons' flesh disguised as game. See note on 663 / 504.

1984 / 1460 *holding on to your gown* Clytemnestra earlier thought that she might save Iphigeneia's life by this gesture (1832–34 / 1367), and it certainly seems an appropriate one, whether or not it will do any good. Nevertheless, Clytemnestra now lets herself be dissuaded from it, as from those other actions of pathos and protest which are proposed but not performed: Iphigeneia's dramatic supplication of Achilles (1360–61 / 992), and Clytemnestra's passionate search for him through the camp (1406–7 / 1026–27).

2006–58 / 1475–1531 *Kommos* (lyric lament among actors and Chorus) in lieu of a final stasimon.

2006–7 / 1475–76 *I who will conquer Troy / and bring down the city of Ilion* These words, repeated at 2039–40 / 1510–11, allude unmistakably to the striking choral passage in Aeschylus' *Agamemnon* where it is suggested that Helen's name spells "death of ships, death of men, death of the city": *helenas, helandros, heleptolis* (689 / 520). Iphigeneia has tried to disassociate herself from Helen in every way (1919–26 / 1416–20), but by calling herself *heleptolis* here as she leaves the stage she makes us realize that by letting herself be sacrificed she has become as responsible as Helen is for the tragedy of the Trojan War. It is no exaggeration to say that she might better hang herself than incur responsibility for the sack of Troy. Like many another noble and devoted young person in similar circumstances, she has been duped by false patriotism, "and that," to paraphrase Aeschylus' Kassandra in another connection, "is far the saddest thing of all."

2028–29 / 1500–1501 *the city of Perseus / which the Cyclopes built...* By a plausible etymology, Perseus means "he who destroys." There is an obvious clash between this significance and Iphigeneia's belief, expressed three lines below, that the city of Perseus has brought her up to be "the light of

Greece." The savagery of the Cyclopes has been remarked in the note on **190–91 / 152.**

2059–184 / 1532–629 *Exodos*

2103–5 / 1568–69 *And Peleus' son / took the basket and the lustral water / and circled the altar...* Achilles performs the role we have been led to expect that Agamemnon will play (**563–66 / 435–36, 2002–3 / 1471–72, 2046–47 / 1517–18**). This is not a forger's clumsy inconsistency, but a masterstroke of irony. We recognize instantly that Achilles' interest in the glory to be won at Troy is even greater than Agamemnon's, and that he has never thought for a moment, in his confidence in the power of destiny in these matters, that he would have to keep his extravagant promises to save Iphigeneia's life (**1285ff. / 935ff., 1302ff. / 948ff., 1335ff. / 970ff., 1377ff. / 1003ff.**).

2108 / 1571 *your gleaming star...* The moon. Artemis, while not exactly the moon-goddess (Selene, whose name means simply "moon," is that), is often associated with it.

2147–48 / 1601–2 *nothing / of the victim but ashes...* It will be difficult for anyone to determine, after the fact, whether it was an animal or a girl that was sacrificed. Or so a bystander familiar with Pelopid and Spartan chicanery might conclude.

2167–70 / 1616–18 *How can I be sure... / that this is not all a lie, made up / to quiet my bitter grieving?* Clytemnestra never became sure. Every member of Euripides' audience knew how in her anger over Iphigeneia's death she murdered Agamemnon when he returned home from Troy, just as she predicted she would in our play (**1586–88 / 1180–82**).

2171–72 / 1619–20 *Here comes King Agamemnon. He will tell you / the same thing* The Chorus by now has come to recognize Agamemnon's way of doing things.

2176 / 1623 *this young calf here...* Agamemnon was prepared to treat Iphigeneia like a calf also. Compare **1455–67 / 1080–88, 1492–94 / 1113–14.**

2178–79 / 1625–26 *My greetings will be slow / in reaching you from Troy* This is probably an ironic allusion to the chain of beacons by which Clytemnestra arranged to hear of Agamemnon's victory, and therefore of his return, almost before he knew of it himself. In this way she had time to prepare his murder.

GLOSSARY

ACHAIANS: Collective name for the Greeks in epic and drama.

ACHILLES: Son of Peleus and Thetis, the greatest Greek warrior at
            Troy, killer of Hector and eventually slain by Paris. At Aulis,
            as the Greek expedition was setting out, he unwittingly became
            the pretended fiancé of Iphigeneia.

AEROPE: Daughter of Katreus, king of Crete. Married to Atreus, she
          became the mother of Agamemnon and Menelaos but com-
          mitted adultery with her husband's brother Thyestes.

AGAMEMNON: Son of Atreus and brother of Menelaos, king of Mycenae
             and Argos, leader of the expedition against Troy. He was the
             husband of Clytemnestra and the father of Iphigeneia, whom
             he sacrificed at Aulis, Electra, and Orestes. After the Trojan
             War, he was murdered by his wife and her lover, Aigisthos.

AIAKOS: Grandfather of Achilles.

AIAS: The name of two separate heroes of the Trojan saga, one the son
        of Oïleus of Lokris (the "lesser" Aias), the other of Telamon of
        Salamis. The usual English spelling is "Ajax" from the Latin
        "Aiax."

AIGINA: A nymph, daughter of the river-god Asopos, who gave her
          name to the island in the Saronic Gulf off Attica. Great-grand-
          mother of Achilles.

AIGISTHOS: His father, Thyestes, was killed by Agamemnon's father,
             Atreus. He became the lover of Agamemnon's wife, Clytemnestra,

while Agamemnon was away at Troy and helped her kill him and seize the throne on his return. He was killed in turn by Orestes, Agamemnon's son.

AINIAN: Adjective from the district of Ainis in north-central Greece.

ALEXANDROS (ALEXANDER):   Name given to Paris when he was raised unrecognized among the shepherds of Mount Ida. See note on *Iphigeneia at Aulis*, 1722–23.

ALPHEIOS: River of the western Peloponnesos.

AMPHITRITE: Goddess, wife of Poseidon.

APHRODITE: Goddess of love, rewarded Paris with Helen when he gave her the victory in her contest with Hera and Athena, and supported the Trojans.

APIDANO: River in Thessaly.

APOLLO: Son of Zeus and Leto, god of healing, music, and prophecy. His most famous oracle was at Delphi.

AREOPAGOS: The hill of Ares at Athens, which gave its name to the city's most ancient law court.

ARES: God of war.

ARETHOUSA: Name of a spring at Chalkis.

ARGIVE: Adjective from the place-name Argos; citizen of Argos. "Argives" is used as a collective name for the Greeks in general.

ARGOS: Most precisely, a city near Mycenae in southern Greece. Ancient writers, including Euripides, use the name interchangeably with Mycenae, and it often designates the district in which both cities were situated, the area ruled by Agamemnon. By extension, since Agamemnon was the supreme leader of the Greeks at the time of the Trojan War, it can also refer to Greece in general.

ARKADIA (ARCADIA):   A mountainous region in southern Greece.

ARTEMIS: Daughter of Leto, sister of Apollo, goddess of wild animals, and of the young of all creatures, especially human beings. Hence, she is the goddess who presides over both virginity and childbirth. In Greek legend, she was worshiped among the Taurians with human sacrifice.

ASOPOS: A river-god.

ATHENA: Born full-grown from the head of Zeus, Athena was a warrior goddess, but also goddess of wisdom and various forms of women's work, such as weaving.

ATREUS: King of Mycenae, son of Pelops, and husband of Aerope, who bears him Agamemnon and Menelaos. He is best known for the revenge he took on his brother Thyestes, who seduced Aerope: pretending reconciliation, he fed the unsuspecting Thyestes the flesh of his own children. This became the justification for the part played in the murder of Agamemnon by Thyestes' surviving son, Aigisthos.

ATTICA: Region in which Athens is situated.

AULIS: The gathering place for the Greek ships that were to set out against Troy, on the coast of Boiotia, across the Euripos straits from the city of Chalkis on the island of Euboia. Aulis was the site of a grove sacred to Artemis, who was said in her anger at its violation by Agamemnon to have demanded the sacrifice of Iphigeneia.

BAKCHOS (BACCHUS): Another name for Dionysos, god of ecstasy and wine.

BOIOTIA: Region of the Greek mainland north of Attica.

BRAURON: Place in Attica, site of a sanctuary of Artemis, the final destination of Iphigeneia.

CASTOR (KASTOR): Twin brother of Polydeukes; in Euripides, spokesmen for the two. See also DIOSCURI.

CHALKIS: City on the island of Euboia.

CHEIRON: A centaur (half man, half horse). He lived in a cave on Mount Pelion and was tutor to many Greek heroes.

CLASHING ROCKS: Also known as the Black Rocks, a landmark at the entrance to the Black Sea.

CLYTEMNESTRA: Daughter of Tyndareos and Leda, sister of Helen and the Dioscuri, wife of King Agamemnon, to whom she bore Iphigeneia, Electra, and Orestes. She murdered her husband Agamemnon on his return from Troy and ruled Mycenae with her paramour Aigisthos until she was killed by Orestes to avenge his father.

CYCLOPEAN: Adjective used for cities such as Mycenae and Tiryns and their great walls, said to have been built by the Cyclopes.

CYCLOPES: A race of giants characterized by having only one eye, located in the center of their foreheads.

CYNTHIAN: Adjective from the hill Cynthos on Delos. Cynthia was a byname for Artemis because of her birth on Delos.

CYPRIS or THE CYPRIAN: Bynames of the goddess Aphrodite stemming from her worship on the island of Cyprus.

DANAANS: Collective term for the Greeks, particularly those who fought at Troy, from the name of Danaos, an early settler at Argos.

DARDANOS: Son of Zeus and founder of the Trojan royal line.

DELOS: The sacred island in the Aegean Sea where Apollo and Artemis were born.

DELPHI: Seat of the famous oracle of Apollo on Mount Parnassus, about two thousand feet above the Gulf of Corinth. See also PYTHIAN.

DIKTYNNA: Foreign (Cretan) name for Artemis.

DIOMEDES: From Argos, Greek hero at Troy.

DIONYSOS: God of wine, madness, and theatrical transformations; also known as Bakchos.

DIOSCURI (DIOSKOUROI): "Sons (kouroi) of Zeus (Dios)," Castor (Kastor) and Polydeukes (Pollux to the Romans), offspring of Zeus' encounter with Leda. Deified, they often returned, riding on horseback through the skies, to save sailors from shipwreck.

DIRKE: Spring and river of Thebes.

ECHINAI: Islands off the mouth of the Gulf of Corinth, to the north; also called Echinades.

ELECTRA (ELEKTRA):   Daughter of Agamemnon and Clytemnestra, sister of Orestes and Iphigeneia. She helps Orestes kill Clytemnestra and becomes wife of his friend Pylades.

ELIS: City-state in western Peloponnesos.

EPEIANS: Greek tribe in the district of Elis.

EROS: God of sexual desire.

EUBOIA: Large and long island across from Aulis on the northeastern shore of the Greek mainland.

EUMELOS: Son of Admetos son of Pheres; according to Homer his horses were the most beautiful of all that belonged to the Greeks at Troy, after those of Achilles.

EUMENIDES: The "kindly ones," a euphemism for the Erinyes, dread powers of the underworld. See FURIES.

EURIPOS: Narrows between Aulis in Boiotia and the city of Chalkis on the island of Euboia.

EUROTAS: The river of Sparta.

EURYTOS: Leader of the Epeians.

EUXINE: The Black Sea.

FURIES: Called Erinyes in Greek, they are Daughters of Earth according to Hesiod, of Night according to Aeschylus. Avengers of crimes committed against kindred, they pursue and madden Orestes after he murders his mother. According to Aeschylus, they are transformed into Eumenides ("kindly ones") when Orestes is acquitted of his crime.

GANYMEDE: Son of the eponymous Tros of Troy. Smitten with his beauty, Zeus took the form of an eagle and carried him off from his father's pastures to Olympos, home of the gods.

GERENIAN: Adjective from the city of Gerenon in Messenia. Nestor, king of Pylos, is frequently called the "Geranian horseman," presumably because as a young lad he was being raised in Geranon and was away from home when his family was destroyed by Herakles.

GORGON: One of three sisters, killed by Perseus. Her name was Medusa, and her snake-haired head, even after death, turned beholders to stone.

GOUNEUS: King of the Ainians. He is mentioned by Homer only in the Catalogue of Ships (*Iliad*, Book 2).

HADES: Brother of Zeus and Poseidon, his realm is death and the dead, and his name is thus used also for the underworld, the place of the dead.

HALAI: Place in Attica, site of the sanctuary to which the image of Artemis is to be carried in *Iphigenia in Tauris*.

HECTOR: Eldest son of Priam and Hecuba, husband of Andromache and father of Astyanax. The greatest champion of Troy, he was killed by Achilles.

HELEN: Daughter of Leda and Zeus (or Tyndareos), sister of Clytemnestra and the Dioscuri, wife of Menelaos. Her elopement with Paris led to the Trojan War.

HEPHAISTOS: God of the fire and the forge, patron of early technology. He made divine armor for Achilles at Thetis' request.

HERA: Sister and consort of Zeus, queen of the gods, patroness of Argos.

HERMES: The messenger god, helper of heroes and tricksters, patron of trade, travel, and heralds.

HERMIONE: Daughter of Helen and Menelaos.

HIPPODAMEIA: Wife of Pelops; for her story, see OINOMAOS.

HYADES: "The rainy ones," five stars in Taurus.

IDA: Mountain near Troy.

ILION: Name of the citadel at Troy, and thus another name for Troy.

INACHOS: River-god, king, and ancestor of the people of Argos.

IO: Daughter of Inachos, beloved by Zeus and persecuted by Hera.

IPHIGENIA (IPHIGENEIA):   Daughter of Agamemnon and Clytemnestra. Her father sacrificed her at Aulis to Artemis to secure favorable winds for the journey of the Greek fleet to Troy. In some versions of the tale, a hind was substituted for her at the last moment. In *Iphigenia in Tauris*, she lives on in the land of the Taurians as priestess of Artemis.

KADMOS: A Phoenician who came to Greece as founder and first king of Thebes in Boiotia. He slew a dragon and sowed its teeth, from which a race of Theban warriors arose.

KALCHAS: Soothsayer for Agamemnon and the Greek army at Troy.

KAPANEUS: The most hubristic of the hubristic "Seven against Thebes"; father of Sthenelos.

KARYSTIAN: Adjective from Karystos, a town on Euboia opposite Halai and Brauron in Attica.

KASSANDRA (CASSANDRA):   Daughter of Priam and Hecuba, whom Apollo loved and to whom he gave the power of prophecy. When she refused his advances, however, he made her prophecies incredible to all who heard them.

KASTALIAN: Adjective from the sacred spring, Kastalia, at Delphi.

KASTOR: See CASTOR.

LAËRTES: Father of Odysseus.

LEDA: Daughter of Thestios, wife of Tyndareos, beloved of Zeus, mother of Helen, Clytemnestra, and the Dioscuri.

LEITOS: Theban warrior and commander of the Boiotians, a descendant of the dragon's teeth sown by Kadmos.

LETO: Goddess who bore Apollo and Artemis to Zeus at Delos.

LEUKOTHEA: "White Goddess," the name given Ino, a daughter of Kadmos, when transformed into a sea goddess; see note on *Iphigenia in Tauris* 262–66.

LOKRIS: Region of northern Greece.

LOXIAS: "Crooked one," a byname of Apollo.

LYDIAN: Adjective from Lydia, a country near Troy allied with the Trojans.

MEGES: Leader of the Taphians; a fighter of some prominence in the *Iliad*.

MEKISTEUS: Son of Talaos and the leader of the contingent sent to Troy from Argos in the narrower sense (SEE ARGOS).

MENELAOS: Son of Atreus, brother of Agamemnon, husband of Helen. As husband of Helen, Menelaos is lord of Sparta.

MERIONES: Leader of the Cretans in the Greek army at Troy.

MYCENAE: City dominating the Argive plain at the head of the Argolic gulf in the eastern Peloponnesos. It lies a few miles north of Argos, with which it is often confused in Greek tragedy.

MYRMIDONS: Warriors of Phthia, commanded by Achilles at Troy.

MYRTILOS: Son of Hermes and charioteer of Oinomaos; with his connivance Oinomaos' chariot was sabotaged to allow Pelops to win his race. Pelops, however, later cast Myrtilos to his death in the sea.

NAUPLIA: The port of Argos.

NEREIDS: Sea-nymph or sea-goddess, one of the fifty daughters of Nereus. The most famous Nereid was Thetis, Achilles' mother.

NEREUS: Sea-god, father of the fifty Nereids, among whom was Thetis, the mother of Achilles.

NESTOR: King of Pylos, an elder statesman and leader of the Greeks at Troy.

NIREUS: Named by Homer as the handsomest of the Achaians at Troy, next to Achilles.

ODYSSEUS: King of Ithaca and a leader of the Greeks at Troy, a master of stratagems and persuasion.

OILEUS: Ruler of Lokris, father of the lesser Aias.

OINOMAOS: King of Pisa, father of Hippodameia. Her suitors had to attempt to escape with her in a chariot. Oinomaos pursued, overtook, and killed them all, until Pelops, aided by Oinomaos' treacherous charioteer, Myrtilos, and treacherous daughter, managed to sabotage his chariot and cause his death. Hippodameia then became Pelops' wife.

OINONE: Ancient name of the island of Aigina.

OLYMPOS: Mythical Trojan singer.

ORESTES: Only son of Agamemnon and Clytemnestra. As a young boy he was smuggled away to Phokis, the kingdom of his relative Strophios. As a young man, he returned to kill his mother and thus avenge her murder of his father.

ORPHEUS: Legendary musician. The power of his music would have served to bring back his wife Eurydice from the dead, had he not disobeyed the ruler of the underworld by looking back to see her.

OSSA: Mountain in Thessaly.

PALAIMON: Deified son of Leukothea.

PALAMEDES: Son of Nauplios, grandson of Poseidon, Greek hero at Troy treacherously murdered through the cunning of Odysseus. He was said to have made numerous important inventions (e.g., currency, weights and measures, dice).

PALLAS: Byname of Athena.

PAN: God of wild places, flocks, and shepherds; inventor and master of musical pipes.

PARIS: Son of King Priam of Troy to whom Aphrodite awarded Helen, which led in turn to the Trojan War. See also ALEXANDROS.

PARNASSOS: The great mountain above Delphi.

PEGASOS: Winged horse, sprung from the Gorgon's blood.

PELASGIA: Traditional name for Argos, connected in myth to a king named Pelasgos, but implying little more than great antiquity, the Pelasgians being pre-Hellenic inhabitants of Greece.

PELEUS: Thessalian king, mortal married to the divine Thetis, father of Achilles.

PELION: Mountain in Thessaly.

PELOPS: Son of Tantalos and Dione, father of Atreus and Thyestes; he is the heroic ancestor of Orestes, Electra, and Iphigeneia, and the Peloponnesos ("island of Pelops") is named after him.

PERGAMOS: A name for the citadel of Troy.

PERSEUS: Son of Zeus and Danae, and one of the most successful of heroes. Among other feats, he killed the Gorgon Medusa and turned his enemies to stone with it.

PHARSALIA: City of Thessaly.

PHERES: Grandfather of Eumelos, who was one of the Greeks at Troy.

PHINEUS: Hero connected with the Argonaut legend who was plagued by Harpies ("Snatchers"), winged female demons who constantly stole all his food.

PHOCIANS: The people of Phocis.

PHOCIS (PHOKIS):   Region of central Greece, in the vicinity of Mount Parnassus, whose king, Strophios, took the young Orestes into his home. Strophios' son Pylades became Orestes' best friend and helper.

PHOIBE: Sister of Helen and Clytemnestra, daughter of Leda and Tyndareos.

PHOIBOS: "The bright one," a byname of Apollo.

PHRYGIA: Region of northwest Asia Minor in which Troy was situated.

PHTHIA: Region of Thessaly in northern Greece, home of Peleus and Achilles.

PHYLEUS: Father of Meges, who led the Taphian fighters at Troy.

PISA: City in western Peloponnesos. The area controlled by Pisa, the kingdom of Oinomaos, included Olympia but was subjugated by Elis in 572 B.C.

PLEIADES: A constellation of seven stars, sometimes pictured as doves (*peleiai* or *peleiades*), and thus appropriately pursued by the hunter Orion.

POLYDEUKES: Twin brother of Castor. See DIOSCURI.

POSEIDON: God of the sea, earthquake, and horses.

PRIAM: Last king of Troy, husband of Hecuba, father of Hector, Paris, Kassandra, and many others.

PROTESILAOS: A Greek hero, member of the expedition to Troy and the first to set foot on Trojan soil.

PYLADES: Son of Strophios, cousin and steadfast friend of Orestes; eventual husband of Electra.

PYLOS: Nestor's capital city, situated in Messenia in western Peloponnesos.

PYTHIAN: Adjective from of Pytho (Delphi), originally the name of the chthonian serpent goddess who ruled Delphi before being ousted by Apollo. Pythian is thus an epithet of Apollo as god of the oracle at Delphi, and of the Pythian games, held there.

SALAMIS: Island in the Saronic Gulf, near Athens.

SIMOÏS: River at Troy.

SIPYLOS: Mountain on the frontier between Lydia and the Greek cities of the Asia Minor coast.

SIRIUS: The Dog-star, which, together with the constellation of the hunter Orion, pursues the Pleiades through the sky at night.

SISYPHOS: Founder and king of Corinth and a great rogue who was in every way unscrupulous and for a time outwitted Death himself. Those who wished to speak ill of Odysseus claimed that his real father was not Laertes but Sisyphos.

SPARTA: Chief city of Lacedaemon, the region occupying the Eurotas valley in south-central Peloponnesos; in legend, the kingdom of Tyndareos, Menelaos, and Helen.

SPHINX: A dangerous monster with a female human head and the body of a lion.

STHENELOS: A leader of the Argives, companion of Diomedes.

STROPHIOS: Ruler of Phocis, brother-in-law of Agamemnon and father of Pylades.

TALAOS: Father of Mekisteus.

TALTHYBIOS: Herald of the Greek army.

TANTALIDS: Descendants of Tantalos.

TANTALOS: Son of Zeus, king of Lydia, a land famed for its gold, and an ancient prototype of excessive good fortune issuing in disaster. He was the father of Pelops and progenitor of the unhappy House of Atreus.

TAPHIAN: Adjective from Taphos, one of the Echinades islands in the Ionian Sea off the coast of Acarnania in northwestern Greece. The Taphians were sea-faring and piratical people.

TAURIANS: People of the Crimea, whose land is often, but incorrectly, called Tauris.

TAUROPOLOS: Epithet of Artemis at Halai, of uncertain significance, but variously taken to mean "bull-handler," "pulled by bulls," or "worshipped by Taurians."

TELAMON: King of Salamis, father of the greater Aias.

THEMIS: Titan goddess of law and order, who first presided over Delphi. For the story of her dispossession, see note on *Iphigenia in Tauris* 1211–56.

THESEUS: The greatest hero and king of Athens.

THESSALY: Broad horse-breeding region in northern Greece.

THESTIOS: King of Aetolia, father of Leda.

THETIS: One of the Nereids (sea-nymph daughters of Nereus), married to the mortal Peleus, mother of Achilles.

THOAS: King of the Taurians.

THRONION: City in Lokris, about ten miles east of Thermopylai.

THYESTES: Son of Pelops, brother of Atreus whose wife, Aerope, he seduced. Atreus in revenge tricked him into eating the flesh of his own sons, but a surviving son, Aigisthos, became his avenger in the next generation through his part in killing Agamemnon.

TITANS: The generation of gods before the Olympians, overthrown by them.

TROY: City in northwestern Asia Minor, site of the Trojan War fought by the Greeks to retrieve Helen.

TYNDAREOS: King of Sparta and husband of Leda, mother of Helen, Clytemnestra, and the Dioscuri.

TYNDARIDAI: Refers to Castor and Polydeukes as sons of Tyndareos, though, like Helen, they are also said to be children of Zeus.

ZEUS: Sky-god and chief divinity of the Greek pantheon; "father of gods and men," both figuratively and as the literal progenitor of numerous mortals and immortals.

FOR FURTHER READING

EURIPIDES

Desmond J. Conacher. *Euripidean Drama: Myth, Theme, and Structure*. Toronto: University of Toronto Press, 1967. Still the most useful play-by-play study of Euripides.

Helene P. Foley. *Ritual Irony: Poetry and Sacrifice in Euripides*. Ithaca, N.Y.: Cornell University Press, 1985. Important study of the uses of ritual in Euripidean tragedy, particularly female self-sacrifice, with a chapter on *Iphigenia at Aulis*.

Ann N. Michelini. *Euripides and the Tragic Tradition*. Madison: University of Wisconsin Press, 1987. A broadly based study of Euripides and the history of Euripidean criticism, with a long chapter on *Electra*.

Donald J. Mastronarde. *The Art of Euripides: Dramatic Technique and Social Context*. Cambridge: Cambridge University Press, 2010. A new assessment of the entire Euripidean corpus, employing a variety of perspectives.

James Morwood. *The Plays of Euripides*. London: Bristol Classical Press, 2002. Brief, personal discussions of all the surviving plays.

Judith Mossman, ed. *Euripides*. Oxford: Oxford University Press, 2003. A collection of influential critical essays, including important papers on *Electra* and *Orestes*.

Note: Among the volumes available in the Duckworth Companions to Greek and Roman Tragedy series are *Iphigenia at Aulis* (Pantelis Michelakis) and *Orestes* (Matthew Wright). These are reliable introductions with full and up-to-date bibliographies.

ELECTRA

Barbara Goff. "Try to Make It Real Compared to What? Euripides' *Electra* and the Play of Genres." *Illinois Classical Studies* 24–25 (1999–2000): 95–105. An analysis of the concept of "realism" to show that certain characteristics of Greek comic drama in this play breach generic boundaries.

David Konstan. "*Philia* in Euripides' *Electra*." *Philologus* 129 (1985): 176–85. A study of significant ambiguity of the term "friendship" in this play.

Judith Mossman. "Women's Speech in Greek Tragedy: The Case of Electra and Clytemnestra in Euripides' *Electra*." *Classical Journal* 51 (2001): 374–84.

IPHIGENIA IN TAURIS

Elizabeth S. Belfiore. "Averting Fratricide: Euripides' *Iphigenia in Tauris*." In *Murder among Friends: Violation of Philia in Greek Tragedy*. New York: Oxford University Press, 2000: "Averting Fratricide: Euripides' *Iphigenia in Tauris*," 21–38.

———. "Aristotle and Iphigenia." In Amélie Oksenberg Rorty, ed., *Essays on Aristotle's Poetics*. Princeton: Princeton University Press, 1992, 359–77. Two complementary and helpful interpretative essays.

Caroline P. Trieschnigg. "Iphigenia's Dream in Euripides' *Iphigenia Taurica*." *Classical Quarterly* 58 (2008): 461–78. An interesting treatment of the ostensibly "false" dream and its significance within the drama.

Christian Wolff. "Euripides' *Iphigenia among the Taurians*: Aetiology, Ritual, and Myth." *Classical Antiquity* 11 (1992): 308–34. Analysis of the play in the light of the etiologies of the final scene.

ORESTES

Francis Dunn. "Comic and Tragic License in Euripides' *Orestes*." *Classical Antiquity* 8 (1989): 238–51. Discusses the mixture of tragic and comic speech patterns in the play.

J. Peter Euben. "Political Corruption in Euripides' *Orestes*." In J. P. Euben, ed., *Greek Tragedy and Political Theory*. Berkeley: University of California Press, 1986, 222–51. A reading of the play as both reflecting the crisis of contemporary Athens and embodying the crisis of the tragic genre.

Froma I. Zeitlin. "The Closet of Masks: Role-playing and Myth-making in the *Orestes* of Euripides." *Ramus* 9 (1980): 51–77. Figures in a mythical landscape in which mythical identities are no longer adequate and heroic action is reduced to parody.

IPHIGENIA AT AULIS

Celia A. E. Luschnig. *Tragic Aporia: A Study of Euripides' "Iphigenia in Aulis"* (*Ramus* Monograph 3). Berwick, Australia, 1988. A book-length literary study of this drama.

David Sansone. "Iphigeneia Changes Her Mind." *Illinois Classical Studies* 16 (1991): 161–72. Iphigenia's choice of willing self-sacrifice as influenced by Achilles' words and reflecting a positive idea of shared compassion.

Christine E. Sorum. "Myth, Choice, and Meaning in Euripides' *Iphigenia at Aulis*." *American Journal of Philology* 113 (1992): 527–42. The relation of choices made in the play to a mythic tradition that meets with resistance but always reasserts itself.

CPSIA information can be obtained at www.ICGtesting.com
Printed in the USA
LVOW11s2100181213

365838LV00001B/3/P

9 780195 388695